1992

To: Hope
and ~~Irene~~
Corrigan,
Fellow parishoners:
All the best
Ed Rowny

IT TAKES ONE
TO TANGO

IT TAKES ONE
TO TANGO

AMBASSADOR EDWARD L. ROWNY

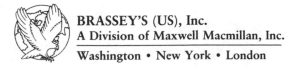

BRASSEY'S (US), Inc.
A Division of Maxwell Macmillan, Inc.

Washington • New York • London

Brassey's (US), Inc.

Editorial Offices	Order Department
Brassey's (US), Inc.	Brassey's Book Orders
8000 Westpark Drive	% Macmillan Publishing Co.
First Floor	100 Front Street, Box 500
McLean, Virginia 22102	Riverside, New Jersey 08075

Brassey's (US), Inc., books are available at special discounts for bulk purchases for sales promotions, premiums, fund-raising, or educational use through the Special Sales Director, Macmillan Publishing Company, 866 Third Avenue, New York, New York 10022.

Library of Congress Cataloging-in-Publication Data

Rowny, Edward, L., 1917–
    It takes one to tango / Edward L. Rowny.
        p.   cm.
    Includes index.
    ISBN 0–02–881037–6
    1. Arms control—United States. 2. Arms control—Soviet Union.
3. United States—National security. 4. United States—Foreign
relations—1945– 5. Rowny, Edward L., 1917– . I. Title.
JX1974.R648 1992
327.1'74—dc20   92–17135
                                                              CIP

10 9 8 7 6 5 4 3 2 1
Printed in the United States of America

To Betty

Contents

Preface   ix

Acknowledgments   xiii

1   Life Before Arms Control   1

2   The Nixon Years: A Close Call   21

3   Ford's Brief Reign: Standing Firm   64

4   The Carter Years: Averting Disaster   93

5   Reagan's First Term: Turnabout   134

6   Reagan's Second Term: Results at Last   164

7   President Bush: A Lack of Conviction   210

8   Negotiating in a Changing World   247

Index   265

Preface

"IT TAKES ONE TO TANGO"

During the SALT II negotiations in 1974, I became exasperated with the stalling tactics of one of my Soviet military counterparts, Col. Gen. Ivan Beletsky. He kept repeating the same statements and would not enter into a serious discussion of the merits of our respective positions.

I told Beletsky that I was elaborating on the rationale for our position and that he should do the same with respect to theirs. "It takes two to tango," I said.

"No," retorted Beletsky, "it takes one to tango." He then told me about the way young men met young women in his hometown: "In my day, we went to Saturday night dances looking for a date. All the young women seated themselves along the walls of the dance hall. Rather than ask one of them to dance, a young man would pick up a chair and dance with it.

"As I danced the tango, I kept looking at the expressions on the young women's faces. When one smiled and nodded approvingly, I knew I had gained her favor. I then asked her to dance, and we became friends.

"It's the same in our dealings with you," he continued. "We simply keep repeating our positions, expecting that one of you will smile or nod approvingly.

"So you see," he concluded, "it takes one to tango."

You can best understand me and the story told in this book if you understand that I spent almost twenty years of my life trying to resist the temptation to smile or nod at my Soviet "dancing partners." While representing America's interests at innumerable conference tables, I acquired the public reputation of being very demanding, perhaps even hard-nosed, in my insistence on equitable and verifiable arms control agreements.

The idea to report my observations and experiences in a book goes

back more than ten years. On June 14, 1979, when the SALT II
Treaty limiting strategic weapons was initialed, I resigned in protest
from my post as the Joint Chiefs of Staff representative to the U.S.
negotiating team. I was convinced that the SALT II Treaty would be
detrimental to the security of the United States and the Senate agreed,
forcing President Carter to withdraw the treaty. During the following
year, while a scholar at the Smithsonian's Woodrow Wilson Center
in Washington, D.C., I wrote a book about my experiences at the
SALT II negotiations. The text demonstrated that the United States
had negotiated poorly at a time when the Soviet Union was still
expanding its empire. I laid out a series of lessons learned from our
negotiating experiences and proposed guidelines that I felt would
help prevent us from coming out second-best at the negotiating table.

While my book was being put into final form, President Reagan
appointed me his chief negotiator for strategic arms control, with the
stipulation, however, that I not publish the book. The administration
felt that the contents and the subsequent publicity would put me at
a disadvantage in negotiating with the Soviets and that enumerating
our shortcomings would encourage the Soviets to exploit them before we had instituted corrective action. I agreed, and over the next
ten years I served in both the Reagan and Bush administrations.

After I resigned from the government in June 1990, I felt that it
would still be worthwhile to publish a book about my negotiating
experiences. The international situation had, of course, changed dramatically since my first writing effort, forcing me to rewrite portions
of my original manuscript. I was strongly encouraged by friends and
colleagues to complete this book and to include more of my insights
and personal observations of what went on behind the scenes. They
pointed out that few Americans at my level had served five presidents
and their administrations for almost two decades. They convinced
me that it was important to record for history my impressions of how
U.S. and Soviet leaders responded to negotiating about life and death
on this planet. I have done this to the best of my ability—trying to
present the important and sometimes even the amusing happenings I
observed.

You will find many references to prominent people whose names
you will recognize. Some references are flattering, some are not. I am
told that this book may be particularly "hard" on Henry Kissinger,
the Carter administration, and President George Bush. I have carefully checked my memory by referring to my notes and consulting
with my former colleagues, and I have tried to be fair. I believe you

will find little rancor or anger. I know you will find unique insights into the personalities, policies, and motives of five administrations as they dealt with arms control. You will also find that I was unwilling to "dance" with the Soviets unless they were willing to dance with us. You can make your own judgment about my approach and whether it was justified.

I do not believe, as some do, that we face the end of history. Rather, we are entering a new phase. By better understanding the mistakes of the past, we can avoid similar mishaps in the complex negotiating world we are now entering. This book is intended to help achieve that goal.

Acknowledgments

I am indebted to a large number of friends who have given me ideas and otherwise helped me with this book. Among these are Herb Cohen, Kirk Lewis, Bill McCaffrey, Sven Kraemer, Fritz Kraemer, Leona Schecter, Frank Jenkins, Monte Mallin, Sam Watson, and Kerry Karchner. I am especially indebted to Bertram Brown, who provided me with insights, advice, and encouragement. My warm thanks to Georgie Anne Geyer, who suggested the title.

Persons who did research and helped with the writing include Susan Munro and Patricia Barwinczak. Richard Smith not only did basic research but helped immeasurably with ideas and writing. Alvin Sanoff did extensive editing to the entire manuscript, pruning it and making many difficult portions readable. Typing of numerous drafts was painstakingly and efficiently done by Virginia McGuire.

I was encouraged along the way by Tom Clancy, Bill Safire, Peggy Noonan, Herb Cohen, Larry King, and Joe Fromm. Frank Margiotta, my publisher, was enthusiastic about the book from the beginning. His associates Don McKeon and Vicki Chamlee were also helpful and supportive. I am grateful to James Piereson and the John M. Olin Foundation for the generous grant that has helped me with

xiii

this book and for getting colleges and universities to teach international negotiating. Others who gave me support were my late wife, Rita; my children and their spouses; and my sister-in-law Carolyn Leyko. Elizabeth (Betty) Ladd, to whom the book is dedicated, would not let me quit when the going got tough. I must end with the usual disclaimer that errors in fact and matters of judgment are mine.

CHAPTER 1

Life Before Arms Control

In 1973 I was dragooned into the SALT II negotiations by one of my closest friends, Senator Henry M. ("Scoop") Jackson of Washington State. I was, at the time, deputy chairman of the Military Committee of the North Atlantic Treaty Organization (NATO) and the head of the team setting up the negotiations on Mutual and Balanced Force Reductions (MBFR). I believed that MBFR, which aimed to reduce conventional weapons, was more important than SALT, the negotiation of strategic arms limitations. I thought I was on a fast track toward achieving the lifelong goal of every officer, being promoted to four stars. I knew that if I joined the SALT II team I would never advance beyond my three-star rank because the U.S. Army reserves its few four-star positions for its top command jobs. To Jackson, however, my ideas about the relative importance of MBFR and SALT and my ambitions made no difference. He felt I was uniquely qualified for the job of strategic arms negotiator. As patriotic as I was ambitious, I had to admit that he was right. But I never suspected that I would spend the rest of my career as an arms negotiator.

What in retrospect seems a series of related events propelled me inexorably to the negotiating table. The first had occurred almost

1

forty years earlier when I was a junior at Johns Hopkins University preparing for a career in engineering. During the summer of 1936, while on a scholarship in Europe, I went to the Berlin Olympics where I saw Jesse Owens win four gold medals. I was impressed with his achievements, but I was even more impressed with the stridency and fervor of Hitler's SS and youth brigades. The vitriolic Nazi zeal and Hitler's obvious grand designs convinced me that war was rapidly approaching and that the United States would inevitably become involved.

Perhaps my family background made me more sensitive to events in Europe. My father immigrated to the United States from a small village near Warsaw, Poland, in 1912 when he was seventeen. He volunteered to serve in the U.S. Army at the outbreak of World War I but was turned down because he was a ship's carpenter and was considered more valuable on the home front. He was hardworking and ambitious, always looking for new and different ways to perform jobs more efficiently. He was also very independent-minded. He inculcated these traits into me at an early age, traits I later recognized I owed to his guidance and example. One of our family stories concerning his independent ways had to do with his becoming a U.S. citizen. When he went for his examination, the local judge asked him the usual question about the separation of powers under the Constitution. When my father rattled off the answer, the judge said, "Okay, you know all this stuff. What ship did you come over on?" Sensing that the judge was not very alert, my father said, "The Mayflower." He got away with that quiet joke. Later on, my friends thought I should apply for membership in the General Society of Mayflower Descendants, which is restricted to descendants of the Mayflower's passengers, who landed in the United States.

When I was six years old, my mother became seriously ill and I was sent to live with her parents. My grandfather, also from Poland, had served as a noncommissioned officer in the tsar's army. He filled me with stories about the adventure and glamour of serving in the military. After he died, my grandmother repeated the same stories, but she added to them a considerable amount of moralizing. To her, the military was necessary not only to preserve law and order but also to guarantee liberty and individual rights. She and my grandfather instilled in me great respect for the military as an honorable profession.

I received my bachelor of science degree from Johns Hopkins in 1937 and shortly after was commissioned a second lieutenant in the army reserves. But being favorably disposed toward a military career, and wanting to prepare myself thoroughly for the war I saw coming, I resigned my commission and started over. I entered the United States Military Academy as a plebe. At West Point, one of my teachers was Capt. George ("Abe") Lincoln, a political science professor who later became Gen. George C. Marshall's chief planner in World War II. Lincoln took a personal interest in me and made me a member of the prestigious "Lincoln's Brigade," officers he watched over and helped place in important assignments. Captain Lincoln kindled in me a lifelong interest in and enthusiasm for international relations.

My first assignment as a second lieutenant in the regular Army was to the 41st Combat Engineer Regiment commanded by Col. Joseph ("Smokey Joe") Wood, a highly capable officer who was also an innovative maverick. In the fall of 1941, when the United States was still not involved in the fighting in Europe, he forecast that we would soon enter World War II. To prepare us for the war he believed was imminent, he trained us hard, introducing a number of ideas that were ahead of the times. For example, he felt that soldiers should spend 100 percent of their time preparing for combat and should not perform "fatigue" duties. To free up time for training, he hired civilians to cook and do KP and charwomen to sweep the barracks and pick up cigarette butts. Wood believed that he and his officers were the best trainers in the U.S. Army and repeatedly volunteered his best soldiers to form cadres for new units.

This left our regiment with a higher proportion of substandard soldiers with physical and mental deficiencies. The poorest of these soldiers Wood formed into "J" Company (there were no "J" companies in the U.S. Army since the time one had mutinied in the Civil War) and assigned it to me. He challenged me to turn the company into a fighting unit.

It was indeed a challenge. For three months we worked around the clock, using Wood's training and motivational techniques. Competing with the other twelve companies of the regiment, "J" Company won ten first places out of thirteen categories. Wood recommended to the Department of the Army that I skip a grade and be immediately promoted to captain. Although the Army turned down his request, Wood saw to it that I was promoted ahead of my contemporaries. In less than three years, while most of my classmates were still captains, I was wearing the silver leaves of a lieutenant colonel. Wood's example as an innovator and risk-taker influenced the direction of my career and my subsequent style as a negotiator.

Wood's prediction that the United States would enter the war was right, of course, and on December 8, 1941, the United States declared war on Japan and Germany. Because of its high state of combat readiness, Wood's regiment was the first engineer unit deployed overseas. In May of 1942, we arrived in Liberia, charged with establishing a base to support the war in North Africa and to build an airfield to enable the United States to airlift supplies to the Soviet Union. When Colonel Wood was promoted to brigadier general in the fall of 1942, he brought me back to the United States with him to help form a new unit, the 92d Infantry Division. When the division completed its training, we were sent to Italy in the spring of 1944, where I served with the division until V-E Day in 1945.

Initially, I commanded an engineer combat battalion of about 900 men. The division suffered heavy casualties, especially among its officers. In late 1944, we lost seven of our nine infantry battalion commanders in one week. As a result, I was assigned command of an infantry battalion and later a unit of approximately 1,200 men, which was called Task Force Rowny. Fighting in northern Italy became intense in January of 1945. My unit was decimated; only about 125 men survived. Personally, I was extremely fortunate. When an artillery shell hit my command group of ten men, three were killed, six were wounded. I was the only one unharmed.

Toward the end of hostilities, I had my first experience as a negotiator. Our division, of which I was then operations officer (G-3), moved to what our maps indicated was the French-Italian border. The French moved their troops around our flank some fifteen kilometers to the south of us in an attempt to reclaim territory they said belonged to France. Without the authority to resolve the issue myself, I referred it to Washington. President Truman acted immediately and cut off the flow of U.S. fuel to the French army. The French government, faced with this prompt and resolute action, pulled its troops back. It was a minor dispute, but it gave me a taste of the dynamics of negotiating. It taught me that quick and decisive action at the highest levels is the best way to resolve disputes.

The day after the war ended in Europe, in May 1945, Abe Lincoln, now a brigadier general and the U.S. Army's chief planner, asked that I be assigned to Washington to the Strategic Plans Section (SPS) of the Operations Division (OPD). SPS was a highly select group, one of the most prestigious in the U.S. Army, consisting of only twelve officers. Eleven of the twelve were well entrenched; I was given the opportunity to become the twelfth. Three officers had in recent months tried and failed to capture the post. My task was to develop a portion of the plan for the final invasion of Japan. Because it was such a daunting task, I asked a friend from cadet days, Col. (later General) Andrew Goodpaster, to look over my work.

"Your ideas are fine," he said, "but they're not presented in a way that will satisfy General Marshall." He edited my plan, and I submitted it for approval. The next day Marshall sent for me and said, "Colonel Rowny, I've been trying to find the proper person to occupy the remaining seat in the Strategic Plans Section, and I've found him. The position is yours."

"General," I said, "I must tell you in all honesty that the ideas in the plan are mine, but it was edited heavily by Colonel Goodpaster."

"Young man," Marshall said, "I wasn't born yesterday. Obviously Goodpaster rewrote it. But anyone who can get Goodpaster to work for him is good enough for me and deserves the billet."

That plan to which I had contributed was, happily, not implemented. I felt especially fortunate because, as I found out later, one of General MacArthur's policies was for the planners to land in the first waves of an invasion. He believed that knowing that would "sharpen their minds" in the planning stage. My portion of the plan included building an artificial harbor in Tokyo Bay where landing craft and supply ships could find protection in the event of a severe storm. Early in July 1945, I received a message that read: "Your request for steel for the artificial harbor in Sagami Wan (Tokyo Bay) disapproved. Signed: Manhattan District Engineer." Indignant that some "New York engineer" was interfering with my project, I stormed into General Lincoln's office. He, too, was incensed and told me to take the message straightaway to General Marshall. Marshall was not in, but I complained bitterly to his deputy, Gen. Thomas Handy. Handy said, "Colonel, whatever the Manhattan District Engineer wants is automatically approved." Dejected, I went back to work on an alternate plan for the artificial harbor without the benefit of steel piles to act as moorings. It was not until the day the United States dropped an atomic bomb on Hiroshima that I learned that *Manhattan District Engineer* was the code name for the atomic bomb project. The secret had been so well kept that not even General Lincoln, the Army planner, had known about it.

Later in the fall of 1945, after V-J Day, General Lincoln made me the desk officer responsible for staffing General MacArthur's plans for postwar control of Japan. Reviewing and coordinating General MacArthur's plans in the Pentagon gave me unique insight into his foresight, brilliance, and courage. Most officials in Washington were at the time debating whether the Emperor of Japan should be jailed, hanged, or shot. MacArthur's answer was: "None of the above. We'll need the prestige and authority of the Emperor to control postwar Japan." He insisted that the Emperor not be publicly humiliated but instead be made the conduit through which instructions would be issued to the Japanese military and civilian authorities. It proved a wise decision.

Later in 1945 I began to work directly for Lt. Gen. Lauris C. Norstad, who took over the Operations Division of the Army. Abe Lincoln at this point left the Pentagon. He chose to give up a second star and revert to the rank of colonel (the highest rank professors at West Point could hold) so he could resume teaching at the U.S. Military Academy. Norstad, my new boss, was an uncommonly long-range global thinker. He organized frequent freewheeling, brainstorming sessions in which he challenged us to develop imaginative ideas for the future. Out of Norstad's "dream sessions" emerged such ideas as the development of land-based intercontinental ballistic missiles, missiles to be fired from submarines, and putting a man on the moon.

Norstad thought that several of us serving in his Strategic Plans Section should broaden our educations. He arranged to have four of us sent to universities (Harvard, Columbia, Princeton, and Yale) to study international relations. There was, however, one serious hitch. The Corps of Engineers, the branch of Army service to which we all belonged, believed we should study engineering, not international relations. An exception was made only for Goodpaster, who went to Princeton; the rest of us were required to study engineering. Not wanting to confine my studies to engineering, I took additional courses in international relations. As a result, during my two-year stay at Yale, I earned a master's degree in engineering and a master's degree in international relations. At that time, Yale had the country's largest stable of first-rate political thinkers including such prominent theoreticians as Arnold Wolfers, William T. R. Fox, Bernard Brodie, Klauss Knorr, and William Kaufman. It was an exhilarating atmosphere in which to study because our teachers worked closely with the Pentagon on developing the postwar nuclear policies of the United States.

While at Yale, it became obvious that the Soviet Union would be the principal military rival of the United States for the foreseeable future; so I studied Russian history, culture, and language. In what turned out to be a foreshadowing of my later career, I became particularly interested in Soviet negotiating behavior. I thoroughly researched the available literature on U.S.-Soviet negotiations and interviewed several individuals who had been directly involved in negotiations with the Soviets, such as Maj. Gen. John R. Deane, who was a member of the team negotiating U.S. lend-lease to the Soviet Union, and Gen. Lucius Clay, who headed the U.S. team negotiating the quadripartite occupation of Berlin at the end of World War II. I tried to determine why the United States always seemed to come out on the short end of negotiations with the Soviet Union. After reviewing some twenty-five books, a pattern became apparent. I developed a list of the ten most important "do's" and "don'ts" that U.S. negotiators should follow to ensure more positive outcomes; I had no idea how important these would someday be.

1. *Above all, remember the objective.* Americans are problem-solvers—inheritors of the Greek rationalist tradition—who believe that all problems have solutions if only we try hard enough. The Soviets did not accept this notion. They had defined goals, while our goals were often fuzzy.

2. *Be patient.* Moscow placed its objectives in a larger context and longer time-frame than Washington. Americans want to rush into things—to "get on with it." Americans played poker; the Soviets, chess. As a result, the Soviets traditionally succeeded in treaty negotiations by simply waiting us out.

3. *Keep secrets.* In stark contrast to the United States, the Soviet Union was a closed and secretive society. Political leaders in Moscow jealously guarded negotiating positions—even from their own delegates—until the very last moment. We, on the other hand, tend to debate even our most sensitive initiatives on the front pages of major newspapers. Combined with the propensity of U.S. officials to "leak" sensitive information in order to advocate their own proposals at the expense of competing bureaucratic agencies, it was virtually impossible for the Americans to enter into negotiations with the Soviets without them having prior knowledge of our bottom line.

4. *Bear in mind the difference in the two political structures.* It is obvious, but the obvious was often overlooked. The Soviets had a centralized authority, with nothing comparable to our independent legislative and judicial checks and balances. Our political structure requires us to consider carefully congressional perspectives in our negotiating positions. The Soviets had no such constraints.

5. *Beware of "Greeks" bearing gifts.* The Soviets viewed compromise as weakness. They tended to follow the maxim that "what

is mine is mine, what is yours is negotiable." When they grudgingly acknowledged the necessity of trading negotiating points, they insisted that it be to their advantage. On those rare occasions when the Soviets willingly offered concessions, Americans needed to respond with extreme caution. Such gifts invariably had strings attached that called for greater repayment somewhere down the line.

6. *Remember that to the Soviets, form is substance.* The Soviets believed that setting the negotiating agenda in advance, the physical size of the table, and having a greater number of representatives in their delegations were highly important. Americans tend to minimize the importance of form. As a result, we are often put at a disadvantage. The Soviets regarded compliance with agreements as simply a matter of form, whereas Americans regard it as a matter of substance.

7. *Don't be deceived by the Soviet "fear of being invaded."* From an early age, Soviet children had been taught to have an inordinate fear of foreign invasion as a rationalization for their nation's extremely large military forces. Granted, the Soviet Union, and Russia before it, had suffered invasions. But in 1898 the Russian general staff concluded that of the thirty-eight major wars in which Russia had been involved, thirty-six were offensive and only two were defensive. The Soviet Union had not come to occupy one-sixth of the world's land mass by fighting only defensive actions.

8. *Don't be deceived by words.* The Soviets' words meant only what they wanted them to mean. To them, democracy meant voting for a single candidate, not a legitimate contest between individuals with competing points of view. The Soviets consistently applied their own self-serving definitions to words and phrases fundamental to the American lexicon. They sought to corrupt concepts like freedom, equality, and reciprocity to their advantage.

9. *Beware of agreements in principle.* A device that the Soviets used to mask their true intentions was called an "agreement in principle." This negotiating tactic entailed getting the United States to lend its support to a seemingly reasonable, if ill-defined, goal. But agreements in principle never spelled out the appropriate means to the desired end. Consequently, the Soviets inevitably tried to impose their own interpretation on the United States, crying foul and refusing to negotiate when we objected to their self-serving and manipulative ways.

10. *Beware of negotiating at the eleventh hour.* The Soviets were masters of last-minute negotiations. They waited until the very end,

hoping to put pressure on us to make concessions simply to complete an agreement.

In the fall of 1949, after I finished my studies at Yale, I was sent to Japan to join General MacArthur's planning staff. When I got to Tokyo I learned that signals had gotten crossed, and I had arrived a month earlier than expected. Not knowing what else to do with me, the Army gave me an open ticket to travel throughout Japan by boat, plane, and train. I was extremely fortunate in teaming up on my trip with Prof. Douglas Morrow, an anthropologist and agronomist from the University of Wisconsin who was working on a land reform policy for Japan. A delightful traveling companion, Morrow acted as my tour guide and taught me a great deal about Japanese history and culture. On our trip, I observed that there were U.S. soldiers occupying most of Japan's cities, villages, and hamlets. It was not clear to me what these soldiers were accomplishing; they were certainly not needed for security reasons. In fact, they seemed to be interfering with Japan's political and economic recovery. It was easy to see that they were causing resentment among the Japanese, who had quickly reestablished a governing hierarchy after the war and were faithfully carrying out MacArthur's wishes, which were issued throughout Japan in the name of the Emperor.

When I returned to Tokyo, I wrote a report to MacArthur's chief of staff recommending that the United States pull back its forces and consolidate them into combat units at several former Japanese army camps. Although most officers on MacArthur's staff disagreed with me, Gen. Edward (Ned) Almond, who had been my division commander in Italy and was now MacArthur's chief of staff, agreed with my recommendations and sent them on to the supreme commander. General MacArthur liked the ideas and assigned me the task of consolidating U.S. troops in Japan. He also directed me to draw up a scheme under which the Japanese could assure law and order in the event of unrest or national disasters. This resulted in my writing a plan for the formation of a Japanese Self Defense Force (JSDF), patterned after the National Guard in the United States. Developing these plans required me to work closely with Japanese civilian and military officials. They found my ideas to their liking and I became quite popular in official Japanese circles.

In the spring of 1950, my position on General MacArthur's planning staff gave me the opportunity to read reporting cables from Korea. The North Koreans were emboldened by a speech delivered by U.S. Secretary of State Dean Acheson, in which he unfortunately signaled that the defense of U.S. interests in Asia would no longer include the protection of Korea. Convinced that the North Koreans would invade South Korea, I wrote a report saying so. Gen. Charles A. Willoughby, MacArthur's G-2 (chief of intelligence), took exception to my prediction of a North Korean attack and demanded that I be ordered not to write any further "intelligence analyses." General Almond ignored Willoughby's objection and sent my report to General MacArthur. After reading it, MacArthur ordered Gen. Walton K. Walker, commander of the Eighth Army in Japan, to accelerate the withdrawal of U.S. forces from occupation duties, consolidate them, and train them for combat. This move came none too soon. On June 25, 1950, the North Koreans marched into Seoul. General MacArthur immediately asked President Truman to appeal to the United Nations (UN) for help. The UN responded rapidly, and eventually, fifteen nations in addition to the United States and South Korea provided sea, land, or air forces to Korea. It was fortunate that on the day the U.S. request for help was put to the UN Security Council Ambassador Jacob Malik, the Soviet representative, was absent. Otherwise, we would certainly have been faced with a veto.

On June 26, the day after the invasion, General MacArthur's spokesman (whose name I shall omit to save him embarrassment) had a few drinks too many to calm his nerves before briefing the press corps. Several hours later I received a short directive from the supreme commander. It read:

Subject: Appointment of Official Spokesman
To: Lt. Col. Edward L. Rowny
    1.   Effective immediately, you will act as my official spokesman. You will do this in addition to your normal duties.
    2.   You will tell the press everything they need to know and nothing they need not know.

Signed: MacArthur

The next six weeks proved a harrowing experience. Several of the top U.S. journalists flew to Tokyo, and while not as demanding as the Sam Donaldsons and Helen Thomases of the 1990s, they were, to say the least, difficult to deal with. Moreover, I was heavily involved with my "normal duties," which included working on a plan to relieve the pressure on our beleaguered forces that had been pushed far down in the south of the peninsula.

I was one of three officers assigned the job of planning an invasion on the west coast of Korea. General MacArthur directed each of us to present our own concepts to him personally. One of my colleagues called for an invasion at the border between U.S. and North Korean forces, the classical "hinge" where an attack is usually made. The second officer planned a deeper invasion, some five kilometers to the north of the front line. His idea was to take the enemy by surprise, even though it would deny attackers full fire support. My plan was to land ten kilometers to the north. Although it would deny the invading forces any artillery support, it would capitalize on a higher element of surprise.

General MacArthur let us finish without interrupting. He then went to a map of Korea and drew a large arrow through Inchon right to Seoul. It was more than 200 kilometers to the north of the front line.

"You're all pusillanimous," he said. "Here's where we're going to land: Inchon. Always go for the objective." He added, "And the objective is Seoul, Korea's capital. Anything wrong with that?" he asked.

One of my colleagues said that the attack was too deep; there was no way to provide artillery support and it was too far to permit a rapid linkup with our frontline forces.

The other said that the beach at Inchon was reportedly heavily fortified with mines and underwater obstacles.

I pointed out that the tides at Inchon were thirty-one feet, among the highest tides in the world (second only to the thirty-two-foot tides at the Bay of Fundy), and once our landing ships came in at high tide we would have to wait twelve hours for another high tide to land further waves of invading troops and support forces. MacArthur dismissed all our objections, admonishing us sternly: "Don't take counsel of your fears."

The three of us joined forces and worked up a plan for the invasion. MacArthur made a few minor changes, approved it, and sent it to Washington. The Pentagon promptly rejected the plan. MacArthur, not to be put off, took the unusual and audacious step of asking the Joint Chiefs of Staff to come to Tokyo so that he could "explain personally why Inchon was the proper place to land."

I sat in the back row when General MacArthur presented the plan to the chairman and four chiefs of staff. The Army chief of staff spoke up first, saying that the Army did not have enough trained forces to make the landing.

"Then we'll augment them with Marines," MacArthur said.

"It still won't be enough," said the commandant of the Marine Corps.

The chief of Naval Operations (CNO) said Inchon was a poor place to land because of the high tides, mines, and underwater obstacles. MacArthur gave the CNO the same lecture he had given us about not taking counsel of one's fears.

The chief of staff of the Air Force suggested, not too diplomatically, that an invasion need not take place at all. He maintained that a sustained air bombardment would force the enemy to surrender.

MacArthur dismissed his objection tersely: "Air forces do not take and hold ground."

Gen. J. Lawton Collins, chairman of the Joint Chiefs of Staff, then spoke up, saying that each of the chiefs had a reason for not landing at Inchon. Therefore, he said, the sum total of their objections made the landing too great a military risk.

For the next several hours, I witnessed the most masterful presentation I have ever seen. MacArthur addressed each argument in turn. He combined references to famous world battles with detailed knowledge of the comparative North and South Korean military capabilities and their political strengths and weaknesses. It was a performance that rivaled any that John Barrymore could have made. Although he answered each individual chief's objections, he concentrated on the chairman, calculating that if he could turn him around the others would follow. It worked. When General Collins said he thought the Inchon invasion had a chance to succeed, the other chiefs fell in line.

Following his meeting with the chiefs, General MacArthur called me and the other planners into his office. He gave each of us a warm hug and said, "Inchon will go down in history as the 22d famous battle of the world." (At West Point we had studied the eighteen famous battles of the world. I did not know until MacArthur mentioned it that three more had been added.)

I was relieved to know that I could shortly turn my assignment as official spokesman over to someone else. As soon as the final touches were placed on the plan, around August 15, I was appointed engineer officer for X Corps, the invading force. Although still a lieutenant colonel, I was given a temporary rank of brigadier general, two grades higher.

The Inchon invasion proved even easier than MacArthur had predicted. We landed on September 15, and five days later were on the south side of the Han River, only a short distance from Seoul. Enemy resistance had been light and the mines and underwater obstacles overrated. The invasion was a complete success. I have not discovered any historian who has designated Inchon the 22d famous battle of the world. In my opinion someone should. MacArthur's boldness instilled in me a conviction that only bold actions lead to big successes.

Flushed with success and full of confidence, General MacArthur made the mistake of ordering the X Corps to make a second landing, on the east coast of Korea. This time the harbor at Wonsan was heavily mined and it took several weeks to clear the mines sufficiently to allow the 1st Marine Division to come ashore on October 25. The 7th Army Division landed farther to the north at the port of Iwan and marched overland to the Chinese border, reaching the Yalu River, which separated Korea and China, on November 17.

Meanwhile, we had been receiving fragmentary intelligence reports that the Chinese had moved into North Korea, perhaps as early as October 14. General Willoughby, MacArthur's G-2, discounted these reports and continued to insist that the Chinese would not enter the war. On October 29, the Republic of Korea Capital Division encountered the Chinese and captured sixteen prisoners. Willoughby, still skeptical, flew to Wonsan to have a personal look at the prisoners. The American interrogator, convinced that the prisoners were Chinese, was frustrated that Willoughby refused to believe it. Trying to help the interrogator, I said, "You can tell they're Chinese; look at the epicanthic fold of their eyelids." Willoughby, annoyed that I was still interfering in "his business," and remembering my association with the anthropologist Douglas Morrow, said sarcastically, "Don't give me any of that anthropological jazz."

The Chinese broke contact with the Korean forces, and Willoughby became more confident that he was correct. However, when the Chinese struck the 31st Regimental Combat Team of the 7th Division in force on the evening of November 24, Willoughby had to swallow his words.

After the Chinese attack, the Eighth Army began to crumble. I continued to be very much involved in the action. When Col. Lewis ("Chesty") Puller's regiment was cut off by the Chinese at the plateau near the Chosin Reservoir, I directed construction of an airfield to deliver supplies to Puller's surrounded regiment and evacuate hundreds of his frostbitten and wounded Marines. I also planned and executed the airdrop of a prefabricated bridge, which permitted the Marines to span the chasm at the reservoir and to break out and withdraw to the low land. I was then placed in charge of evacuating U.S. troops and supplies from Hungnam and was the last person to leave the port.

I won't recount in detail the devastating effects of our ill-fated east coast invasion. Suffice it to say that the second lesson I learned from MacArthur was that big risks can also result in colossal failures.

Having rejoined X Corps, which had redeployed to the southern part of Korea, I was assigned as second in command of the 38th Infantry (Rock of the Marne) Regiment. Six months later I was placed in command of the regiment, and we participated in several very bloody battles. On September 15, 1951, my regiment was ordered to capture Hill 1215. This hill, 1,215 meters high, was the key to winning other battles on lower hills to our flank. I mobilized every clerk, cook, and even tank crew to backpack ammunition around-the-clock for seventy-two hours to fire bases on the spurs of Hill 1215. It took the soldiers six hours to climb up to the fire bases and two hours to come down, after which I allowed them to rest for four hours. Some soldiers dropped from sheer fatigue, but most continued to build up stockpiles of thousands of rounds of mortar and rocket ammunition. This allowed us to put down an unusually heavy and unexpected amount of firepower—about ten times the normal amount—on the enemy defending the hill. Although more than 200 Chinese soldiers were killed or wounded, our regiment did not suffer a single fatality. Criticized by some for wasting ammunition, I considered September 15, 1951, the proudest day of my Army career.

The next six months proved highly frustrating. Negotiations concerning a cease-fire had begun, and my regiment was ordered to patrol actively to determine the enemy's intentions so we would not be surprised if he attacked. Yet, because Washington wanted to avoid criticism of prejudicing the negotiations, I was not permitted to commit more than a platoon of thirty men to any operation. Under a great deal of pressure by my division commander to show some tangible results from our patrolling, I ordered a platoon-size attack on a hill between the enemy's front line and our own, where we could see that several Chinese soldiers had established a listening post forward of our position. During the attack, we received an unexpected amount of enemy fire, which pinned down my platoon. The troops could not advance and suffered casualties when they tried to withdraw. The temperature had dropped to 20 degrees below zero and the troops were freezing in their immobile positions. To break the stalemate, I ordered the remainder of the company, about 100 men, to attack through the pinned-down platoon, seize any enemy soldiers who might still be at their listening post, and return. The attack was successful, and the company captured two prisoners.

Several hours later, Brig. Gen. Hayden Boatner, the acting division commander, arrived at my regimental command post. He told me he had been instructed by Washington to relieve me of command because I had committed more than a platoon to combat. When I explained to Boatner what had happened, he told me I had done the only sensible thing and that my violation of orders was a technical one. Boatner sent a message to Washington explaining what had happened, adding that he was reinstating me in command. Several hours later, Boatner received a second message from Washington instructing him to carry out his original orders. Boatner wired back: "Colonel Rowny took the proper action under the circumstances. I have reinstated him in command and will not relieve him. If you must relieve someone, relieve me." Faced with Boatner's forthright and courageous action, Washington relented and wired back that he should disregard its messages.

During my remaining months in Korea, I took an interest in the cease-fire negotiations. Although I was not directly involved, I followed the talks closely and made several trips to Panmunjom to speak to Adm. C. Turner Joy and our other negotiators. I learned that the North Korean negotiating team was following the tactics and techniques prescribed by Moscow. The North Korean negotiators tried to control the agenda, they stalled, and they built in loopholes. They used every negotiating trick in the Soviet book.

Following the Korean War, I was assigned to the Infantry School at Fort Benning, Georgia, to help revise Army tactics in light of the Korean experience. I explored new ideas such as the use of helicopters as weapons platforms and the possible use of tactical atomic weapons. Since both of these ideas went beyond approved doctrine and cut across the lines of service responsibilities, I developed them in off-duty, voluntary sessions, which I called PROFIT (Professional Improvement Time). One of these sessions was attended by a remarkably well-informed captain of the Army reserves who was undergoing a two-week obligated tour of duty. He was Congressman Henry ("Scoop") Jackson from the state of Washington. Jackson liked what he heard and several days later called to tell me he had reported to the chief of staff of the Army that my ideas should become Army doctrine. Several days later, I was summoned to Washington. Expecting to be praised, I was instead admonished for "exacerbating inter-Service rivalries." I was ordered to shut down my PROFIT sessions. My teaching was to reflect only "approved doctrine" and be conducted in regularly scheduled programs. Apparently I had learned too well from my former bosses, most of whom set strong examples as innovators and risk-takers. What I lacked was four stars of power.

A year later, General Norstad "rescued" me from my difficult situation at Fort Benning and asked that I be assigned to NATO headquarters, where he was deputy to Gen. Alfred Gruenther, the Supreme Allied Commander in Europe (SACEUR). There I contributed to the revision of U.S. nuclear policy, which at the time was based solely on massive retaliation in response to an atomic attack. Norstad was developing the strategy of flexible response and forward defense, a strategy that called for deploying troops to the front in the event of a ground attack and responding with measured steps. If necessary, these steps would include the selective use of tactical nuclear weapons. My participation in the formulation of these new policies stood me in good stead during my later negotiations with the Soviets.

In 1961, I was awarded my first star and as a newly promoted brigadier general became assistant division commander of the 82d Airborne Division. Several months later, Secretary of Defense Robert McNamara directed the Army to assemble all of its fixed- and rotary-wing aircraft at Fort Bragg, North Carolina. Gen. Hamilton ("Ham") Howze was instructed to devise ways to maximize the potential of Army aviation by improving the Army's mobility and firepower. I was made the director of tests for the Howze Board and conducted experiments with Army aviation in three types of operations. The first employed helicopters in conjunction with possible use of tactical nuclear weapons. I had developed this idea, which I called Swarm of Bees, during the PROFIT sessions at Fort Benning. The aim was to land soldiers dressed in protective clothing into the "eye" of an atomic burst. The notion was that troops could quickly take over while the enemy was still in a state of shock. The second type of experiments became known as "Sky Cav" operations. The idea was simple—outflank and outmaneuver the enemy by transporting troops by helicopter instead of vehicles. The third set of experiments explored the use of helicopters to fight terrorists and insurgents. By flying fast and low, helicopters could land troops to the flanks or in the rear of the guerrillas and capture them. Weapons on helicopter platforms could successfully deliver accurate and discriminating firepower, in contrast to the less accurate bombs delivered by Air Force fixed-wing aircraft.

The Howze Board tests were highly successful. In 1962, after they were finished, I was nominated for a second star and assigned to command the 1st Cavalry Division in Korea. I never got there, and in fact my promotion was delayed because Cyrus Vance, then secretary of the Army, decided to send me to Vietnam to introduce armed helicopters into combat against the Vietcong.

This was not an easy assignment, largely because I was caught in the middle of a roles-and-missions fight among the services. The Air Force considered that any firepower delivered from an airborne platform was solely within its area of responsibility. The Navy, although it had control of aircraft on its carriers, feared that the Army's moves would eventually encroach on the Navy's prerogatives, and therefore backed the Air Force. One would have expected me to have the backing of the Army. But that was not the case. The Army's top military leadership was at that time dominated by officers who backed the expanded use of armor. To them, in an era of limited resources, each helicopter the Army bought would be at the expense of a tank. Moreover, Gen. Earle ("Bus") Wheeler, the chief of staff of the Army, was ambitious to become chairman of the Joint Chiefs of Staff. Apparently he felt that the best way to accomplish this was to appear nonparochial, so he bent over backwards and backed the Air Force and Navy. Despite this lack of support from any of the services, the experiments with helicopters in Vietnam were successful and led to the subsequent deployment of the Army's air assault divisions in Vietnam.

Although later promoted to two-star rank, I paid a price for my success with helicopters in Vietnam. Gen. Harold K. Johnson, who succeeded Wheeler as chief of staff of the Army, continued to support the notion that every helicopter acquired by the Army meant one less tank. Also like Wheeler, he wanted to avoid being considered parochial. He did not like what I was doing and told me that "over his dead body" would I ever be promoted. He was true to his word; not until after he was replaced as chief of staff by Gen. William Westmoreland some four years later was I promoted to three-star rank.

As a three-star general, I was assigned in 1971 to NATO as deputy to Gen. Johannes Steinhoff, a German Air Force officer. Steinhoff was a highly competent and courageous officer. During World War II he was one of Germany's top aces and was assigned to command the first group of jet-propelled fighter aircraft. Fighting against English bombers during the day and American bombers at night, Steinhoff found himself defending an ever-shrinking Third Reich. In January 1945, when Reichsmarshall Hermann Göring ordered the use of Me 262 jet fighters as bombers, Steinhoff and five other officers tried to remove Göring from his command. Not able to get to see Adolf Hitler, they decided to confront Göring himself. Göring listened to what they had to say but terminated the discussion by calling their action a mutiny and threatened to have their spokesman, Oberst Franz Lütsow, shot. They went back to their units to do the best they could until the end of the war. Several days before the war ended, Steinhoff's jet aircraft crashed, and he was badly burned.

Steinhoff's courage was exemplified by the way he handled his injuries. He lost his ears, nose, lips, and eyelids in the crash. Over a twenty-year period and more than twenty operations, he had his face rebuilt by plastic surgery. Although he did not lose his eyesight, he had to put eyedrops in his eyes every hour. Despite his handicaps, Steinhoff rose to become chief of Germany's postwar Luftwaffe and subsequently the first German appointed chairman of NATO's Military Committee.

Several NATO countries, remembering their treatment at the hands of the Nazis, objected to a German heading the Military Committee. Steinhoff, for example, was never permitted to visit NATO troops in Norway. He took these slights and insults in good grace. "If I were in their shoes," he told me, "I too might resent seeing a German at the head of the Military Committee."

When I arrived in Brussels, Steinhoff put me in charge of drawing up plans for Mutual and Balanced Force Reductions. Two years earlier, in 1969, Soviet General Secretary Leonid Brezhnev had announced that he would like to "taste the wine" and explore reductions of conventional forces. The United States was not ready at that time to reduce conventional forces in Europe. By placing me, a U.S. officer, in charge of developing MBFR and making me the head of a working group involving all NATO countries, Steinhoff outmaneuvered the United States and forced it to cooperate. A year later, the United States changed its policy and backed MBFR.

In early 1973 I was summoned to Washington to report to Adm. Tom Moorer, chairman of the Joint Chiefs of Staff (JCS). I thought I had been called back to report on the progress of MBFR. Instead, Admiral Moorer told me that Henry Kissinger, then Richard Nixon's national security advisor, said that I was to be the Joint Chiefs' representative to the Strategic Arms Limitations Talks (SALT). I told Moorer I would prefer to remain in my NATO job, that I liked working for Steinhoff and believed that advancing MBFR was more important than joining SALT.

"That's fine," said Moorer. "I have a Navy admiral in mind for the job. Besides, no one is going to tell me who I should have as my representative at the SALT talks. Over my dead body will you be my representative."

I was delighted, but the next day he sent for me again. When I went into his office, he leaned back in his chair, extended his arms, and said, "I'm dead." Moorer told me what he had learned—Kissinger and Jackson had made a deal in the summer of 1972 whereby Jackson would support the Antiballistic Missile (ABM) treaty and I would become the JCS representative to SALT. Moorer said that he also learned that Kissinger had "gone to the president with the deal and 'the German' got his way."

I went to see my friend Scoop Jackson. "Why are you doing this to me?" I asked. "Why are you again interfering with my career?"

"Because you're the best qualified U.S. officer for the job," he said. "You've studied nuclear policy and deterrence theory, you've studied the Soviets, you know how they negotiate, and you speak Russian." His lecture on duty, honor, country and sincere commitment to national security left me with no rebuttal, even though I knew that if I became JCS representative I would never achieve my lifelong goal of pinning on a fourth star.

As my career had evolved over the years, I had indeed become uniquely qualified for a job as arms negotiator. My education and knowledge of the Soviet mind-set, my experience in war and dealings with foreign governments and peoples, and my assignment to NATO and to force planning and doctrine tasks provided me with a solid framework for becoming a player in the arms control game. And my personal relationship with Senator Scoop Jackson, a very powerful influence in the U.S. government at the time, was the key to unlocking the door to the career that would dominate the rest of my life. It was a career that would put me into close contact with five American presidents.

I would discover that I often had to spend as much time negotiating with the strong personalities within the U.S. government as I did with the implacable Soviets. I was, at times, appalled by the lack of judgment and knowledge displayed by a president or secretary of state. On other occasions, I was heartened by the wisdom shown by the nation's leaders.

In taking up my new career during the often tumultuous days of

Richard Nixon's second term, I would find myself dealing with two of the most intriguing characters in modern U.S. history, Richard Nixon and Henry Kissinger. Each of them already had a formidable record in foreign policy; Nixon had a more mixed record on the home front. I would soon gain unexpected insights into both their policies and their personalities.

CHAPTER 2

The Nixon Years: A Close Call

R ichard Nixon was the first president to espouse "linkage" as a component of U.S. foreign policy. He believed—incorrectly, as it turned out—that the Soviets' desire to reach an arms control agreement was so strong that they would cooperate in other areas of international competition, particularly Vietnam, in return for U.S. participation in arms control negotiations. He outlined this concept in his first presidential press conference on January 27, 1969. After making it clear that the Nixon administration would encourage negotiations on strategic arms, he added an important condition: talks had to occur in a way that would "promote, if possible, progress on outstanding political problems at the same time."

Nixon fully understood that the Soviet Union's desire for an arms control agreement with the United States was based on calculations of self-interest. He knew they believed that lessening strategic tensions with the United States would result in a much-needed infusion of Western trade and technology into the stagnant Soviet economy. Furthermore, Nixon understood the Soviets' primary international goals and methods of operation. He knew they sought to use the process of arms control to give legitimacy to their claim of superpower status, and to foster the impression that they were in the vanguard of promoting international peace. Nixon reasoned that he could use these Soviet tactics to his advantage. But the Soviets had other priorities. They understood that Nixon's desire to disentangle the United States from Vietnam gave them bargaining leverage that they could use to perpetuate the process of arms control without actually making substantive progress or linking the negotiations to cooperation in other areas.

Immediately prior to Nixon's inaugural, the man he had chosen to be his national security advisor, Henry Kissinger, received a favorable response from Moscow to an unofficial probe outlining the new policy of linkage. In Kissinger's words, "The Soviet leaders recognized that our relations would be favorably affected by a settlement of the Vietnam problem, a political solution in the Middle East, and a 'realistic approach' in Europe. . . ." When Secretary of State William Rogers first met with Soviet Ambassador Anatoli Dobrynin a month later, however, Dobrynin told him that although the Soviets were prepared to move ahead on SALT, they were unhappy with the idea that the United States wanted to tie progress in the negotiations to advances in other areas. The Soviets gave no explanation as to why they shifted their position. Nevertheless, Nixon continued to believe that the Soviets would realize the advantages of linkage and would eventually become more cooperative. Nixon persisted even though he knew that his efforts would run into opposition with an American public that did not want to see any obstacles placed in the way of an arms control agreement.

From his previous political experience, most notably his service as Dwight Eisenhower's vice president, Nixon had developed an abiding distrust of government bureaucrats. He went so far as to question their commitment to implementing presidential policies. He was convinced that if his initiatives were to meet with success, he and Henry Kissinger would need to maintain complete control over the foreign policy apparatus, and to operate in utmost secrecy. Accordingly, he told Ambassador Dobrynin on February 17, 1969, that all matters of "special sensitivity" were to be handled secretly through a private channel with Kissinger rather than through the State Department. This opened a Pandora's box of events that backfired on Nixon. Kissinger began to use the back-channel extensively—and subsequently to excess—resulting in an unprecedented and dangerous concentration of power in the hands of a nonelected official.

The back-channel was first used several weeks later, when Kissinger told Dobrynin that U.S.-Soviet relations were "at a crossroads" and that the United States was "prepared to make progress . . . on a broad front." He emphasized that the Vietnam War was a major obstacle to such progress and that the United States wanted Soviet assistance in bringing about negotiations to end the war. Kissinger proposed to send Cyrus Vance (later President Jimmy Carter's secretary of state) to Moscow, ostensibly to discuss SALT but in fact to meet secretly with North Vietnamese representatives to lay the groundwork for a peace settlement. Kissinger added, rather ominously, that if U.S. moves to end the war were not reciprocated, the United States would have no choice but to escalate the war rapidly, causing U.S.-Soviet relations to suffer. "A settlement on Vietnam was the key to everything," Kissinger said.

Dobrynin asked him point-blank if the United States was making resolution of the Vietnam War a precondition for progress on SALT. Kissinger hedged, afraid that if he pressed too hard for linkage it would jeopardize the dialogue he was trying to establish on arms control. He simply replied that progress in U.S.-Soviet relations would be more rapid if the Vietnam War were brought to a close. Ambassador Dobrynin countered with the disingenuous assertion that the Soviet Union had only limited influence over North Vietnam and that it was China that was seeking to poison U.S.-Soviet relations. Escalation of the war, he said, would only serve Chinese interests. He assured Kissinger that he would forward his views to higher authority, but Moscow never replied to Kissinger's proposal on the Vance mission.

A month later, realizing that his initial attempt to link the SALT negotiations to an end to the war in Vietnam had gone nowhere, Nixon resorted to public diplomacy. In a speech on May 14, 1969, he appealed directly to the North Vietnamese to bring the war to a close. He did not mention the Soviet Union or China directly, but he did say that if the United States were to unilaterally withdraw and permit a military victory by the North, international confrontation would escalate and the "era of negotiations" would be jeopardized.

Although Nixon was willing to be patient and give linkage additional time to work, mounting public pressure in the United States for opening SALT negotiations forced his hand. Unable to convince his domestic critics that he was not stalling, on June 11, 1969, he instructed Secretary of State William Rogers to notify Moscow that the United States was prepared to begin talks on limiting arms.

Even before he made that decision, Nixon realized that to avoid a situation where public opinion might pressure him into accepting an unfavorable arms control agreement, he would need to acquire additional negotiating leverage. After much careful study, Nixon announced in March 1969 that he would ask Congress to authorize the Safeguard antiballistic missile system. Unlike its predecessor, Sentinel, which was originally designed to protect U.S. cities from a limited Chinese nuclear attack, Safeguard's primary mission was to defend U.S. land-based missiles from a possible Soviet first strike. Nixon was aware that Safeguard would not accomplish that mission without a greater commitment of funds than the Congress would support.

To placate growing criticism that he was abandoning the defense of American cities, Nixon's Safeguard proposal called for twelve interceptor sites as well as comprehensive radar coverage of the continental United States. The true value of Safeguard, Nixon reasoned, was to gain negotiating leverage over the Soviets, who were moving ahead with an ABM system of their own. He forwarded his request to the Senate where the debate, as expected, was intense. Finally, by a margin of only one vote (cast by Vice President Spiro Agnew), the Senate approved the deployment of Safeguard. The Senate's irresolute backing for an ABM system was a clear signal to the Soviets that Nixon's domestic support was weak and would serve to undermine his policy of linkage.

THE CHINA CARD

Nixon's approach to negotiating with the Soviet Union was complicated by a determination to simultaneously rebuild relations with the People's Republic of China (PRC). A careful observer might have discerned a new approach to the PRC formulating in Nixon's mind. A year before his election, Nixon had written a significant article for *Foreign Affairs* suggesting a new initiative aimed at Communist China. He concluded, "Taking the long view, we simply cannot afford to leave China forever outside the family of nations." Nixon believed that by opening diplomatic relations with the PRC he could capitalize on deteriorating Sino-Soviet relations and gain leverage he could exchange for Soviet cooperation on Vietnam. The Soviets and the Chinese had engaged in a series of armed border clashes from March to December 1969, and tensions were high in both capitals.

In the first months of his administration, Nixon had done little to help his own cause of liberalizing relations with China. In fact, numerous confusing policy statements alluding to the "Chinese threat" caused relations to deteriorate. The Sino-Soviet border clashes provided the opportunity he sought to bring about closer ties with the PRC.

Although Kissinger later claimed a large part of the credit, he did not originally share Nixon's enthusiasm for expanded relations with China, a point which Kissinger acknowledges in his writings. The China initiative was Nixon's brainchild alone, based largely on his perception that he could reap gains from Sino-Soviet tension. Kissinger was more interested in improving U.S.-Soviet relations and feared that playing China and the Soviet Union against one another would upset our relationship with the Soviet Union. But being "present at the creation" of a historic moment was simply too good an opportunity for Kissinger to turn his back on.

In the summer of 1969, Nixon embarked on a multination tour. During his travels, he cautiously and carefully let it be known that the United States was interested in improving relations with the PRC. Diplomatic back-channels were opened to Peking through Romania and Pakistan, among the few countries on good terms with both the United States and China. By the end of the year, the groundwork had been laid, and the Washington-Beijing-Moscow diplomatic triangle began to take shape. Nixon moved adroitly and took great pains to assure the world, particularly Moscow, that improved U.S.-Chinese relations were not intended to be achieved at the expense of any other country. But the meaning of Nixon's overtures to China were not lost on Moscow, and there can be little doubt that they stimulated Soviet cooperation in arms control later that year.

NIXON DOCTRINE

In the fall of 1969, after Nixon returned from his tour, he turned his attention to his major preoccupation, resolving the Vietnam War. One of Nixon's primary campaign promises had been to end the war and bring U.S. troops home. Although he had begun to accomplish the latter goal with the return of 25,000 troops in June, a permanent peace remained elusive.

Secretary of Defense Melvin Laird had coined the awkward term *Vietnamization* in March of 1969 to justify reducing U.S. troop levels in Asia. Although the effort met with public support in the United States, the prospect of a complete American troop withdrawal caused concern internationally. It was perceived as a unilateral reduction of

U.S. overseas commitments and an abdication of international responsibility.

Nixon moved to stem that concern by formulating a comprehensive new approach to American obligations abroad. The Nixon doctrine emphasized U.S. economic and material aid, and narrowed the conditions under which large contingents of U.S. troops would be committed to overseas operations. The plan envisioned the development of regional power centers, which, with U.S. assistance, would contain low-intensity conflicts in their respective spheres of interest. The United States would exercise a certain degree of control over those centers by manipulating levels of economic and military aid.

While the theory looked good on paper, it had a number of drawbacks when applied directly to the war in Vietnam. First and foremost, it severely curtailed Nixon's negotiating room with the North Vietnamese. If the leaders in Hanoi were to take Nixon at his word, why should they negotiate a peace treaty when it would only be a matter of time before all U.S. troops were evacuated?

But Nixon had no intention of completely abandoning the South Vietnamese. He was convinced that a gradual reduction in U.S. forces could be balanced by a combination of massive military aid to the South and extensive deployment of U.S. tactical air power and conventionally armed B-52 heavy bombers. The trick was to convince the North, as well as the Soviets, that he was ready to use such force in the face of the predictably negative impact it would have on U. S. public opinion.

Meanwhile, Nixon's efforts on China and his pursuit of antiballistic missile defenses began to pay dividends. On October 20, 1969, Ambassador Dobrynin informed the president that the Soviets were prepared to begin strategic arms talks. Nixon, euphoric over the apparent success of his maneuvering, once again tried to link the talks to the Vietnam War. He instructed Kissinger to put pressure on the Soviets, through the back-channel, to address the Vietnamese situation. He told Kissinger to say that the United States was willing to resort to extreme measures to bring the war to an end. Kissinger, knowing that the United States had no plans to escalate the conflict and fearing that such a heavy-handed ploy would disrupt the budding SALT negotiations, ignored Nixon's instructions. This marked the beginning of growing tensions between Nixon and his national security advisor. When I became an arms negotiator in 1973, I heard

Kissinger's staff say on several occasions that their boss thought Nixon was going down the wrong track on arms control.

Shortly before joining Nixon's staff, Kissinger, too, had written a piece for *Foreign Affairs*. In the article, Kissinger made clear his skepticism that a military victory in Vietnam could be won and encouraged turning over a larger share of combat responsibility to the South Vietnamese. Nixon's attempts to link Vietnam with SALT seem only to have reaffirmed Kissinger's beliefs and increased his disenchantment with linkage. Moreover, his frequent discussions with Ambassador Dobrynin and Foreign Minister Andrei Gromyko led Kissinger to conclude that arms control negotiations with the Soviets were more critical to U.S. interests than an early end to the war in Southeast Asia.

Dobrynin, closely following what was going on in the White House, sensed the direction of Nixon's efforts despite Kissinger's failure to convey the president's warning. When the Soviet ambassador informed Nixon of Moscow's willingness to begin negotiations, he slipped in the barb that Nixon's proposed method of solving the Vietnam question by using force was extremely dangerous. Dobrynin, also aware of Nixon's overtures to the PRC, added that if the United States was tempted to profit from deteriorating Sino-Soviet relations at the Soviet Union's expense, it would prove to be a serious miscalculation.

Dobrynin's remarks got Nixon's back up, and his response was equally blunt. In his autobiography, *R. N.*, Nixon said he told Dobrynin that "the only beneficiary of U.S.-Soviet disagreement over Vietnam is China and that now was the last opportunity of settling the Vietnam War." Becoming almost hysterical, Nixon added, "You may think that you can break me. . . . You may believe that the American domestic situation is unmanageable, [but] I want you to understand that the Soviet Union is going to be stuck with me for the next three years and three months. If the Soviet Union will not help us get peace, then we will have to pursue our own methods of bringing the war to an end."

Despite this tension, arms control negotiations got underway in Helsinki, Finland, on November 17, 1969. They lasted two-and-one-half years and encompassed seven separate rounds of talks. During the first round of SALT, the Soviets appeared willing to discuss placing limits on highly destabilizing land-based intercontinental ballistic missiles (ICBMs), the primary U.S. objective. But at the second round of negotiations, in April 1970 in Vienna, the Soviets reversed the thrust of their previous proposals and sought to exclude ICBMs from the negotiations. The new Soviet agenda called exclusively for limiting defense-oriented antiballistic missile systems.

The United States insisted that placing limits on ICBMs was paramount. Any constraint on defensive systems would need to be accompanied by simultaneous limits on strategic offensive arms. The Soviets, while unwilling to put limits on the numbers, size, and throw-weight of offensive missiles, indicated that they would be willing to place limits on the number of multiple independently targetable reentry vehicles (MIRVs) a missile could carry. They realized that the United States was ahead of them in MIRV technology. Putting limits on MIRVs would allow them to maintain their lead in strategic offensive capability. It was precisely for this reason that the Pentagon did not want to see a ban on MIRVs and convinced President Nixon to back its position. Thus, while the United States was unwilling to place limits on strategic defenses unless they were accompanied by limits on offensive weapons, we wanted such limits to be restricted to the numbers, size, and throw-weight of ballistic missiles and not to the number of warheads they could carry.

HENRY WHO?

The Nixon-Kissinger relationship was a critical factor in the president's approach to foreign policy. Kissinger was brilliant and energetic, but mercurial and enigmatic. Almost instantly, he could shift from being withdrawn and melancholy to being outgoing and effusive.

I first heard about Kissinger from officers who studied at Harvard University in the early 1960s where he taught international relations and nuclear diplomacy. I also heard a great deal about Kissinger from my close friend, Dr. Fritz Kraemer, who served as a foreign policy advisor to the secretaries of defense in the 1960s and 1970s. Kraemer and I were classmates at the National War College in 1958. In the final semester, I had the good fortune of sharing first place with Kraemer in the annual term paper competition. It was customary for the winner to present his paper to the class, and we were both called upon to do so. Kraemer gave a brilliant presentation; he acted out the four protagonists of his paper, each in a different language. Like my fellow classmates, I was spellbound and forgot most of what I wanted to say about my own paper.

Kraemer, a Prussian by birth and temperament, had left Germany for the United States in the late 1930s when he could do no more to prevent Hitler's rise to power. Kraemer was forced to leave behind his Swedish-born wife, Britta, and their infant son, Sven. (Later, Sven, already in the NSC, became a member of Kissinger's staff after Kissinger became national security advisor to the president.)

Fritz Kraemer arrived in the United States in 1939, with little money and few friends. He moved from job to job while trying to earn his U.S. citizenship and convince the FBI that he was not a German spy. Finally, in 1943, on the same day that he became a citizen of his adopted country, Kraemer was inducted into the U.S. Army. Anxious to join the war against those who had forced him from his ancestral home, he won his arguments against those in the United States who thought he should not be sent to fight in the European theater. Kraemer further proved his Prussian stubbornness by insisting that he be permitted to wear a monocle while in uniform. He was the only soldier in the U.S. armed forces to be granted that right.

In the last days of the war in Europe, Kraemer, who was then in the 84th Infantry Division, learned that a unit of General Patton's Third Army had liberated the village where Kraemer's wife and son had taken refuge in the family's hunting lodge. Kraemer wrote a memorandum to General Patton, through channels, asking that his family be sought out and protected. A man of high principle, Kraemer considered it improper to leave his own unit while it was engaged in combat. On V-E Day, Kraemer asked for and was granted a week's leave. A day later he drove into the village and spotted his wife. Not wanting to create a scene, Kraemer had his driver take him to the outskirts of the village. He then had his driver go back for Mrs. Kraemer and bring her to his location, where they were joyfully reunited after a six-and-one-half-year separation.

Kraemer "discovered" Kissinger under rather unusual circumstances. During World War II, Kissinger was a private in the Army assigned to a special unit of soldiers with very high IQs. The Army was searching for ways to use the talents of these highly gifted draftees and had grouped them in one battalion with the intention of sending them to school, an idea that was later abandoned. Kraemer and Kissinger met when they were assigned to the 84th Division for standard military training.

Kraemer, despite his gifted intellect and numerous advanced academic degrees, was at the time also a private. Later, he was to be awarded a battlefield commission and become a lieutenant, the oldest soldier in the Army to receive such a distinction. Because of Kraemer's background, he was able to convince his commanding officer to allow him to address the special group of gifted soldiers on U.S. war aims. He found the unit resting during a march at its Louisiana training grounds in 1944, and for the next twenty minutes gave them a stirring "why we fight" talk. As one of those present later told me, Kraemer delivered an impassioned speech from the hood of a jeep. Animated and perspiring, he received a standing ovation.

That afternoon, Kraemer received a letter of appreciation from a "Pvt. H. Kissinger." Kissinger asked to meet with Kraemer to discuss the finer points of his presentation. Kraemer obligingly looked him up, and the two had an hour-long conversation. "My first impression of Kissinger," Kraemer told me, "was that he was brilliant—obviously a gifted person. He knew nothing but understood everything."

The chance meeting started a long friendship between the two. Kissinger told Kraemer that he hoped to become an accountant. Kraemer suggested to the young soldier that he could do much better and should set his sights on higher goals. Kraemer did not then know that he had stung Kissinger's sensibilities. Kissinger's father was an accountant, and Henry wanted to follow in his footsteps. But Kraemer counseled his young protégé to pursue studies in foreign affairs. Kissinger took Kraemer's advice and was awarded a scholarship to attend Harvard University to study international relations.

After receiving his undergraduate degree, Kissinger remained at Harvard to pursue graduate studies. His doctoral dissertation, *A World Restored*, was subsequently published and is considered by many to be his most enduring intellectual effort. Author and former Kissinger aide Roger Morris described it as "a penetrating, sometimes wry study of the diplomats and diplomacy of the decade after the Napoleonic Wars, [that] was obviously a labor of intellectual love. Into it, Kissinger poured his most creative and practical insights about the politics of foreign policy."

In 1957, when he was thirty-four years old, Kissinger, then teaching at Harvard, became instantly famous for his prize-winning book, *Nuclear Weapons and Foreign Policy*. He had written it while chairing a study group on nuclear policy for the prestigious Council on Foreign Relations. Kissinger persuaded the council to let him edit and expand upon the group's recommendations. In the resulting book, Kissinger disclosed that his approach to international relations was a blend of cynicism and pragmatic idealism.

In 1958 Kissinger prepared another special report on national security issues, this time for the Rockefeller Brothers Fund. Through this effort, he became acquainted with Nelson Rockefeller, who became his lifelong friend and benefactor. That same year, he was appointed associate director of Harvard's highly regarded Center for International Affairs.

Kissinger's first experience in government came in 1961 when for a short time he was a consultant to the National Security Council during the Kennedy administration. It was not a happy experience for the young academic. He described it in his book, *White House Years:*

> The very nature of an outside consultancy, and my own academic self-centeredness, as yet untempered by exposure to the daily pressures of the Presidency, combined to make this a frustrating experience on all sides. . . . With little understanding then of how the Presidency worked, I consumed my energies in offering unwanted advice and, in our infrequent contact, inflicting on President Kennedy learned disquisitions about which he could have done nothing even in the unlikely event that they aroused his interest.

Ironically, Kissinger emerged from this frustrating experience having learned a lesson of critical importance about being near the center of power. He later told journalist Oriana Fallaci, "What interests me is what you can do with power." When he came to work for Nixon, his first priority was to move quickly into a position where he could gain and hold the president's confidence.

Shortly after Nixon was elected, his staff called Kissinger and arranged for the two to meet at Nixon's office in the Hotel Pierre in New York. Kissinger, with the approval of Nelson Rockefeller, whom Nixon had defeated for the Republican presidential nomination, provided the president-elect with an elaborate set of briefing papers on various foreign policy issues that had been prepared originally for the Rockefeller campaign. Not sure of the purpose of the meeting, Kissinger hoped at best to be offered the job as head of the Policy Planning Group at the State Department. To Kissinger's great surprise, particularly in light of Nixon's unfamiliarity with Kissinger and his well-known antipathy toward the "liberal Eastern establishment," Nixon asked Kissinger to become his national security advisor.

By offering Kissinger the job, Nixon sought the respectability that an advisor from the Ivy League would bring his administration. For his part, Kissinger craved the power and prestige that would flow from a highly placed position in the administration. *New York Times* columnist William Safire, then a Nixon speechwriter, was quoted on this odd but reciprocal relationship in Marvin L. Kalb and Bernard Kalb's book, *Kissinger:*

> You've got to remember that Nixon was not always sought after by intellectuals, to put it mildly. He'd heard about Kissinger, one of the crown jewels in the Rockefeller diadem. He knew that he needed intellectual content in his administration. And he was rich—rich in power. He could offer Kissinger something that Kissinger couldn't refuse, to use "Godfather" terminology. He could offer him the action, the power, the center, and there was nothing he could offer before that could get Kissinger away from Rockefeller. He took a certain delight in that.

Kissinger accepted Nixon's offer with alacrity despite his earlier bad experience as a consultant. He had once confided to a Harvard classmate: "Washington is a terrible place. Everyone cuts everybody else's throat. Only a son-of-a-bitch can succeed." It wasn't too long afterwards, this classmate told me, that Kissinger began living up to his own prescription for success.

Kissinger had a knack for choosing friends who could help his career. He would add to the ranks of his associates those who could be of assistance, while discarding those who were no longer useful. "The secret of my success," Kissinger once said, "is I forget my old friends."

Between the time he met Nixon in New York and the inaugural, Kissinger devised an ingenious scheme under which the national security advisor would tower over the State and Defense Departments in the formulation of U.S. foreign policy. His plan centered on placing himself between the cabinet members (and the bureaucracies they represented) and the president. All foreign policy recommendations would be passed along to Kissinger, who would then add his own judgments and opinions before submitting them to the president.

Under Secretary of State for Political Affairs U. Alexis Johnson, the number-three man at the State Department, realized that Kissinger was engineering a clever bureaucratic end run, and tried to prevent the plan from being instituted. Kissinger, anticipating such resistance, asked Gen. Andrew Goodpaster, who had administered the

National Security Council (NSC) for President Eisenhower, to give the plan his blessing. Goodpaster's reputation was so distinguished that Melvin Laird and William Rogers, the secretaries of defense and state, bowed to Goodpaster's judgment when he okayed the scheme. I am certain my old friend and former colleague had no idea at the time that he would be instrumental in setting up procedures that would ultimately be exploited by Kissinger to gain full control of the foreign policy apparatus.

Once Nixon brought him to Washington, Kissinger became a weekly visitor to Fritz Kraemer's home, where he sought Kraemer's advice and poured out his most intimate hopes and fears. Kraemer had high regard for Kissinger's brilliance as a diplomatic historian. Their long discussions of such historically pivotal personalities as Bismarck and Metternich were a constant source of intellectual satisfaction for both men. Although Kraemer never shared Kissinger's confidences with me, he nevertheless told me a great deal about this complex man. To Kraemer, Kissinger was Machiavelli (because of his love of intrigue), Talleyrand (because of his passion for negotiation), and Rasputin (because of his hold on the lives of others) all rolled into one.

Kissinger was a difficult person to work with and an impossible person to work for. His temper and brusque manner were legendary. On one occasion, I was seated next to a State Department official at a sub-cabinet level meeting where we were developing a proposal on how to deal with the Soviets' large inventory of heavy missiles. During the discussion, my neighbor passed me a note: "Are Henry's statements correct?"

"No," I wrote back. "He's wrong."

"Shall I correct him?" he scribbled.

"Only if you want to get fired," I whispered. "Tell him privately, later. If you tell him now, Henry will blow up; he can't stomach criticism."

My friend ignored the advice. He suggested, in a carefully worded and respectful manner, that Kissinger might want to check his facts. Kissinger's face momentarily went white. Then, after regaining his composure, he coolly thanked him. The next day my friend learned that he was being unceremoniously detailed to a foreign assignment.

Soon after becoming the JCS representative to SALT in March 1973, I became the JCS chairman's principal advisor on arms control and had ample opportunity to witness first-hand Kissinger's volatile personality. I attended all National Security Council meetings on arms control and saw that Kissinger routinely ran roughshod over those who disagreed with his views, including his most trusted advisors—Bill Hyland, Larry Eagleburger, and Hal Sonnenfeld.

Kissinger had his own ideas about how to use staff experts, analysts, and planners. Like Nixon, he considered such bureaucrats necessary evils. For Kissinger, the bureaucracy was useful only in fostering the illusion that various government agencies were being consulted and their recommendations taken into account. In fact, Kissinger brooked no outside interference in what he considered his personal domain. More often than not, he would put the bureaucracy to work on tangentially relevant, but ultimately meaningless, aspects of important issues.

It is an understatement to say that, in his dealings with others, Kissinger did not suffer fools (or anyone for that matter) gladly. He felt intellectually superior to most and so classified them as incompetents, including Bill Clements, Nixon's original deputy secretary of defense. Clements was respectful and deferential to Kissinger, but his willingness to take a back seat made him all the more vulnerable to Kissinger's mean streak.

At a cabinet meeting in 1974 soon after Kissinger had returned from a successful meeting with Soviet Foreign Minister Andrei Gromyko, Clements congratulated Kissinger. "Henry," he said, "you did a fine job in Moscow."

Kissinger turned on his heels and snapped sarcastically, "Don't think you can butter me up with flattery." I thought Kissinger was joking, but he did not crack a smile. It was obvious to all of us present that he was putting Clements down. A stunned and flustered Clements could think of no response. He had learned that when dealing with the venerable Dr. Kissinger, even a simple compliment was dangerous.

Kissinger's personal idiosyncrasies notwithstanding, I retain a great deal of admiration and respect for him. I always found Kissinger to be smart, aggressive, able to keep a number of balls in the air at the same time, and an innovative thinker who could always be counted upon to come up with a new angle on any issue. My admiration for Kissinger was made easier because he never saw fit to castigate me as he did others. In part, I believe he treated me differently because he retained a certain amount of respect for senior military officers as a result of his wartime experiences. I noticed that Kissinger always treated his military assistants, Alexander Haig and Brent Scowcroft, better than his civilian staff. Kissinger's benevolence may also have been due in part to my friendship with Senator Scoop Jackson. Kissinger was ever mindful of the need to stroke Congress, and he had no desire to alienate the powerful senator from the state of Washington.

As a negotiating team, Nixon and Kissinger complemented each other. Nixon understood the Soviet mind-set and rapidly assimilated the broad aspects of arms control, while Kissinger mastered the many intricate details. On occasion Nixon would engage Kissinger in discussions on specific details of the negotiations, but he strictly avoided challenging Kissinger on technical issues. Some members of Kissinger's personal staff believed that Nixon avoided such confrontations because he felt intellectually inferior to Kissinger, but I do not subscribe to that view. Although Nixon was notoriously insecure, he was highly intelligent in his own right. (He had graduated at the top of his class from both college and law school.) Fritz Kraemer, who knew them both well, considered Nixon Kissinger's intellectual peer. Nixon simply lacked the temperament needed to deal with the finer points of complicated U.S. arms control proposals. After all, that is why he hired Kissinger.

The president treated Kissinger deferentially. He rarely criticized him and never in public. Kissinger, on the other hand, regularly ridiculed Nixon behind his back. On one occasion in 1973, while Kissinger was being briefed by his staff prior to an NSC meeting, Nixon sent for him. A close advisor to Kissinger later told me that Kissinger replied, "You tell our meathead President I'll be there in a few minutes." But to Nixon's face, Kissinger uttered only praise.

Use of back-channel communications fit with both Nixon's and Kissinger's love for secrecy and pathological need for control. When used sparingly and judiciously, the back-channel can be an effective and even necessary mechanism for moving negotiations along. But that was not Kissinger's main purpose in maintaining secret lines of communication with Moscow. Simply put, Kissinger was trying to bypass the entire arms negotiating process so that he could not only control what was being negotiated but also have complete freedom to develop the U.S. position in these negotiations. Both he and Nixon justified this approach as critical to linkage, but it was widely understood that the real reason was that neither man trusted the bureaucrats.

There were several critical drawbacks to this highly secretive approach. First, it kept the U.S. negotiating team in the dark as to what was being discussed at higher levels. Soviet ambassador Dobrynin, with whom Kissinger usually communicated, often informed the Soviet delegation about what was being discussed in the back-channel. This put U.S. negotiators at a tremendous disadvantage in dealing with their Soviet counterparts, who often seemed to be more in tune with shifts in U.S. policy than we were.

Second, although the Soviet negotiating team was informed about what was going on, it seldom received instructions from Moscow to implement the decisions Kissinger thought he had arrived at with Dobrynin. The U.S. negotiators, because they were kept in the dark, were unable to press the Soviets into carrying out the agreements Kissinger and Dobrynin had reached. The practical effect was that little productive work was accomplished at the negotiating table in translating back-channel agreements into treaty language.

Finally, there were certain occasions when Kissinger took it upon himself to exceed the president's instructions, discussing or even settling issues that he was not authorized to deal with. This was particularly true for certain aspects of the final agreement of SALT I in 1972.

Ambassador Gerard Smith and the State Department representative on his SALT I team, Raymond Garthoff, were both highly critical of Kissinger's back-channel approach. Smith's unhappiness was understandable, given the way he, the chief negotiator, was bypassed and kept in the dark. Garthoff observed that the back-channel suited Kissinger's style and acknowledged that at times Kissinger had acted brilliantly, but he said that Kissinger "failed to recognize the role that professional . . . diplomats could play." Kissinger's failure to get "needed advice" meant that "U.S. interests suffered."

Helmut Sonnenfeld, a member of Kissinger's personal staff, disagreed with Garthoff's criticisms, basing his arguments largely on constitutional grounds. He wrote that ". . . it is really quite absurd to suggest that the President of the United States, given his constitutional position, is somehow not entitled to deal in his own channels with other heads of government, or that the Secretary of State on behalf of the President of the United States is not entitled to deal with . . . foreign ministers . . . of other governments." However, I do not believe that the question Sonnenfeld raised is one of constitutional authority. The president and his representative clearly have the authority to deal confidentially with other governments. Rather, I believe it is a question of whether the secrecy involved, carried to extremes, ran the risks of saddling the United States with potentially disadvantageous agreements. Sonnenfeld himself seemed to suggest the solution by acknowledging the importance of keeping "front-and back-channels . . . in some kind of harmony." During Nixon's and Kissinger's time the two approaches were simply not in balance.

The relationship between Nixon and Kissinger was initially harmonious. Their first serious disagreement was about holding an early arms control summit with the Soviets. By his nature, Nixon was skeptical that presidential summits could ever meet the high expectations set by the American public. He was too much of a political realist not to understand that long-standing ideological differences were rarely resolved in the high-pressure atmosphere created by face-to-face negotiations. Nonetheless, in the spring of 1970 Nixon decided to pursue the idea of a summit. He believed that he could outmaneuver anti–Vietnam War demonstrators with a dramatic peace initiative and that such a bold gesture would help put Republican candidates into office in the next congressional elections.

Kissinger disagreed. He felt that conditions were not right for a face-to-face meeting. In the first place, the future of arms control negotiations was still up in the air. Second, the Soviets had provided no assistance in resolving issues in Southeast Asia and were dramatically escalating tensions in the Middle East. Finally, although Kissinger did not say so to Nixon directly, he told his aides that he did not believe the president was up to the test of a face-to-face summit with Soviet leader Leonid Brezhnev.

Nixon persisted in his desire to meet with the Soviets and told Kissinger to explore through the back-channel with Dobrynin the possibilities of a summit. It was at this time that the Soviets decided to play their own version of the China card. In late June 1970, the chief Soviet negotiator in Vienna, Vladimir Semenov, indiscreetly suggested to the head of the U.S. arms delegation, Gerard Smith, that if a nuclear provocation were "being prepared by a third country," the United States and the Soviet Union should notify each other of the imminent crisis. He added that if such an act resulted in an actual attack, each party would be obligated to take retaliatory action against the offender. The Soviet Union, in effect, was proposing a U.S.-Soviet security condominium against China. Sino-Soviet relations at the time were dangerously contentious, and the United States's overture to China was still in its embryonic stages. Nixon was quick to see what the Soviets were up to and instructed Smith to rebuff Semenov's suggestion.

A few years later, soon after I joined the SALT II delegation, I personally witnessed the fear and visceral hatred the Soviets had of the Chinese. During a cocktail party conversation with Soviet Col. Gen. Ivan Beletsky, Boris Klosson, the State Department representative to the arms control talks, quipped that the Soviets were too sensitive about a possible Chinese threat. "When Napoleon attacked Russia," he said, "the Russians burned all their cities between the East-West border and Moscow. Think of how many cities would have to be burned between the Chinese border and Moscow." The lump on Beletsky's forehead, the result of a World War II injury, turned red and began to blink like a tilt light on a pinball machine. Klosson quickly changed the subject.

As soon as the Soviets received a firm "no" to their China ploy, Dobrynin said the Soviets were interested in a summit and asked Kissinger to furnish him a draft agenda for meeting. Kissinger said that the United States sought to discuss SALT but also wished to discuss European security and the rising tensions in the Middle East. The Soviets appeared prepared to hold a summit on arms control but saw no reason for discussing European security and the Middle East because events in these areas were, from their point of view, progressing satisfactorily. The United States once again did not possess sufficient leverage to make linkage work, and the summit did not take place.

SALT I

In June 1970 the United States began deploying MIRVs on its Minuteman III ICBMs. These missiles, each carrying three warheads that could be aimed at separate targets, greatly improved U.S. offensive capabilities. These deployments triggered a year-long series of back-channel negotiations between Kissinger and Dobrynin. The Soviets, obviously concerned, labored intensely and successfully to redress what they perceived as strategic inferiority. They worked hard to reach numerical parity with the United States in ICBMs and showed every intention of surpassing us. Their new missiles were not only larger but also more powerful than ours.

The United States chose not to enter the race to see who could deploy more missiles. It unilaterally froze the deployment of new ICBMs and focused on "MIRVing" existing missiles. This, combined with proposed deployment of an ABM system, was designed to offset the Soviets' determination to attain and maintain greater numbers of more powerful missiles. The Soviets' insistence on limiting only defense in an ABM treaty had little to do with the alleged destabilizing effects of defense systems. Rather, they wanted to get us to limit our defenses without limiting the number or power of their offensive missiles. Meanwhile, to further increase their offensive lead, they were developing their own MIRV technology.

The United States continued to seek limits on both offensive and defensive systems but was unwilling to constrain its MIRV technology unless the Soviets were willing to commit to an overall balance in offensive power. On May 20, 1971, what was described as a compromise was announced. Both nations committed themselves to working out a limit on ABMs and agreeing to "certain measures with respect to the limitations of offensive strategic weapons." It was a rather precarious compromise because it did not make clear what was meant by "certain measures" applicable to offensive systems. The so-called compromise highly favored the Soviet Union. It proposed to place limits on defenses, where the United States was ahead, in return for promises to limit Soviet offensive capabilities.

Very little was achieved during the months following the purported compromise. To try to get the ball rolling, Nixon decided once again to pursue holding a summit with the Soviets. At first, he was willing to hold a summit even if arms control was the only topic on the agenda. Nixon believed that if he could get the Soviets to meet with him, he could broaden the discussions and get them to address a possible resolution in Vietnam. This time Kissinger agreed, convinced that the rapport he had established with Dobrynin and Gromyko would lead to a satisfactory agreement on strategic arms. A successful arms control summit would bring credit to the United States and, not incidentally, to himself.

In April 1972, just five days prior to Kissinger's departure for Moscow to pave the way for a May summit, U.S.-Soviet relations were put to a serious test. On April 15, 1972, in response to a major North Vietnamese offensive, Nixon authorized the bombing of military targets in the area around the North Vietnamese cities of Hanoi and Haiphong. In contrast to the 1969 bombing of Communist sanctuaries in Cambodia, this action was in direct contravention of Lyndon Johnson's November 1968 prohibition against bombing targets in the North. It represented a major reescalation of the war. Nixon's priorities were clear: Vietnam first, arms control second. Despite Nixon's actions, his national security advisor proceeded to do what he thought was best; he placed arms control first on the agenda for the May summit.

In Kissinger's defense, the Soviets had made it clear to him that

Vietnam would not be the main topic at the summit. Although they condemned the bombing, the Soviets let it be known that the summit should proceed as planned. The prospect of improved superpower relations and a possible arms control agreement with the United States was more important to the Soviets than demonstrating their displeasure over Vietnam.

On April 20, 1972, Kissinger arrived in Moscow for secret talks prior to the planned summit. He not only bypassed the Washington bureaucracy but also kept Jacob Beam, our ambassador in Moscow, in the dark. Without Beam's prior knowledge, Kissinger came complete with a staff and limousine. Beam was furious because he had not been informed of Kissinger's impending arrival and felt that his position as the U.S. representative in Moscow had been undermined. This highly irregular diplomatic conduct was, by now, nothing unusual for Kissinger. It not only placed him in complete charge but was totally in keeping with his love of surprise, intrigue, and conspiracy.

By the time Kissinger arrived in Moscow, Nixon had changed his mind on the agenda. Convinced that Moscow held the key to his problems in Southeast Asia, Nixon was not willing to leave it to chance that discussions on arms control would lead to the subject he wanted to discuss. He issued Kissinger explicit instructions to arrange an agenda that specifically addressed Vietnam and only later addressed arms control. He told Kissinger that if the Soviets were not forthcoming, he was to "pack [his] bags and come home." But while Nixon was apparently prepared to torpedo the summit, Kissinger was not. Convinced that the Soviets were unwilling to discuss Vietnam, he ignored Nixon's instructions and confined his discussions to arms control.

Much of what was discussed during Kissinger's April meetings with Gromyko and Brezhnev had already been settled through the back-channel with Dobrynin. For example, it was agreed that both sides would limit their ABM deployments to only two sites, one at the National Command Authority (NCA)—Washington, D.C., and Moscow, respectively—and another at an ICBM field of their own choosing. That was the easy part; the hard part, dealing with offensive arms, was yet to come.

Kissinger was very much aware of negative opinions in the United States about the failure of the earlier compromise to be more specific about limiting strategic offensive arms. The Pentagon, in particular, had voiced its concern, causing Kissinger to insist with Dobrynin that there should be finite restrictions on offensive missiles. Dobrynin proposed a freeze on ICBMs for a period of time to be determined later. But submarine-launched ballistic missiles (SLBMs) were not mentioned.

Pentagon officials were outraged when news of the proposed freeze surfaced. What good would a freeze on offensive missiles be, they asked, if SLBMs were excluded? The Soviets were engaged in an aggressive effort to build new, more sophisticated submarines, while the United States had postponed missile submarine production. Any freeze on offensive systems that failed to include SLBMs was clearly to the Soviets' advantage. The Washington bureaucracy was in open revolt. Somehow Kissinger had to find a way to include SLBMs in the agreement without causing the Soviets to walk out.

While Kissinger was still trying to figure out how to bring the Soviets around, they surprised him and suddenly came to his rescue. They said they would agree to a freeze on offensive ICBM systems for five years and would limit their deployment of SLBMs to 950 missiles on 62 submarines. They would do so, however, only if they were assured that they could continue to expand their current SLBM force of 740 missiles in exchange for phasing out older ICBMs and SLBMs. Seizing on the opportunity to limit SLBMs, Kissinger agreed.

After Kissinger returned to Washington, and shortly before the summit was to convene, Nixon once again risked antagonizing the Soviets. On May 8, he announced the mining of Haiphong harbor and intensified the bombing of North Vietnam. It was further proof that Nixon's determination to end the war exceeded his wish for a summit. Despite the loss of Soviet sailors and ships as a result of Nixon's action, Moscow refused to let events in Vietnam derail a summit. To the Soviets, resolving the Vietnam War was of limited relevance to their long-term goals. But to Nixon, the war in Indochina was the linchpin of linkage and represented his abiding determination not to be the first U.S. president to lose a war.

Kissinger, having reached the conclusion that there was little chance of resolving the war on terms favorable to the United States, was more determined than ever to put Vietnam on the back burner. He wanted to move on to what he considered the more important foreign policy issue, improved relations with the Soviet Union. Kissinger believed that pursuing détente, the relaxation of tensions with the Soviet Union, was the highest priority of U.S. foreign policy. He was convinced that pursuing détente could check the growing power of the Soviet Union and limit the risk of nuclear war. Finally, he believed, quite mistakenly, that détente would induce the Soviets to accept the existing world order and abandon their expansionist activities.

Senator Scoop Jackson and other prominent U.S. conservatives disagreed with Kissinger. They believed that the Soviets were using détente as a diplomatic cover for pressuring the United States into accepting the Brezhnev doctrine, which held that it was legitimate for the Soviet Union to militarily advance its brand of "socialism" in other countries. By refusing to acknowledge linkage, and by manipulating the administration's growing interest in an arms control agreement, the Soviets sought to turn the tables on Nixon.

Secretary of Defense Melvin Laird and chairman of the JCS Adm. Thomas Moorer agreed with Jackson and the conservatives on détente. Nixon found himself being whipsawed between two camps. Wanting above all else to extricate the United States from Vietnam, Nixon adopted a dual policy, allowing Kissinger to pursue détente while at the same time supporting the tough stance of the Department of Defense and the Joint Chiefs. Nixon thought this "carrot and stick" approach would lead to an acceptable conclusion in Vietnam. Kissinger's détente was the carrot; the military's stick was the threat that the United States would employ its entire military might to defeat a Soviet ally.

Against this backdrop of internal division, the SALT I summit began in Moscow on May 22, 1972. There followed four days of hectic negotiations between Kissinger and Gromyko, who periodically reported their results to Nixon and Brezhnev but kept their own negotiators in the dark. These meetings were the most bizarre in U.S.-Soviet negotiating history. Gerard Smith, the chief U.S. negotiator at the SALT talks, wrote, "The Moscow summit phase is still somewhat murky." This was a colossal understatement, given that negotiations were going on between the U.S. and Soviet delegations in Helsinki at the same time that negotiations were going on between Kissinger and Gromyko in Moscow. There is no accurate record of what officially transpired during the Moscow talks because no U.S. interpreters were present; that in itself was a big mistake, because the verbatim notes of interpreters are traditionally the best record of negotiation proceedings.

Kissinger did send occasional cables to Smith and vice versa, but for the most part the two talked past one another. In some instances, the negotiations in Moscow raised issues that had already been agreed to in Helsinki. In other instances, the Moscow negotiations broke new ground. Smith described what took place in Moscow as "a case of the negotiations being too important to be left to the negotiators."

An important difference arose over the SLBM freeze limit agreed to by Kissinger during his April trip to Moscow. The draft treaty stipulated that the Soviet Union would be limited to 950 submarine launchers on 62 submarines, while the United States would be limited to 710 missiles on 44 submarines. There were at least two serious questions, however, about the proposed ceilings. First, there was confusion as to how many SLBM submarines the Soviet Union had operational or under construction. The Soviets said that the number was 48; the U.S. intelligence community estimated that the actual number was between 41 and 43. If the U.S. estimate was correct (the number later proved to be 42), allowing a Soviet ceiling of 62 submarines was a significant concession. This raised concerns that Kissinger had, in order to save face, negotiated an SLBM ceiling that was almost 50 percent higher than the U.S. estimates of Soviet submarines and at the same time so high that it would not interfere with the planned Soviet SLBM buildup.

The second stumbling block was whether 100 older Soviet SLBMs on their G- and H-class submarines would be included in the count of strategic missiles. The United States wanted to include them; the Soviet Union did not. A compromise was struck under which the 30 SLBMs on the H-class submarines would be included under the 950 ceiling, but not the 70 missiles on the older G-class boats.

There was also a major dispute over the size of land-based ICBM silos. The United States wanted to keep the Soviet silos at their present size to prevent the Soviets from replacing light missiles with heavier, more powerful ones. While the U.S. delegation in Helsinki was against any increase, Kissinger had agreed to the rather nebulous formulation of "no significant increase" in silo size. *Significant*, to Kissinger, meant anything over 10 to 15 percent. What was not pinned down was whether the increase would be in one dimension, length, or in two dimensions, both length and diameter. If it were only in length, then the increase in volume could be no more than 15 percent. If, however, increases could be made in both dimensions, the increase in volume could be as large as 37.5 percent. The situation was further confused because the delegations in Helsinki were talking about the size of silos, whereas the Moscow negotiations were concentrating on missile volumes.

Smith later said that if we had accepted the Moscow formula on missile volume, the United States would not have been able to modernize its Minuteman III missile because its planned size was more than 15 percent greater than that of Minuteman I. Smith wrote that "it would have been the major irony of SALT and of arms control history if the leaders had inadvertently stumbled into MIRV controls. . . ." Even though the possibility of foreclosing our option to "MIRV" our Minuteman III proved to be a false alarm, Kissinger shifted to the Helsinki formula of specifying silo dimensions. At least then the two delegations were talking on the same wavelength.

To Gerard Smith's credit, he took a courageous stand at Helsinki. Recognizing the U.S. desire to limit strategic offensive arms, Smith attached a unilateral statement to the ABM Treaty that provided the United States with a very important escape clause. It read: "If an agreement providing for more complete strategic arms limitations were not achieved within five years, U.S. supreme interests could be jeopardized. Should that occur, it would constitute a basis for the withdrawal from the ABM Treaty." In hindsight, it is unfortunate that the United States did not invoke Smith's unilateral statement at the first or second five-year review of the ABM Treaty. Even though we were able to get only a provisional agreement on offensive arms, we were not willing to jeopardize the ABM Treaty, which, as the years passed, took on an importance all its own.

Meanwhile, the Soviets, resorting to one of their favorite techniques, introduced an element of surprise into the summit. On May 25, Brezhnev asked Nixon to drive to his dacha in the afternoon so that they could have some time alone before dinner. Brezhnev took Nixon for a wild ride on the Moskva River in his hydrofoil, then he suggested that they meet to discuss business. For the next three hours, Nixon said, Brezhnev shifted from affability to toughness. Nixon wrote that he

> pounded me bitterly and emotionally about Vietnam. I momentarily thought of Dr. Jekyll and Mr. Hyde when Brezhnev, who had just been laughing and slapping me on the back, started shouting angrily that instead of honestly working to end the Vietnam war, I was trying to use the Chinese as a means of bringing pressure on the Soviets to intervene with the North Vietnamese. At dinner there was much laughing and joking and storytelling—as if the acrimonious session downstairs had never occurred.

It was after midnight before Nixon and Kissinger got back to the Kremlin, at which point Kissinger and Gromyko went to work on the remaining unresolved issues. Around 1:00 A.M. Kissinger reported to Nixon that the Soviets were continuing to hold out for their positions, apparently believing that domestic pressures on Nixon would force him to make additional concessions. Nixon told Kissinger not to give in, and by morning Kissinger and Gromyko broke up their meeting with negotiations still deadlocked. Later that day, Dobrynin arrived at Nixon's apartment with the news that the politburo had met and agreed to the U.S. proposals. Nixon's patience had paid off.

Ambassador Smith was notified that he was to arrive in Moscow at 6:30 P.M. that evening for an 8:00 P.M. signing ceremony that same night, May 26, 1972. He was told he could invite Vladimir Semenov, his Soviet counterpart, to fly to Moscow with him. On the plane, the two heads of delegation read and initialed the ABM Treaty and Interim Agreement on offensive weapons. Despite their careful reading, however, they missed several errors, requiring the treaty to be signed a second time. It was just as well, because the treaty had been typed on ordinary paper and not the watermarked parchment on which treaties are traditionally recorded.

On the flight from Helsinki to Moscow, Smith and Semenov were having a beer when turbulent air caused the drinks to spill. They had visions of having to deliver beer-soaked documents to their leaders.

Because they had worked on the final text of the agreements past the time they were scheduled to leave Helsinki, Smith and Semenov did not get to Moscow until 9:00 P.M. When they arrived, Smith was handed a message from Secretary of State Rogers instructing him to attend a press conference at 10:00 P.M. at the U.S. Embassy. Soviet officials meeting the plane, however, told Smith that he was expected at the Kremlin immediately. When Smith arrived there, no one from the American delegation was around, and nobody could tell him why he had been summoned. Realizing that a mistake had been made, he went to Spaso House (the U.S. ambassador's residence), where the official dinner celebrating the treaty was winding up. Not wanting to interrupt the festivities, Smith went to the embassy to await the beginning of the press conference.

Shortly after ten o'clock, Kissinger arrived and unexpectedly told the reporters that Smith would give the briefing. A surprised Smith attempted to do so but soon realized that he was not certain about what had been worked out in Moscow concerning the SLBM freeze.

When several reporters accused him of evading their questions, Smith tried to finesse the matter, saying that it dealt with sensitive material. At this point, Kissinger arrogantly upstaged the tired and frustrated Smith. He stepped forward and told the reporters that he did not feel as constrained as Smith, and lest an atmosphere of mystery be built up around the submarine issue, he would address it at a second press conference later that evening.

Smith, humiliated and dejected, returned to the Kremlin to witness the official signing ceremony. As Nixon and Brezhnev were signing the documents, Kissinger further infuriated Smith by whispering angrily to him, "What were you trying to do, cause a panic?"

Fatigued, hungry, and emotionally drained, Smith found out the worst was yet to come. Herb Klein, the head of White House communications, told Smith that the president did not want him to take part in the second press conference. When the astonished Smith asked if this was the president's personal decision, Klein told him that "it was and that it had been checked with Kissinger." Smith, convinced that Kissinger did not want to risk being contradicted, surmised that he had gone to Nixon and told him he preferred to deal with reporters alone. Smith, seeing no way of appealing the decision, returned to Spaso House and went to bed.

The press conference was held in the early hours of the next morning in a poorly lit, smoke-filled bar in a downtown Moscow hotel. Although Kissinger adroitly danced around the SLBM issue, he was unable to conceal from some of the more astute members of the press the loophole created by a failure to include the Soviet G-class submarine SLBMs in the treaty's counting rules.

The end result of SALT I was that the United States agreed to limit its ABMs in return for a promissory note that the Soviet Union would agree, within five years, to equal levels of strategic offensive arms. It was a promissory note that the Soviets never honored. Kissinger had his deal, at the expense of everyone who had negotiated for years. Worse, he had his deal at the risk of jeopardizing U.S. interests.

DOMESTIC REACTION

The treaty provoked prolonged congressional debate, which revealed that a number of senators were, at a minimum, apprehensive about the agreements. Scoop Jackson, fearful that the Soviets would take advantage of the United States, introduced legislation on September 30, 1972, that became known as the "Jackson Amendment." The bill, which subsequently passed Congress, was a congressional mandate to seek "more permanent and comprehensive agreements that would not limit the United States to levels of intercontinental strategic forces inferior . . . to the Soviet Union." The Jackson Amendment became the basis of U.S. arms control policy for the next decade.

Subsequently, Senator Jackson told me that he initially supported Nixon's initiatives and wanted to work with the president in a spirit of bipartisanship. He liked the way Nixon had repudiated what he thought was Lyndon Johnson's soft approach to the Soviet Union. Jackson, however, became increasingly unhappy with Kissinger, who he felt was steering Nixon toward unwarranted accommodation. Jackson confided in me that he would have liked to continue to back Nixon, but he was unable to do so in view of Kissinger's strong hold on the president.

In the end, the Senate voted 88 to 2 in favor of ratification of the treaty. The Jackson Amendment, however, put both Nixon and Kissinger on notice that Congress would not approve a future agreement that failed to limit both sides to equal levels of strategic offensive arms.

I was in Brussels in a NATO post during the negotiations on SALT I and its subsequent ratification in the Senate. I visited Washington frequently during that time and kept in touch with the Joint Chiefs of Staff, Scoop Jackson, and others. I had little inkling that I would soon be drawn into the SALT negotiations.

On November 7, 1972, Nixon was reelected in a landslide victory over Senator George McGovern. Early the next month, Kissinger commenced a fresh round of talks with North Vietnamese politburo member Le Duc Tho. Regrettably, the talks soon broke down. Intent on bringing Tho back to the table and anxious to bring the war to a close, Nixon resumed the bombing of Hanoi and Haiphong. The "Christmas bombings" of 1972, which lasted for eleven days, finally had their intended effect. The North Vietnamese announced their willingness to return to the negotiating table in January 1973.

From January 8 to January 23, Kissinger and Tho negotiated around the clock. Finally, a compromise was reached under which the North was allowed to maintain troops already in place in the South, and in return, the North rescinded its demand for the ouster of South Vietnamese president Nguyen Van Thieu. A cease-fire went into effect on January 27, and the last U.S. troops were withdrawn two months later. Nixon was finally free of his albatross. He could now proceed with arms control without feeling obliged to link progress in the talks to Vietnam.

JOINING THE SALT II TEAM

After Nixon's reelection, Gerard Smith resigned as head of the U.S. negotiating team and was replaced by U. Alexis Johnson, the career diplomat who had unsuccessfully tried to thwart Kissinger's earlier end run around the State Department. Smarting from criticism that the United States had concluded an ABM Treaty but had only reached an interim agreement on strategic offensive arms, Nixon wanted to begin talks immediately on a more permanent agreement on offensive arms. General Secretary Brezhnev was scheduled to visit Washington in June 1973, and Nixon wanted a new treaty ready at that time.

After applying considerable pressure in the back-channel, Kissinger was able to get the Soviets to agree to commence negotiations on SALT II. It soon became clear, however, that no agreement on offensive arms would be quickly forthcoming. The United States, in keeping with the Jackson Amendment, wanted a treaty based on equality in the aggregate number of "central" strategic delivery systems. The Soviets, on the other hand, wanted to keep the numerical advantages they had won in SALT I and to codify those advantages in a permanent treaty.

I joined the SALT II team as its military representative on March 1, 1973. I learned that Scoop Jackson had been unhappy with the way my predecessor, Lt. Gen. Royal B. Allison, had represented the military's interests in SALT I.

I spent several weeks getting briefed by the staffs of the Joint Chiefs and the military services. One of my predecessor's primary difficulties with the Joint Chiefs had been his lack of a close rapport with them, something I took immediate steps to correct. I quickly learned that the chiefs were very nervous about what was going on at the negotiating table; they feared that U.S. military capabilities would be sacrificed without a corresponding diminution of the Soviet threat.

I assured the Joint Chiefs of Staff that, in addition to following their advice and keeping them informed on the status of the negotiations, I would not permit unilateral reductions in U.S. military capabilities. I told them that, while I favored entering into an arms control agreement with the Soviets, the agreement had to be evenhanded and verifiable to gain my support. Otherwise, I would resign my post and go public.

By the time I arrived at the talks they had been going on for several months and had settled into a routine. Sessions in Geneva lasted eight to ten weeks, and then the negotiators returned to their home bases for roughly an equal length of time.

We usually held two formal meetings a week, generally every Tuesday and Thursday. While this does not sound like a demanding schedule, in reality the workweek was long and arduous. Mondays were usually spent transforming a portion of our broadly worded instructions from Washington into a carefully worded official statement that we would read to the Soviets the next day. On Tuesdays, reading our official statements took about two hours, counting the translation time. This was followed by informal discussions that lasted from two to four hours. Our team then spent the rest of Tuesday discussing among ourselves what the Soviets had said and sending our reports back to Washington. On Wednesdays and Thursdays we repeated the Monday-Tuesday routine. Fridays we devoted to finishing what was left undone and consulting with our experts. Fridays were also the days normally set aside for creative thinking and planning what we wanted to do the following week. We often spent Saturdays, and occasionally Sundays, entertaining visitors, who included large numbers of senators, congressmen, and their staffs.

The basic idea of keeping members of Congress informed was good, but most of our visitors from Washington were more interested in using the negotiations as an excuse for junkets. Geneva was a picturesque place, only an hour by car from good ski slopes and within two hours' flight time of Paris and London. Perhaps one in five of our visitors was seriously interested in staying abreast of the negotiations. But even the others felt constrained to meet us for short conversations and briefings in order to keep their consciences clear that they had come to Geneva "on business." With these demands on our time, it was clear that no more than two formal meetings could be held in any one week.

We alternated meeting places. Tuesday sessions were held in the office building where the U.S. delegation worked and Thursday sessions in the enclosed prison-like Soviet compound. The atmosphere seemed to change when we moved from the cheery and spacious rooms at our complex, which looked out on beautiful Lake Geneva, to the crowded, windowless Soviet building.

Many of our most difficult negotiations took place not with the Soviets but among the members of our own team. Aside from the chief negotiator, each member of the U.S. team represented an agency: the Department of State, the Defense Department, the Arms Control and Disarmament Agency, and the Joint Chiefs of Staff. An interpreter and a notetaker rounded out our team. The chief U.S. negotiator received only broadly worded guidance from Washington, which provided each team member with the opportunity to get his own interpretations incorporated into the proposals we gave the Soviets. Ambassador U. Alexis Johnson, trying to be fair-minded, found himself whipsawed by members of his team, myself included, each an advocate of a different agency. At times, in an effort to strike a compromise, Johnson agreed to formulations that were ambiguous. In 1982, when I became the chief negotiator, I tried to reduce the amount of time we spent negotiating among ourselves and kept on my desk as a reminder the famous "Pogo" cartoon: "We have met the enemy and he is us."

At our meetings with the Soviets, they always sat where they could watch the door. Their chief negotiator, Vladimir Semenov, explained that this gave the Soviets the opportunity to see who was entering and leaving the room. When we tried to break this routine and have them sit with their backs to the entrance, they simply ignored us and sat where they pleased. This arrangement made little difference in the windowless Soviet compound, but at our meeting place it proved a mixed blessing. On the one hand, because of the glare from the windows, we could not see the expressions on the Soviets' faces. But, on the other hand, we enjoyed looking out on Lake Geneva and, on a clear day, Mont Blanc. Minister Semenov insisted on sitting on a higher chair at both locations. "We're all equal," he said with a straight face. "But I'm more equal than others." He even boasted that he came to the meetings in a leased Mercedes, while his subordinates had to travel in Volkswagens.

In the U.S. meeting place, we offered our counterparts fresh orange juice, a rare treat for the Soviets. When they were hosts, they offered us warm mineral water that smelled and tasted of sulfur. It was hard to convince them that we preferred tap water.

After shaking hands, we would take our seats. The guests would speak first and begin by reading a prepared statement. Our statements were crafted in Geneva based on the guidance we received from Washington. The Soviets' statements, however, were written for them in Moscow. During SALT I, U.S. draft statements had to be approved by Washington prior to their presentation. But, when Ambassador Johnson took over SALT II in late 1972, he said he would not serve as the chief negotiator if his statements had to be second-guessed back home. He was a "big boy," he added, "a senior State Department officer, . . . as qualified as any of the weenies in Washington to interpret the president's instructions." Johnson said that if Washington disagreed, it should simply find another negotiator. Since most of the changes made by Washington amounted to mere word-smithing, officials were delighted that someone had finally decided to take charge. It relieved them of the need to respond to Geneva on short deadlines and to haggle endlessly by long-distance phone on whether a statement ought to read *should* or *could*. This practice of approving our statements in Geneva without referring them to Washington was continued during my tenure as chief negotiator for START.

These formal written statements became part of the official record that was binding on our governments and could be referred to by both sides to reinforce or dispute the interpretation of a given treaty provision. These records proved essential for the negotiators working on the ABM Treaty. The Soviets claimed that our statements reinforced a narrow interpretation of the type of testing that was allowed under the provisions of the treaty whereas we claimed that the statements backed up a broad interpretation.

On Tuesdays and Thursdays, after the chief negotiators read their formal statements, we would break up into informal groups. At the informal meetings both sides served coffee, tea, cookies, and peanuts. Their coffee and tea were strong, and their cookies and peanuts usually stale. In both meeting places the bowls of peanuts were continually replenished; I calculated that I ate from one-half pound to a pound of peanuts per session, depending on the length of the meeting. During SALT I, alcohol had been served during the informal meetings; the Soviets were as fond of our bourbon and Scotch as we were of their vodka. Not surprisingly, some of these sessions had reportedly become quite boisterous and incoherent. This practice was carried over into SALT II, but when Ambassador Johnson, who appreciated good Scotch as much as anyone, realized after the first several sessions that the Soviets could hold their liquor and their tongues better than we could, he decided not to serve alcohol.

During the informal discussions, "bilats" as we called them, negotiations ranged over a wide variety of subjects. At times they concentrated on some point covered in the formal statements. At other times, we went into greater detail on some issue we had raised previously. The bilats, unlike the plenary statements, were considered exploratory; they were not part of the official record and were not binding on our governments. If either side wished to have any of the points discussed in these informal meetings subject to future reference, they had to include them in the next official statement.

At the informal discussions, the Soviets usually simply repeated what had been said in their formal statements. Their motto seemed to be "repeat, repeat, and then repeat again." We, in contrast, tried to move beyond the formal statements, either to explore what the Soviets thought about some new idea or to elaborate further on the rationale underlying our own positions. The discussions soon became a one-way street because the Soviet delegates allowed themselves no new or original thought. Obviously on a short leash, they had to await instructions from Moscow before reacting to anything we said.

In addition to the negotiating sessions, we usually met about once a week at "social functions." I put the term in quotes because a social function with the Soviets is a contradiction in terms. Only on rare occasions was a social event a relaxed affair. The Soviets invariably considered them working sessions and were quick to bring up substantive matters.

On one occasion, I invited the Soviets to take an excursion boat ride on Lake Geneva. Unable to get them to relax, I took out my harmonica. When I played "Pelushke Pole" (a children's song), they began to hum. When I played "Pod Moskovia Vechiera" ("Moscow Nights"), they began to dance. In response to my rendering of "Mi Communisti" ("We Are the Communists"), they formed a conga line and stomped around the boat.

Afterwards, Minister Vladimir Semenov took up a collection of dollars, rubles, and Swiss and French francs from astonished onlookers. "We'll divide 50–50," he said. But when I stretched out my hand he put all the money in his pocket. "You had 100 percent of the pleasure of playing. I'll have 100 percent of the pleasure of spending the money," he said, "50–50." This was their idea of fairness.

My two three-star military counterparts at the talks were Col. Gen. Konstantin Trusov and Col. Gen. Ivan Beletsky. Trusov was from the Russian republic, Beletsky from the Ukraine. Although Beletsky was promoted to his rank earlier than Trusov, the latter acted as spokesman. When I once asked Beletsky about this, he said ruefully, "I'm only a lowly Ukrainian, not a Russian," an admission that there was a definite hierarchy among Soviet nationalities. Trusov, soft-spoken and careful in his choice of words, was a weapons expert who had risen through the staff ranks. Beletsky, who was loud and subject to emotional outbursts, was a troop commander who had fought as a lieutenant of horse cavalry against the Germans in 1943 and 1944. Trusov and Beletsky could not have been more different, yet they complemented each other well. They provided double coverage on me, and when one hit me high the other hit me low.

During my early years at the negotiations I tried hard to identify issues on which there was no hard-and-fast Moscow "party line." I listened attentively to what my counterparts said and carefully studied their body language, but it seemed that Moscow had a party line on every single issue. After some long and exhausting sessions, I found myself wondering why I continued to play along with what seemed to be senseless gamesmanship. Would it not be easier simply to exchange plenary statements and let it go at that? If we did it that way, the Soviets would know our official positions and have fewer opportunities to drive wedges among us. But I knew, deep down, that we would continue to go through the same motions. We Americans feel derelict in our duty when we fall silent. Talking makes us feel that we are at least trying to accomplish something.

The Soviets always opened negotiations with extreme positions, while we traditionally opened with proposals closer to the final outcome we sought. I once tried to explain to General Trusov how Americans developed their opening positions. We would appoint two teams, I said, one representing U.S. interests and the other advocating what we thought would be the Soviet point of view. After debating the matter, the U.S. team would leave some negotiating room but would come to the table with a position close to our desired outcome. We wanted to appear reasonable and fair. "Let us assume that the best outcome for both of us lies in the middle of this room," I explained. "While we enter with a position a meter from the middle, you Soviets come in with a position over at that wall."

"Don't do us any favors," Trusov said. "If you feel we begin with a position over at that wall, then you should come in at the opposite wall. After all," he said, "we can't go back to Moscow admitting that we gave up more than you did." It was of no use trying to explain to Trusov that Americans were simply unable, psychologically, to enter a negotiation with an extreme position. It was a good example of the cultural gap that divided us.

I once talked to Beletsky during an informal conversation about the six points dividing us on a particular issue. I suggested that the United States could concede the three points that the Soviets felt were most important if the Soviets could give us the three that were of most importance to us. It was, I explained, what analysts call a non-zero sum solution in which both sides gain. Since Beletsky did not disagree with me, I asked my chief, Alex Johnson, to let me put forth the compromise formally.

During the next plenary, Johnson gave me the floor. "On behalf of the United States," I said, "we are prepared to offer you points A, B, and C." On a signal from Beletsky, the Soviets all got up to leave the room.

"Just a minute," I said, "I'm not finished. I haven't talked about D, E, and F, which we want."

"We believe you're finished," Beletsky said. "We're not ready to give up anything."

Having learned my lesson, I opened the next plenary session by saying, "If you will give us D, E, and F, I'll tell you what we're ready to give up."

"*Shtovy dumaete?*" he asked, "*my idioty?*" (What do you think we are, idiots?)

At times, the talks got even more bizarre as the Soviet negotiators resorted to the highly unconventional technique of presenting us with "non-papers." One of the negotiators would say to me as he was leaving a meeting, "Here's a non-paper, you can read it if you wish. But if you attribute it to me, I'll deny it." His expectation was that if the idea appealed to me, I would present it at the next meeting as my own. The Soviets would then send the "American proposal" to Moscow for analysis. If Moscow approved, "our proposal" would be adopted. If Moscow did not agree, the Soviet negotiators could not be accused of having suggested it.

This strange way of negotiating would be further complicated if we thought the idea needed refinement. In such instances, we would give our counterparts a "non-paper reply" to their "non-paper." If we heard nothing back from them, it was a signal that they did not like our changes. But at times, they would respond to our "non-paper" with another "non-paper." It was by such unconventional, and often silly, games that the negotiations moved forward.

PEACEFUL NUCLEAR TESTING

While the SALT II negotiations were in progress, I was assigned the additional task of serving as military member of the U.S. team negotiating with the Soviets on Peaceful Nuclear Explosions (PNE). There were two reasons the United States wanted to prohibit the use of underground nuclear explosions for peaceful purposes. First, a device being tested for peaceful uses could simultaneously be tested as a nuclear weapon. Second, the fallout from such tests threatened not only Soviet citizens but also the rest of the world.

Maj. Gen. Sergei Makharov was my Soviet counterpart. He tried very hard to convince me that the Soviet Union needed to use nuclear detonations to optimize its natural resources. He described an elaborate Soviet scheme to reverse the northerly flow of the Kama River by blasting a canal through a low range of mountains. He estimated that some twenty nuclear explosions were "all that it would take" to get the job done. Reversing the flow of the Kama, he explained, would cause it to flow into the Volga River, providing much-needed water for irrigation and for raising the sinking level of the Caspian Sea. The Caspian was gradually drying up, he said, and the additional water would save the sturgeon and the dwindling caviar industry. I explained to Makharov that these explosions would inevitably release enormous amounts of radiation and contaminated debris into the atmosphere and that the widespread radiation would have devastating effects on large numbers of people within and beyond Soviet borders. I told him that the United States had at one time briefly considered using nuclear charges to blast a sea-level canal through Nicaragua, parallel to the Panama Canal, but the project (on which I had worked) had been abandoned because of the devastating effects of introducing large amounts of radioactive material into the atmosphere.

"You Americans," said Makharov, "are too squeamish. You don't seem to realize that it's permissible to put a few lives at risk if it would result in the greater good for the people as a whole." His entreaties sent a cold chill up my spine and gave me a greater appreciation of the low regard Soviet officials had for the health and well-being of their countrymen. It made me more determined than ever to insist that any nonmilitary uses of nuclear detonations be carefully contained and the environmental risks minimized. I was pleased that we blocked an agreement that would allow peaceful nuclear explosions.

Several years later, at the 1986 summit meeting in Reykjavík, Marshal Sergei Akhromeyev told me that the Soviet Academy of Sciences had convinced Mikhail Gorbachev to abandon the Kama River project. The accident at the nuclear power plant in Chernobyl, where upwards of two million people were affected by nuclear fallout, made Gorbachev acutely aware of the dangers of radiation. Even if it could have been accomplished without the use of nuclear devices, Akhromeyev explained, the ecological unknowns of artificially reversing the flow of the river were too great.

SALT II NEGOTIATIONS

It became clear to me soon after I became involved in SALT II negotiations that the Soviets had a very different idea from the United States about what a comprehensive agreement on offensive weapons should include. The U.S. position was straightforward: we wanted a treaty based on overall equality of strategic delivery systems. The Soviet Union, however, was intent on maintaining the advantage in delivery vehicles it had acquired in SALT I. In addition, the Soviets wanted any permanent treaty to compensate them for U.S. forward-based nuclear systems (FBS) in Europe, as well as British- and French-based nuclear forces capable of striking Soviet territory.

The issue of placing limits on MIRVs became especially contentious. My Soviet counterparts let me know that while they would like to limit our MIRVed systems, they would resist any effort to place limits on their own. Kissinger refused to take them at their word. He felt that since the United States had already mastered the new technology, the Soviets would be anxious to reach an agreement limiting their own MIRVs if it would place limits on ours. It was not the first, and would not be the last, time that Kissinger practiced mirror-imaging, believing that the Soviets would follow what in his own mind was the most logical path.

The Joint Chiefs of Staff were convinced that the Soviets would have no part of an agreement that constrained their own adoption of the new and important MIRV technology. The chiefs wanted to maintain a technological edge, which the intelligence community had convinced them was feasible, in order to help them counteract the Soviets' rapidly increasing quantitative advantage. Moreover, the chiefs could not envision a realistic means of verifying a limit on MIRVs. A ban that could not be verified, and therefore enforced, would simply be an open invitation to the Soviets to cheat.

When the chiefs learned that Kissinger was proposing a MIRV limit through the back-channel, it heightened their concern. They asked me to try to block any agreement on MIRVs that Kissinger might reach via the back-channel. Since I was so strongly opposed to a MIRV ban, it was a task I readily accepted.

The talks moved slowly, and it became apparent that a comprehensive agreement would not be ready by June, when Brezhnev was to visit the United States. Watergate, meanwhile, began to have its effect on foreign relations. Nixon became increasingly diverted from international affairs by his attempts to stem the tide of domestic criticism over the growing scandal. Yet he wanted to demonstrate that relations with the Soviet Union were improving and thus divert attention from Watergate. Nixon and Kissinger, feeling it important that at least some element of a comprehensive settlement be agreed to during the general secretary's visit, cast about for some device that would provide a cosmetic solution. They proposed a set of "Basic Principles of Negotiations on Strategic Arms Limitations," which would be perceived as a road map leading to a comprehensive agreement. Because getting us to agree to a set of vague principles, which they could interpret to their own advantage, played into the Soviets' hands, they seized upon the idea with alacrity.

The Soviets always favored broad guidelines over specific proposals because they felt that they could exploit the more generalized formulations. When I learned from my Soviet counterparts in Geneva that the Basic Principles were being discussed in the back-channel, I alerted the Joint Chiefs of Staff and told them that they should find out what was really going on. They discovered that the Soviets had resurrected an old formula claiming their right to "equality and equal security." This was a none-too-subtle attempt to once again get the treaty language to legitimize their previously rebuffed demand that U.S. forward-based systems be included under SALT II.

The Joint Chiefs of Staff, having successfully flushed into the open Kissinger's back-channel negotiations on the Basic Principles, insisted that an agreement call simply for equality. In the end, a compromise was struck between Kissinger and Dobrynin that read "both sides will be guided by the recognition of each other's equal security interests." It was not what the Joint Chiefs would have preferred, but it did narrow the grounds for misinterpretation. At a minimum, it did not explicitly codify a Soviet advantage.

Secretary General Brezhnev arrived in Washington on June 18, 1973, and the Basic Principles were signed four days later. Since they were too vague to be used as guidelines, their only significance was that they committed the United States and the Soviet Union to attempt to complete a permanent agreement on limiting offensive arms by the end of 1974.

I met Brezhnev for the first time when he came to the Washington summit. He was a big, burly man, with dark bushy eyebrows. After

I greeted him in Russian, he gave me a crushing bear hug. I was prepared for this, having heard that Brezhnev liked to express himself through physical contact. What I was not prepared for was his incredibly bad breath.

"The United States has a secret weapon," he said, "a hawkish general who speaks Russian."

"I'm not a hawk," I told him, trying to soften my hard-line image. "I'm a cross between a chicken and a dove." Brezhnev did not understand my reference to a chicken. His interpreter explained to him that in American slang a chicken means someone who is cowardly or timid. "But why only part dove?" he asked.

"Because," I said, "bird watchers tell us that the dove is the only species of bird that will kill its own kind."

Not content to let the conversation end there, Brezhnev said, "You know, general, that Clemenceau said war was too important to leave to the generals."

"I know," I replied, "and that's why I'm on the negotiating team. Peace is too important to leave to the diplomats."

"*Molodiec!*" Brezhnev exclaimed, the equivalent of "stout fellow." But to his interpreter he said, "Remind me to warn our negotiators about General Rowny. He's not impressed by authority and doesn't give in easily."

Later, in June 1973 we went back to the negotiating table in Geneva, where for the next several months we made almost no progress. Kissinger, meanwhile, continued to pursue his agenda of seeking a MIRV limit, giving it priority over all other U.S. arms control objectives. Kissinger describes his differences with the chiefs and me in his book *Years of Upheaval:*

> . . . the Joint Chiefs of Staff continued to insist adamantly on equal aggregates (that is, equal overall total of delivery vehicles); in return, they remained prepared to drop any attempt to limit MIRVs, thus substituting a Soviet edge in warheads for an advantage in delivery vehicles. The Chiefs maintained this position through the fall; at one point their representative, Lieutenant General Edward Rowny, on November 23 argued that the Chiefs did not see anything they would pay for an MLBM (heavy missile) MIRV testing agreement that would be worth it.

I learned that it was typical of Kissinger to skew an argument to his advantage by framing it in terms of his own assumptions. His faulty reasoning in this case was that if we gave up our demand for equal aggregates of delivery vehicles, the Soviets would not MIRV their heavy missiles. But the Soviets had shown no interest in a deal limiting MIRVs, unless it limited only our MIRVs, and wanted to be allowed both more missiles and more warheads than the United States.

PENTAGON VERSUS KISSINGER

The relationship between the Joint Chiefs of Staff and Kissinger became ever more strained in the fall of 1973. Several members of Kissinger's staff, wanting to bolster their boss's position, told the chiefs that Nixon had authorized Kissinger (who was now secretary of state as well as the national security advisor) to use his own judgment in choosing among the options being considered in SALT II. This rather remarkable abdication of presidential authority made it quite clear that the pressures of Watergate were taking the president's attention away from arms control. Nixon stopped coming to NSC meetings and allowed Kissinger to chair them. Kissinger would write up the comments of others at the meetings and attach his own recommendations. I was told by a person close to Nixon that he often initialed the papers Kissinger put before him without even reading them.

In October 1973 the Egyptians and Syrians attacked Israel. In Washington, attention shifted rapidly from SALT II to the Middle East. The White House ordered a worldwide alert of U.S. strategic and conventional forces. Rumors surfaced that Kissinger had quickly run the idea of a strategic alert by Nixon who, preoccupied with Watergate, had given his approval without giving much thought to the gravity of his action. From what I could learn from my friends in the White House, the rumors appeared to be based on fact. The chiefs, already at loggerheads with Kissinger over arms control, were now worried that he was unduly influencing decisions that should be made only by the commander in chief after close consultations with his principal military advisors. Although the alert was subsequently rescinded, battle lines between the chiefs and Kissinger had been drawn.

In January 1974 James Schlesinger, who replaced Elliott Richardson as secretary of defense, initiated a policy change that further unified the Pentagon in its opposition to Kissinger's repeated attempts to limit MIRVs. Schlesinger announced a new targeting doctrine that would give the United States a broader range of options in dealing with a Soviet nuclear threat. Schlesinger's new policy called for the United States to conduct selected targeting of hardened Soviet ICBM silos and other military targets, not just Soviet cities.

To put teeth into this new approach, additional funds for research and development were needed to increase the accuracy and yield of U.S. missiles to the level needed to destroy hardened targets. Kissinger argued that such a policy would make it even harder for him to reach an agreement with the Soviets. Schlesinger responded that reaching an agreement was secondary; the president of the United States should be provided with the greatest number of options to deter an attack or, if deterrence failed, to prevail in a nuclear war.

The president faced a difficult decision. He liked the idea of making deterrence more credible by increasing his choice of retaliatory options, but he was also anxious to successfully conclude an arms control deal with the Soviets to quiet the growing furor over Watergate. Nixon decided to try and have it both ways. He supported Schlesinger's bid for the funds needed to institute his new policy and simultaneously instructed Kissinger to press for an arms control agreement. To offer something that looked attractive, Nixon proposed to limit the number of missiles the United States would MIRV providing the Soviets agreed to equal aggregates of missile throwweight. The Soviets did not bite on the MIRV proposal.

As Watergate blossomed into a full-blown scandal, Nixon pursued "summitry" in order to divert public opinion from his domestic difficulties. Kissinger, not generally favoring summits, agreed with Nixon's new initiative because he felt it would further his policy of détente and lead to an arms control agreement. Besides, it might allow him to arrest Jackson's criticism that Kissinger had created a loophole in his secret understanding with the Soviets in 1972 over SLBMs. The Soviets agreed to another summit because they believed that a U.S. president facing the prospect of impeachment might make arms control concessions.

The Moscow summit began on June 25, 1974, and ended on July 3. Although I had heard many stories about Foreign Minister Andrei Gromyko's dour nature and Job-like patience, it was not until the second Moscow summit that I witnessed it firsthand. I was well aware that Gromyko had been foreign minister for twenty-seven years and liked to boast that he had "worn out" thirteen U.S. secretaries of state. One story often told about Gromyko, and usually attributed to Nikita Khrushchev, was that Gromyko was so patient he would sit on a cake of ice until it melted. After meeting Gromyko, I knew the story was false—if Gromyko sat on a cake of ice it would never melt; I was convinced he had ice water in his veins.

Desperately seeking a deal, Nixon offered the Soviets an advantage in throw-weight if they would agree to give the United States an advantage in MIRVed missiles. The Soviets quickly rejected the proposal, hoping that Nixon's domestic troubles would result in U.S. concessions.

The Soviets' assessment of Nixon's domestic difficulties was now in the second of three stages. At first, Moscow viewed Watergate as a plot to embarrass Brezhnev that had been designed by opponents of arms control and détente. During the first days of the 1974 summit, realizing that Watergate was not a ruse, they came to believe that Nixon would be forced to make concessions in order to counterbalance his domestic woes. They reasoned that Nixon would make the case that the U.S. electorate needed him to remain in office so as to see a treaty through to completion. Finally, the Soviets came to the realization that Nixon would only go so far in order to get a deal and would not grant the significant concessions that they wanted. They also concluded that even if an agreement with Nixon was reached, it had little chance of gaining congressional approval. Having come full circle, Brezhnev lost interest in an arms control agreement and the Moscow summit went nowhere.

Although I attended several summit sessions within the rarefied confines of the Kremlin, one event in particular stands out in my mind as representative of both the humor and irony found in the Soviet system. I was riding in the third car of a four-car convoy that was stopped by a security guard at the entrance to the Kremlin. The guard refused me entry because I was not displaying my *znatchok,* the lapel pin indicating that I was cleared for entrance. The guard wanted some other *positivno* identification. I told him that I remembered him from the previous day and that he should remember me as well. No dice. I then produced my State Department identification card. The guard examined it and returned it to me. "Many persons have such cards," he said. I next showed him my Pentagon pass hoping that, as a fellow soldier, he would defer to my military rank. "*Nyet,*" was the answer.

The other passengers were getting anxious, fearing that they would be late for the meeting. In desperation I took out my MasterCharge credit card. I put my thumb over the yellow circle so that only the red circle showed.

"*Vot,*" I said to the guard in Russian, "*krasnja y krasivaja*" (Look, it's red and it's beautiful).

At this the guard broke into a wide grin, clicked his heels, gave me a sharp salute, and waved us through.

MasterCard, as it is known today, should adopt a takeoff on the American Express slogan: "If you want to get into the Kremlin, don't leave home without it."

On the last day of the summit, after the meetings had ended in a stalemate, I was preparing to leave for home. Suddenly, I was called back to the Kremlin to take part in renewed negotiations. Nixon and Brezhnev had reportedly reached an agreement on voluntary on-site inspection of nuclear weapons sites.

When we reconvened, I decided that I should learn precisely what Nixon and Brezhnev had agreed to. I asked my Soviet counterpart point-blank, "Just what do you mean by voluntary on-site inspection?"

"What we mean," he said with a straight face, "is that you Americans can volunteer to come inspect us, and we can volunteer to say no." I could not believe my ears. It brought our negotiations to an abrupt halt.

The summit ended with both sides concluding that a permanent agreement on strategic offensive arms by the end of 1974 was impossible. On July 3, Kissinger told the press that a failure to limit MIRVs in the near future would lead to "an explosion of technology and an explosion in the number of missiles, at the end of which we will be lucky if we have the present stability. What in God's name," he asked, "does strategic superiority mean?" Kissinger, having tried his best to get an agreement on MIRVs, was sorely disappointed. Nixon was despondent. His inability to reach an agreement had only exacerbated his troubles at home. He left for Washington to face the consequences of Watergate.

NIXON'S FAILURE

I have no doubt that President Nixon would have liked to have signed a permanent arms control agreement limiting strategic arms as a companion piece to the ABM treaty. To his credit, however, he was not prepared to sacrifice U.S. security interests in order to get a deal. Had he been able to reach an evenhanded agreement, he fully appreciated that it carried with it certain ancillary advantages such as possibly subjecting Soviet forces to greater on-site inspection. This would have provided a higher degree of predictability and stability to the U.S.-Soviet relationship.

Kissinger's goals also went unfulfilled. He wanted more than anything else to be the architect of détente and a historic arms agreement with the Soviet Union. During the summer of 1974, both he and Nixon (but for different reasons) came perilously close to committing the United States to a MIRV agreement that would, in my opinion, have been prejudicial to the long-term interests of the United States. It was fortunate for us that, for reasons of their own, the Soviet leadership demurred.

President Nixon's penchant for secrecy and surprise, his over-reliance on Kissinger, and his refusal to involve elements of his administration and the Congress in his initiatives contributed to the failure of his linkage policy. In the end, Watergate inflicted the fatal wound that destroyed the president's influence and dashed any hope of an agreement with the Soviet Union. It was a sad irony that Nixon, with his sound approach to foreign affairs in general and his knowledge and understanding of the Soviets in particular, should have his policies collapse under the pressure of his own intrigue.

Nixon, of course, was followed by Gerald Ford, who would prove to be much more assertive than many in Washington ever expected. Although Kissinger remained a force, he would find his freedom to maneuver severely curtailed. A new, less freewheeling era in American foreign policy and arms control would be the result.

CHAPTER 3

Ford's Brief Reign: Standing Firm

Gerald Ford was chosen as Richard Nixon's vice president after the resignation of Spiro Agnew in October 1973, largely through the efforts of former Secretary of Defense Melvin Laird. Laird felt that Nixon, in order to broaden his political base, needed a staunch conservative from the Midwest as his new second in command. When Nixon was subsequently forced to resign over Watergate, Ford moved into the Oval Office on August 9, 1974. Ford was more inclined than his predecessor to utilize the vast expertise available to him in the government bureaucracy. As a result, I spent more time in Washington than I had when Nixon was president.

Like Nixon, Ford had a good grasp of the Soviet Union's foreign policy agenda. He believed, as had Nixon, that a strategic arms deal with the Soviet Union was only one of the many foreign policy objectives of the United States. Unlike Nixon, though, Ford was not driven as much by political considerations to seek an agreement with the Soviets. Nor was he as strongly influenced by Henry Kissinger.

Much maligned at the outset of his administration for his lack of knowledge of international affairs, Ford proved his critics wrong. In the area of arms control, he quickly mastered the complex strategic

64

issues. Prior to making a decision, he invariably asked his advisors a fundamental question: "What's in the best interests of the United States?" When Henry Kissinger told him at a National Security Council meeting in late 1974 that American public opinion strongly favored reaching an early agreement with the Soviet Union, Ford was unimpressed. He replied that it was the president's task to "mold, not follow, public opinion."

Although Ford was seen by the American public as bringing honesty and openness back into the White House, most Republican Party leaders, particularly the more conservative ones, were not enthusiastic about his presidency. Many were troubled by his selection of liberal Republican Nelson Rockefeller as his vice president. Others opposed Ford's continued pursuit of détente. In 1975, at the height of his difficulties with Congress, Ford was criticized more by the Senate than Nixon had been at the low point of his political career.

Even before Nixon's resignation, an "Imperial Congress" began to emerge in response to what some saw as Nixon's "Imperial Presidency." The legislative branch was determined to limit the chief executive's freedom to formulate and conduct U.S. foreign policy. In an earlier challenge to the president's authority, Congress had flexed its political muscle in 1973 by passing the War Powers Act. This legislation sharply limited the president's traditionally unrestricted powers as commander in chief to send U.S. forces into combat without prior congressional approval. The legislation put then-Vice President Ford on notice that Congress would no longer tolerate the freewheeling style of international deal-making characteristic of the Nixon-Kissinger era.

Adding to this challenge to presidential authority was the public's growing uneasiness with a president who assumed office without the benefit of a popular election. Ford's sudden and unexpected pardon of Richard Nixon one month after taking office increased his woes. Faced with a precipitous decline in popularity, Ford felt compelled to announce his candidacy for the 1976 elections shortly after moving into the White House. He realized that unless he did so, his domestic support would continue to erode and he would be unable to conduct foreign policy and international negotiations with any measure of public confidence. After witnessing Nixon's political demise, Ford knew that even U.S. presidents did not carry much international clout if their domestic political support was in question.

Most new presidents have a three-month transition period—"100 days"—to acclimate to their new responsibilities and to organize their administration. Ford had no such luxury. Accordingly, he decided to maintain continuity and coherence at the highest levels of government by keeping much of President Nixon's cabinet in place. Although he was particularly keen to keep Henry Kissinger as secretary of state and assistant for national security affairs, Ford moved quickly to assert his own authority. On his second day in office, he instructed Kissinger to assemble the NSC. Kissinger balked and tried to convince the president to postpone meeting with the NSC until a later date. Kissinger told Ford that assembling the NSC so soon after taking office would make the Soviet Union think that a crisis was afoot. Ford was not swayed. Despite Kissinger's objections, he convened the NSC meeting the next day.

Notwithstanding this early signal to Kissinger, the president soon became immersed in domestic policy. For the next several weeks, it appeared to a number of us that Kissinger alone was conducting foreign policy. For example, a series of National Security Memorandums (NSDMs) on arms control issues appeared. These directives on the direction in which arms control was to proceed were issued without prior discussion in NSC meetings and, to our knowledge, without being cleared with the president.

Still, Ford made it known very quickly that he preferred to deal directly and openly with a full range of advisors rather than emulate President Nixon's highly secretive management style. But after six months of trying to coordinate the activities of seven or eight advisors on international affairs, Ford decided to retrench. He realized that while he was handling domestic issues well, he was neglecting foreign affairs and especially arms control. He instructed Donald Rumsfeld, his chief of staff, to screen and coordinate matters before they were brought to his attention.

In keeping with his policy of maintaining continuity, Ford kept James Schlesinger as his secretary of defense. Although several of Ford's former colleagues in Congress reportedly complained to him that Schlesinger gave them short shrift and treated them contemptuously, Ford recognized Schlesinger's valuable expertise in strategic matters. Much to Kissinger's dismay, Ford began consulting his secretary of defense first on military aspects of arms control. While it was understandable that Ford would go first to his secretary of defense for such advice, Kissinger grumbled about it to his staff. He had grown accustomed to providing advice of this kind to Nixon and, only subsequently, having it commented on by the secretary of defense.

Ford particularly liked Schlesinger's approach to U.S. deterrence policy. The "Schlesinger Doctrine" was based on limited retaliation options that allowed the United States to conduct selected nuclear operations against hardened Soviet ICBM silos and other military targets rather than unleash a full-scale nuclear strike in response to a Soviet attack. Although strategic targeting of this nature required sophisticated, accurate, and expensive weapons, the new doctrine provided the president with additional latitude to respond to limited aggression in a way that would not lead to immediate and deadly nuclear escalation.

President Ford knew that the Soviet Union was a dangerous military adversary, but he felt that the Soviet Union, like the United States, did not want to run the risk of initiating a nuclear war. Ford was also aware that the Soviets were trying to capitalize on the American public's growing desire to enter into arms control agreements. To counter this tactic, Ford instructed our team in Geneva to make tough but fair demands on the Soviets. If the Soviet delegation failed to accept them immediately, he said, we should be patient. Eventually, the Soviets would see the futility of their stalling and reason would prevail. I liked Ford's guidance, but I was not convinced that the Soviets would allow reason to prevail.

As we anticipated, the negotiating sessions in Geneva following Ford's swearing-in were not very productive. True to form, the Soviets took a wait-and-see attitude while they tried to get a feel for the new president's policies. But Ford was faced with ever-mounting public pressure to "get on" with arms control. Not wanting to be blamed for holding up progress, Ford, after only two months in office, sent Kissinger to Moscow to see if he could make any headway with Foreign Minister Gromyko on SALT II. Ford instructed Kissinger not to pursue linkage, having decided that the policy had gotten Nixon nowhere. He simply wanted Kissinger to review with Gromyko the two main arms control issues dividing the United States and the Soviet Union and determine if progress was possible.

The first point of discussion concerned the overall number of strategic nuclear delivery systems that both sides would be allowed under the treaty. The second was to see if there was any possibility of agreeing to a limit on "MIRVed" missiles. While still in Moscow, Kissinger cabled the president that, after talking to Gromyko and Brezhnev, the two sides were closer to an agreement than previously thought. Ford was pleased with the news. He instructed Kissinger to explore the possibility of arranging a summit meeting to coincide with his scheduled trip to the Far East the following month. Kissinger did so and preparations for the summit at Vladivostok began in earnest.

The most important goal I hoped we would achieve at Vladivostok was a guarantee that both sides would be permitted an equal number of strategic delivery systems. One of the ways to approach that goal was to broaden the number of weapon-system categories being considered in the negotiations. SALT I had only sought to limit ballistic missiles, an area where the Soviets held an advantage in both size and quantity. In SALT II, the Soviets insisted that heavy bombers, where the United States had the numerical advantage, should also be counted. Our original SALT II position, a stern one, rejected the Soviet demand. We insisted that we would seek equality with the Soviets in terms of ballistic missiles only, leaving heavy bombers out of the equation.

Although ballistic missiles are primarily first-strike weapons, and bombers fit only second-strike or retaliatory scenarios, the Soviet argument was not without merit. Bombers, like ballistic missiles, could inflict significant damage at intercontinental ranges. To include heavy bombers in the count of strategic delivery systems clearly worked to the Soviets' advantage. Even so, the Soviets had so many more ballistic missiles than we that, even if we included our more numerous bombers, the Soviet Union would still have more strategic systems than the United States. If true equality in the number of strategic systems were to be reached, the Soviets would still need to reduce their ballistic missile forces.

The question of U.S.-Soviet equality, military or otherwise, evoked deeply rooted psychological reactions from the Soviet leaders. To them, more and bigger was not only better but imperative. Whether it was the grandeur of their buildings, the expanse of their avenues, or the size of their missiles, the Soviets were never satisfied unless theirs were more numerous and bigger than ours. In an attempt to legitimize this alleged right to superiority, the Soviets resorted to an Orwellian insistence that in order for them to be equal, they had to be more than equal. They answered our demand for equality in strategic delivery systems with a counterdemand that they be afforded "equality plus equal security." In this way they hoped to achieve not only parity with the United States, but also to be equal to any combination of forces from other nations that might be arrayed against them. It was a way of justifying their demand that the United States include French and British nuclear missiles in the total count of strategic delivery systems. It was a classic example of how the Soviets tried to use the "fear of invasion" fallacy to their advantage.

Since the Joint Chiefs of Staff insisted on absolute equality, it fell to me to be the principal proponent of their view on the U.S. negotiating team. I explained to one of my counterparts, Gen. Konstantin Trusov, that the United States would never agree to strategic inequality with the Soviet Union. Every time I pressed for *equality*, Trusov countered with *equality and equal security*. Trying to appeal to his mathematical mind, I went to a blackboard and wrote the following equation:

$$(US)\ E = (USSR)\ E + (USSR)\ ES$$

"This is your formula," I said, "but the equation is clearly unbalanced. Our formula, $(US)\ E = (USSR)\ E$, represents equality. If one subtracts E from each side of your formula, it would read $0 = (USSR)\ ES$. As you can see," I continued, "it would leave nothing on our side and equal security on yours."

I could tell that Trusov realized I had a point, but he would never be able to admit as much. His lame response was, "Everyone knows that international relationships transcend pure mathematics." I sensed, nevertheless, that Trusov and, perhaps, other Soviet negotiators were beginning to understand that the United States would settle for nothing short of equality.

Meanwhile, Kissinger, as usual, was overstepping his bounds. In his presummit preparations, Kissinger failed to share with President Ford the most important results of his negotiations with the Soviet leadership. Just as he had in April 1972, when Nixon had sent him to Moscow, Kissinger reportedly took it upon himself to complete, for all intents and purposes, the details of what was to be discussed at the summit. Kissinger believed that the Soviets would insist on retaining a larger number of strategic launchers to offset the U.S. technological advantage in MIRVed missiles. He nonetheless put forward the equal aggregates option in addition to one that allowed the Soviets to field more numerous strategic launchers if the United States was allowed to deploy a larger number of MIRVed missiles. To Kissinger's surprise, Brezhnev said the Soviets would accept either option. Kissinger, however, reported that Brezhnev had accepted only the proposal that called for higher numbers of launchers for the Soviet Union and higher numbers of launchers with MIRVed missiles for the United States. Schlesinger and the Joint Chiefs of Staff said that they could only accept equal numbers of strategic launchers.

Kissinger, knowing that Brezhnev had already agreed, told Schlesinger and the chiefs that he would negotiate hard for their position. At Vladivostok, Kissinger told Gromyko that the United States, after reconsidering the matter, preferred equal numbers of launchers. He knew, of course, that Brezhnev had already said that he would agree to either option. Kissinger thus made it appear that he had defended and won a hard-fought victory for Schlesinger's and the chiefs' position. It was yet another example of the way Kissinger played games with the Washington bureaucracy.

To make matters worse, Kissinger also assured the Soviets that their Backfire bombers would not be classified as having intercontinental capabilities. In other words, Backfire bombers would not be counted under the limits placed on Soviet strategic weapons. Kissinger's assurance granted the Soviets an unwarranted concession, one which ultimately proved enormously disadvantageous. These episodes were further evidence of the perils of unmonitored back-channel negotiations.

FORD AND VLADIVOSTOK

The summit meeting at Vladivostok was, on the whole, a success. The two leaders agreed to a basic negotiating framework for SALT II and largely mollified the concerns of the U.S. military by agreeing to equal aggregates of strategic systems. Not everyone, however, shared my opinion that Vladivostok was a U.S. triumph. My friend Scoop Jackson argued that the Soviets had hoodwinked the United States into believing that strategic equality had been achieved when in fact the Soviets had codified their strategic superiority. For one thing, he believed the 2,400 aggregate number for strategic delivery systems was too high, that even though the Soviets would have to eliminate several hundred systems, we had no intention of building additional weapons to come up to that number. For another, the 3 to 1 Soviet advantage in aggregate missile megatonnage, Jackson complained, had been swept under the rug. But I was optimistic. Having achieved success on the principle of equality of weapons systems, I believed that the equality of megatonnage could be resolved at a later date.

To my pleasant surprise, the Soviets failed to raise the issue of air-launched cruise missiles (ALCMs) at Vladivostok. There had been a lively debate in Geneva over the Soviet claim that not only should strategic bombers be counted against the proposed ceiling of 2,400 permitted strategic delivery systems but also each ALCM carried by those bombers. Our counterargument was that ALCMs were simply munitions that made a bomber a single strategic system and that each cruise missile carried on a bomber should not be included in the 2,400 total.

The Soviet negotiating team, feeling that Brezhnev should have raised the ALCM issue at the summit, insisted that ALCMs be covered in the final communiqué. By simply deleting the word *ballistic* before *missiles,* the Soviets sought to broaden the scope of the agreement to include cruise missiles, which do not have ballistic trajectories. I objected. After all, the matter had not been discussed in any of the negotiating sessions at Vladivostok and to include it in an official record of the meeting proceedings was completely unwarranted.

For several days after the summit, Kissinger refused to agree to the Soviet version of the communiqué. By inference, if the final version of the communiqué did not contain the word *ballistic*, it included cruise missiles. Finding himself subject to mounting public and media pressure to issue a joint statement, Kissinger's resolve began to wane. Fearful that Vladivostok might be looked upon by the public as a failure, Kissinger finally caved in and did not insist on the word *ballistic* in the communiqué. It allowed the Soviets subsequently to claim that the communiqué covered ALCMs. It introduced an issue that would stay alive for many years, one that would not be resolved until the final negotiations on START in 1991.

At Vladivostok, the question of whether U.S. tactical nuclear weapons and aircraft deployed in Europe should be included in the count of U.S. strategic delivery systems played out in a way that had been previously telegraphed to me by Soviet Gen. Konstantin Trusov.

In Geneva, the forward-based system issue had become a matter of intense debate between General Trusov and me. He claimed that U.S. tactical nuclear weapons and aircraft deployed in NATO Europe, with sufficient range to reach Soviet territory, should be included in the count of U.S. strategic delivery systems. From the outset I explained to Trusov that U.S. weapons of less than intercontinental range were deployed in Europe in response to Soviet conventional superiority as well as the threat posed by Soviet intermediate-range systems. I emphasized that under Article V of the NATO Treaty, an attack against one NATO member was an attack against all. More fundamentally, if the Soviets attacked U.S. forces, it would not matter where our troops were stationed. An attack on U.S. troops anywhere in the world would be tantamount to an attack on the United States.

General Trusov and I had, for over a year, hotly argued the pros and cons of the FBS issue. To my surprise, one day in the summer of 1974, during one of our informal talks in the park out of earshot of any interpreters or other Soviets, General Trusov told me that my arguments had merit. In a manner highly uncharacteristic of Soviet negotiators, he admitted that the FBS issue was a diversionary tactic, one that Moscow would not let interfere with an otherwise satisfactory agreement. He told me that Brezhnev was looking for an arms control deal with the United States, knew how strongly the U.S. military felt about the FBS issue, and would not let it stand in the way of an agreement.

Elated at this breakthrough, I rushed to tell the Joint Chiefs of Staff the good news. The chiefs, however, were highly skeptical. They were convinced that the Soviets had held their views on FBS for so long, and had expressed them so strongly, that they would never concede the issue. I continued to insist that the Soviets had had a change of heart and that Trusov was giving me the straight story. Finally, I received their permission to raise the matter with Secretary of Defense Schlesinger.

Like the chiefs, Schlesinger was highly doubtful that the Soviets would give in on FBS, but he agreed to raise the matter with President Ford. The president, persuaded that FBS should not be counted as strategic systems, instructed Kissinger to rebut the Soviets on FBS and offer no compromise. Kissinger did not like Ford's instructions. He seriously doubted that the Soviets would back down, and if he were in their shoes the FBS issue would be nonnegotiable. His own views notwithstanding, Kissinger followed orders and at Vladivostok vigorously challenged the Soviet FBS arguments. To his great relief and greater surprise, Gromyko did not pursue the matter. Kissinger was able to pocket the windfall. Although several explanations have been offered as to why the Soviets gave in, I remain convinced that the facts were as Trusov had revealed to me. Unlike many others, I was confident that we would eventually win the point if we remained firm—and we did. It was another lesson I learned from negotiating with the Soviets. They would cooperate only when they determined that we were resolute and absolutely committed to our stated position.

The verification provisions of the Vladivostok accord, while not as comprehensive as we would have liked, were better than the nearly nonexistent measures provided for in SALT I. I later learned from several Soviet sources that Brezhnev overrode the objections of his military on verification in order to conclude the agreement. Buoyed by Brezhnev's actions, our hopes were raised that the framework for a SALT II treaty agreed upon at Vladivostok would soon be fleshed out and that complete agreement on a SALT II treaty could be reached by the middle of 1975. It was generally accepted in Washington that if a treaty was not completed by that time, the Ford administration would not be able to see the treaty through the ratification process.

In a fit of euphoria, Ron Nessen, President Ford's press secretary, boasted to the press corps that Ford had done more in three months toward reaching an arms control agreement than Nixon had done in five years. Shortly after Vladivostok, however, Nessen conceded that this was an exaggeration. He admitted that a great deal of work remained before SALT II would be ready for signature. Kissinger made the unwarranted and bewildering statement, unwise in any negotiating process, that the Soviets were responsible for the progress, having made most of the concessions. He echoed Nessen's premature optimism by claiming that SALT II was 90 percent complete. What he refused to realize was that in negotiating with the Soviets, the last 10 percent of a treaty often took more time than the preceding 90 percent.

When President Ford returned to Washington from Vladivostok, we noticed that he was becoming more careful about how much freedom of action he allowed Kissinger. It must have become apparent to the president that in the months preceding Nixon's resignation, Kissinger had become quite independent and had engaged more and more in back-channel communications with Ambassador Dobrynin in Washington and Foreign Minister Gromyko in Moscow. President Ford undoubtedly had heard lurid tales of the uncoordinated 1972 summit, where the two sets of negotiations resulted in the negotiators talking past one another. Kissinger's handling of the joint communiqué following the Vladivostok summit, especially the way he dealt with the ALCM issue, further irritated the president. Ford wanted to avoid such gaffes in the future.

It was not until after Vladivostok that we learned that Kissinger, during the presummit consultations, had accepted the Soviet demand that the Backfire bomber not be counted as a strategic delivery system. Apparently believing the Soviets would never give in on the Backfire issue, Kissinger had "gone off the reservation" and committed the United States to a controversial negotiating position without prior consultations with the president, the Pentagon, or other interested parties. Ford's suspicions were confirmed: Kissinger was a loose cannon, acting on his own.

Kissinger was quick to sense Ford's displeasure with his conspicuous independence. Although the secretary of state remained the chief architect of foreign policy, he realized that prudence required him to be more circumspect. While Kissinger continued to use the back-channels, he did so more sparingly. It was obvious that President Ford wanted to call the tune in foreign policy and equally obvious that Kissinger did not want to risk losing his position as the president's primary foreign policy advisor.

SALT II AND LINKAGE

When negotiations resumed in Geneva in early 1975, the Soviets stonewalled more than usual. They were incensed over the Jackson-Vanik Amendment to the U.S.-Soviet Trade Agreement that linked relaxation of U.S. trade with the Soviet Union to more liberal emigration policies for Soviet Jews.

The Stevenson Amendment to the Export-Import (ExIm) Bank bill proved even more odious to the Soviets. It limited Soviet access to ExIm Bank financial credits to no more than US$300 million over four years. To put this in perspective, in the fifteen months prior to the introduction of this legislation, the Soviets had received almost US$470 million in credits. The Soviets desperately needed periodic infusions of foreign capital because of their nonconvertible currency, few hard currency exports, and rapidly deteriorating industrial base. They viewed the Stevenson Amendment as a deliberate attempt to retard their growth and development and as gross interference with their domestic policies. The Stevenson Amendment, like the Jackson-Vanik Amendment, was a congressional expression of Nixon's policy of linkage, which was always present but seldom discussed.

The Soviets continued to insist that strategic arms negotiations were so important in their own right that progress toward an agreement should not be tied to any other conditions. They dragged their feet because of the Jackson-Vanik and Stevenson amendments, clear evidence that linkage was having a direct and negative impact on the negotiations.

Three primary issues were left hanging by the Soviet decision to stall: (1) verification of MIRVed missiles, (2) limitations on air-launched cruise missiles, and (3) classification of the Backfire bomber as a strategic system.

BACKFIRE

From the outset of SALT II negotiations, I took a strong stand on the Backfire issue. Having had exhaustive studies made of its capabilities, I was convinced that it was a strategic bomber and should be counted in the Soviets' total number of strategic delivery systems. The Joint Chiefs of Staff agreed. The Backfire was a huge aircraft, closer in size to a heavy than a medium bomber, and larger than the planned B-1. The large majority of U.S. intelligence estimates strongly indicated that the Backfire had intercontinental capabilities.

The Soviets tried to refute our assessment of the Backfire on three levels. The first was semantic. They claimed that, in Russian, inanimate objects such as an airplane cannot possess capabilities. Machines, they argued, have no will of their own and are only as capable as the humans who operate them. The Soviets refused, therefore, to discuss the matter of the Backfire's capabilities. I countered that it did not matter whether one referred to the Backfire's performance attributes as capabilities or characteristics, the Soviets would use the Backfire against the United States as an intercontinental bomber in time of war.

The Soviets' second argument was that they could not discuss the characteristics of the Backfire because to do so would divulge military secrets. My rebuttal was simple and straightforward. No arms control negotiation, I said, would ever bear fruit if weapon system characteristics were not openly discussed. Referring to several charts in *Interavia*, a Swiss magazine, I demonstrated to General Trusov that the Backfire had intercontinental capabilities or, in their terminology, intercontinental characteristics. But Trusov would not give in. In the maddening style of Soviet negotiators, he said, "You have not presented objective arguments but only engineers' estimates."

Trying to skewer me with an expression I had often used in reference to the Soviets, he said, "Figures lie and liars figure. Therefore, your ideas are subjective. Leonid Brezhnev himself has said that the USSR will never use the Backfire against the United States, and that is the objective truth." He left me incredulous and speechless.

The Soviets' third rebuttal became known as the "radius versus range" argument. They maintained that the Backfire did not have the ability to take off from a base in the Soviet Union, strike a target in the United States, and then return to its point of origin. We did not deny that the Backfire was unable to perform any such go-and-return mission; no U.S. aircraft could either. I pointed out, however, that ever since Gen. Jimmy Doolittle's time no modern air force flew such missions. Doolittle, a much-decorated World War II aviator, had taken off from an aircraft carrier, hit a target in Japan, and landed in China. Today, I explained, U.S. wartime plans called for bomber missions to strike targets in the Soviet Union and land in third countries such as Turkey or Greece. My argument was that the Backfire could take off from the Soviet Union, strike a target in the United States, and land in Cuba.

The Soviets did not accept this line of reasoning, saying that such plans amounted to suicide or kamikaze missions. At a Moscow diplomatic reception, Marshal Nikolai Ogarkhov, the Soviet chief of staff, chided me for my stand.

"I'll let you take off in a Backfire," he said, "fly over the United States, and head for Cuba. There I'll have your former wife, now your widow, waiting with flowers to strew over your watery grave since you will never get there."

"I'll go," I replied, "provided you come with me. Then I'll know the bomber will take off with a full tank of gas."

Secretary of Defense Schlesinger, initially skeptical about U.S. intelligence assessments of the Backfire's range, asked a group of highly capable and respected analysts to study the problem carefully. After six weeks of exhaustive study, they reported their results to Schlesinger in a six-hour meeting that I attended. He repeatedly challenged them on their data, their assumptions, and their judgments, trying in every way he could to discredit their findings. But in the end, they convinced him that the Backfire bomber did indeed have intercontinental capabilities. This gave me confidence that I could defend my position with State Department skeptics, who had become a bigger obstacle than my intransigent Soviet counterparts.

Arguing over the Backfire gave me the opportunity to have some fun with General Trusov. As the JCS representative, I often used my access to extensive U.S. intelligence estimates to impress the Soviets with the extent of our knowledge of their military assets. On one occasion, however, General Trusov stumped me with a question about the Backfire that I could not answer.

"I'll have to turn to my computer," I said, "and give you the answer after lunch."

During the lunch break, I found the answer I was looking for in a computer printout of the Backfire assessment report prepared for Schlesinger. When we reconvened, I turned to the appropriate page and provided Trusov the answer to his question. He was stunned. He thought that I had queried Washington during lunch and immediately received the information I wanted. I didn't tell Trusov that I had brought the information with me from Washington. I let him believe that we could get instant replies to our inquiries through a computer terminal I had in my office. Trusov, who was only rarely permitted to use the Soviets' most sophisticated piece of office equipment, Minister Semenov's lone copier, was duly impressed. It was one of the many mind games we negotiators liked to play on one another.

The Soviets also played games, some of which were quite sophisticated. Vladimir Pavlichenko, the senior KGB operative on their team, would buttonhole U.S. negotiators and feed them bits of information that were true. Having established some credibility, he would then slip in a significant item that was not true. For example, having gained the confidence of one of our team from the State Department, Pavlichenko told him that Moscow had decided not to make any further modifications to their SS-18 heavy missiles but would allow them to atrophy. The facts were just the opposite. I was chagrined at how often members of our team fell for Pavlichenko's tactic of providing us disinformation.

Perhaps the favorite Soviet mind game was endless repetition of the same theme. After a while, we would catch ourselves believing that something was true simply because we had heard it so often from the Soviets. But for the most part we were onto their game and let them know it. For example, there was the time I recounted to Soviet negotiator Viktor Karpov the scolding I had received from my mother when I was a boy because the soap I had brought home from the store was not Ivory, my mother's favorite brand.

"You didn't buy the right brand," she said. "Don't you know Ivory is 99-44/100 percent pure, so pure that it floats?" She had heard the advertisement so often she believed it was true. "The soap I bought was just as pure," I explained. "Ivory doesn't float because it is pure, but because it has been whipped up." I had learned in my chemistry classes that trapping air in soap makes it less dense and causes it to float.

Karpov took the occasion to remind me of the evils of capitalism, which he said squanders resources in order to sell products that should be bought simply on their own merits. Still, he had learned well the effect Madison Avenue has on Americans. I often felt that, like my mother's favorite soap, Soviet arguments floated only because they had a lot of hot air whipped into them.

A British diplomat who had negotiated with the Soviets said that talking to them was like putting coins into a broken vending machine. You could kick it and shake it, but you could not get it to cough up anything. You could not even get your coin back. Ambassador Alexis Johnson, frustrated by a lack of give-and-take, resorted to asking direct questions. His counterpart, Minister Vladimir Semenov, reacted by searching through a stack of index cards he kept at hand to see if he could answer Johnson's questions. When he found a card that answered a question Moscow had anticipated, he would read it. More often, however, he simply read the answer to a question for which he had an answer, even though it had no relevance to the question asked. When Johnson complained that Semenov was not answering his questions, Semenov, with a straight face, told Johnson he was not asking the right questions. Johnson at one point decided not to let it pass. "I insist," he said, "that I asked the right question."

"Well," said Semenov, "I gave the right answer, but you didn't listen between the lines."

Alex Johnson tried hard to engage Semenov in small talk, but without much success. At one point, Johnson said he was in his late sixties and had suffered a heart attack. Semenov said, "Me, too." Johnson said he limited himself to one cocktail a day, to which Semenov replied, "Me, too."

"Then how do you stay so youthful, so vigorous?" Johnson asked, indulging in a little diplomatic flattery.

"It's easy," said Semenov. "My wife keeps me young; she's a ballet dancer in her twenties." It was a story Johnson hoped would not get back to Mrs. Johnson.

On another occasion Semenov, well versed in period furniture, boasted that his Moscow apartment was furnished with Louis XV pieces. "What period is your furniture?" Semenov asked. "Early Johnsonian," said Alex wryly.

It was as hard to engage the other Soviet negotiators in small talk as it was their chief. On those few occasions when we succeeded, they were uneasy, suspicious, xenophobic, and self-conscious. They were always looking for hidden meanings to things we said. For example, I once mentioned to Gen. Konstantin Trusov that my son, who rowed on a college crew, ate steak and eggs for breakfast every morning. Instead of passing it off as a casual remark, Trusov inferred that I was making an invidious comparison between American and Russian diets. "Don't you know that it takes eight pounds of grain to add a pound to a steer and that less than 10 percent of a steer is steak?" he asked. "Why not raise fowl which requires only two pounds of grain to produce one pound of chicken?" Wasn't my son discriminating against the poor people in America and forcing them to eat sausage? This silly line of questioning made me wish I had never brought up the subject.

I recall another occasion when the Soviet search for hidden meanings came to the fore in bizarre fashion. During a visit to the talks, Senator Charles Mathias of Maryland explained to Minister Semenov that spy satellites and listening devices were insufficient to provide adequate verification of arms control treaties. What was needed, he said, was on-site inspection. To drive home his point, Mathias told Semenov that before Mathias' mother paid for a box of strawberries, she would empty them into a plate. That way she could see if the berries at the bottom of the box were as nice as those on top.

That evening, the senator brought a box of strawberries to a reception we were holding for the Soviets. He cornered Semenov and emptied the strawberries onto a plate. As expected, those at the bottom of the box were inferior to those on top. But Semenov did not get the point. He turned the box over and noticed the stenciling on the bottom: "Product of Israel." Semenov turned to an aide and said, "You see, even U.S. Senators try to send us messages about third countries."

I had a similar experience just before Christmas break when I received a bottle of vodka as a gift from General Trusov. In return, I gave him a Texas Instruments calculator. General Trusov examined the gift suspiciously. He commented that perhaps I did not think the number of Soviet missiles he told us they had was correct, or that I thought he could not count accurately. Not believing that he could be serious, I tried to make light of the matter. But then Trusov noticed that inside the calculator were the words *Made in Japan*. "Are you trying to give me a message about third countries?" he asked. I gave up and decided that in the future I would stick to giving him bourbon. It would be the safest way to exchange gifts.

Throughout the talks, the Soviets, always looking for a psychological edge, would probe for information about how members of our team got along with one another. Gen. Ivan Beletsky knew that I played golf with Alex Johnson on weekends. At our first meeting of the week he often asked about our scores, hoping to learn Ambassador Johnson's mood and hence predict what success the Soviets could expect at the negotiating table. One morning I told Beletsky that I had shot a lower score than Johnson. Incredulous, he asked me, "Did you really beat your boss?" When I confirmed that I had, he said soberly and in all seriousness, "That would never happen on the Soviet team. I'd always find a way to let my boss win."

Although we were usually less interested in the mood swings of Soviet negotiators than they were in ours, I would invariably open my conversations by asking: *"Kak dela?"* This question is similar to the American expression "How's it going?" or the French *"Ça va?"* While Americans and Frenchmen usually answer with some platitude like "Okay" or *"Va bien,"* the Soviets always took the question literally. They felt compelled to give some definitive answer like *"Kharasho"* (good), *"Normalno"* (normal), or *"Ploho"* (poorly).

"Kak dela" became my trademark. Once, when a Soviet negotiator asked me, *"Kak dela?"* I answered in rhyme: *"Kak sazha bela"* (Like soot is white). This was not original; I had picked it up somewhere, but the Soviets credited me with having thought it up and from then on would go out of their way to think of other interesting answers. Once when both negotiating teams were quite busy, I asked, *"Kak dela?"* and received the answer, *"Dela idut, kontora pischet,"* which freely translates into "things are moving, the office is writing furiously." Another time when matters were getting quite complicated, the answer I got to my question was *"Kak generalskie pagony— zigzaggy i splosh propspeykt"* (Like a general's epaulets—zigzaggy and hard to see through). Over the course of the negotiations, I gathered some thirty different answers for my collection.

At times, without even realizing it, the Soviets would provide us with a sobering thought. On one occasion, chief negotiator Semenov told me that he believed timing was everything, in love, in war, and most of all, in attending meetings. He explained that he was once invited, as a member of the Soviet foreign ministry, to attend a meeting called by Lavrenti Beria, the infamous head of the KGB. "I felt in my bones that I should not go," he said, "so I sent someone in my place."

During Beria's meeting, said Semenov, a military squad broke in and arrested the group. Beria was subsequently shot and the others sent to Siberia. "You Americans," he said, "like to say you have to know when to hold your cards and when to fold them. More important, you have to know when to go and when not to go to meetings."

Semenov had studied carefully the King James Bible ("for its literary value only"), Shakespeare, and Bullfinch's *Mythology*. He said that knowing these three Western classics was all that a foreigner need to know to communicate well with Americans.

Semenov often used quotations from his three basic sources to give some indirect or cryptic response to questions he did not want to answer. For example, quoting from the Bible, he once told Johnson to "sweep the house for the talents." At other times he would quote Shakespeare: ". . . to post with such dexterity to incestuous sheets." Semenov's favorite expression was: "The owl of Minerva comes out only at night." At first we found it amusing, but we soon became exasperated by Semenov's calculated evasiveness.

The Soviets at times attempted to justify their positions by attributing them to higher authority. They expected us to be impressed when they announced, seriously and gravely, that what they said "had the approval of Moscow." When it was clear that we were unimpressed, they would trot out some quotation from General Secretary Brezhnev. They seemed disappointed that we did not share their reverence for their leader and that we did not hasten to agree that "it was so because Brezhnev said so." As a last resort they would quote their deity—Lenin. As one of the Soviet negotiators once told me, "We keep a set of quotations on hand. We never get in trouble by citing higher authority."

Even during informal meetings, when we attempted to get a discussion going by asking the Soviets a question about something they had said, they would resort to repeating a canned statement. They would never answer a serious question unless it had first been analyzed and approved in Moscow.

When they wanted to stall negotiations the Soviets would monopolize the discussion, resorting to their maddening technique of repeating their position. Trying to thwart these stultifying Soviet efforts, I once brought along a clock with two timers, the kind used by chess players during official matches to limit the time allowed for each move. Minister Semenov, realizing what was going on, feigned great indignation. He complained that I was treating the serious matter of negotiations as a mere game.

MIRV VERIFICATION

In an attempt to break the deadlock over the verification of MIRVed missiles, Kissinger met with Soviet Foreign Minister Gromyko in Vienna on May 19–20, 1975. The verification problem was compli-

cated because the Soviets had both MIRVed and single-warhead missiles at two of their missile sites—Derazhnya and Pervomaysk (D& P).
Our intelligence analysts had studied satellite photographs but were
unable to differentiate between the two types of missiles. Accordingly, our policy was to assume that all the silos contained
MIRVed missiles.

The Soviets objected. "Only a portion of the missiles are MIRVed,"
they said, adding that we would simply have to take their word for
it that some missiles were MIRVed and others were not. This D&P
problem, as it came to be known, was further complicated by the fact
that we, too, had both MIRVed and single-warhead missiles deployed at Malmstrom Air Force Base in Montana. We informed the
Soviets that the silos at Malmstrom contained both types of missiles.
The headworks of the missile silos were different, we said, and they
should be able to distinguish between them by examining their satellite reconnaissance data. The Soviets replied that their intelligence
capabilities were not as good as we claimed and their analysts could
not tell the two types of silos apart.

In an effort to break the logjam, I asked the Joint Chiefs of Staff for
permission to invite the Soviets to inspect our silos at Malmstrom.
The chiefs, alarmed at the thought, denied my request. They were
concerned that the Soviets would examine our silos and not let us
look at theirs. I told the chiefs that we would insist on a quid pro quo
and that because of the Soviet obsession with secrecy, we stood to
gain if they accepted our offer. In the end, the chiefs gave their
permission.

Back in Geneva, I said to my counterparts, "On behalf of the
United States, I invite Soviet representatives to inspect our silos at
Malmstrom Air Force Base." Before I could add our conditions,
General Trusov said, "Nyet, if we inspect your silos you will want to
inspect ours, and this we will never allow." The chiefs were relieved,
but we had scored another negotiating point; we were willing to be
more open than they were.

Negotiations continued to move slowly during the remainder of
1975. In part, this was because the Soviets were disturbed that former
Secretary of Defense Melvin Laird had published a scathing article in
the July issue of Reader's Digest accusing the Soviets of cheating on
the ABM Treaty and the Interim Agreement. The article charged the
Soviets with deploying high-powered, phased-array radars in a manner that violated the ABM Treaty. Laird also accused them of stuffing
newer and more powerful missiles into the same silos used to house

their predecessors. This, Laird suggested, was a violation of the Interim Agreement on Offensive Weapons. Although in essence correct, Laird's silo assertion was not completely accurate. By putting newer and more powerful missiles into old silos, the Soviets were violating an "understanding" that had been agreed to, but they were not in direct violation of any specific treaty clause. They were, of course, breaching the spirit of the agreement, but this came as no surprise because they had little regard for the spirit of any agreement.

THE DEMISE OF DÉTENTE

Ford and Brezhnev met again in July 1975 in Helsinki at the Conference on Security and Cooperation in Europe (CSCE). Although I had seen them together previously, in Helsinki I was struck by their physical similarity. Both were large men, although Ford was in better condition. Brezhnev's years of chain-smoking and heavy drinking had taken their toll. When Brezhnev got started talking, however, he was the more animated of the two. He was also more wily. On one occasion Brezhnev appeared to be napping during one of Ford's presentations, causing the president to race through his talking points without elaboration. When Ford finished, Brezhnev gave Ford a point-by-point rebuttal on every argument he had made. He apparently had not been asleep at all but simply tricked Ford into lowering his guard and then attacked him furiously.

In an effort to sidestep our proposal regarding on-site inspection, Brezhnev told us that he no longer had serious problems with our proposal on the verification of MIRVed missiles. The Soviets would allow all their launchers at D&P to be counted as MIRVed missile launchers and accept our number of launchers of MIRVed and un-MIRVed missiles at Malmstrom. He noted, though, that serious differences still remained over the cruise missile and Backfire bomber.

Throughout the fall of 1975, we tried to resolve these issues, but the Soviet negotiators continued to stonewall. The Soviet position was undoubtedly influenced by the perception that President Ford was having increased difficulties with Congress. Despite the president's plea for additional aid to counteract Cuban and Soviet intervention in the Angolan civil war, Congress adamantly refused to honor his request. Earlier that year, when South Vietnam faced imminent collapse, Congress had also refused to release designated aid money to assist our former ally. Saigon's subsequent fall in April dramatically illustrated the growing impotence of executive power in the face of an activist Congress. Ford asked the American people to put the war behind them, but he could not help but worry that the collapse of South Vietnam, coupled with the failure to aid Angola, was a clear sign to other U.S. allies that the president did not have the support of Congress. Believing that a weakened president might try to enhance his popularity by concluding an arms control agreement, the Soviets dug in their heels and looked to Ford to make concessions.

It soon became evident that while we had been concentrating on relations with the Soviet Union and China, a new challenge had arisen in the Third World. The United States's willingness to be accommodating in areas other than arms control as an enticement to the Soviets to bring their Third World clients into line simply did not work. Even when direct Soviet complicity in Third World crises was conspicuous, such as the use of Cuban troops in Angola, Congress was not inclined to respond to Soviet belligerence in any constructive fashion. I decided to do what I could at my level to change our détente policy.

I knew Kissinger felt strongly about pursuing détente, and had convinced Nixon that it was the correct policy. He was so persuasive, in fact, that détente came to be regarded more as a foreign policy theology than a strategy for improved relations with the Soviet Union. I believed that détente was playing into Soviet hands and viewed the term as a code word for a policy of unwarranted accommodation. In the West, it was often assumed that we and the Soviets shared the same foreign policy goals: a rapprochement based on mutual restraint and the maintenance of the international status quo. But the Soviets did not view détente as having any bearing on their relationships with countries other than the United States. As a result, détente served as a constraint only on the policies of the United States.

I was reinforced in this view by Dr. Wynfred Joshua, a tough-minded intelligence analyst who had studied the matter closely. I took a summary of her findings to Secretary of Defense Schlesinger. He agreed that the arguments against détente had merit. "But," he said, "you're dealing with one of Henry's sacred cows. He believes he invented the concept and will never give it up." I nevertheless continued to pursue the matter, and Schlesinger finally arranged a briefing for President Ford.

Schlesinger convincingly laid out the arguments showing that détente was not furthering our foreign policy interests and worked only to the Soviets' advantage. The president was impressed. It may have been that he had already come to the same conclusion, or that he had seen the mounting congressional dissatisfaction with the policy as handwriting on the wall; it was impossible to tell. Soon afterward, the president phoned Kissinger and told him that the Ford administration would no longer pursue a policy of détente. He also instructed Kissinger that U.S. officials were no longer to use the term in any speeches or communications but to substitute for it other language, such as the phrase *peace through strength*. Kissinger, as Schlesinger had predicted, was furious. Détente was the foundation upon which his concept of dealing with the Soviet Union was based. The president remained firm, and Kissinger did his bidding. Early the next year, détente was dropped completely from the Ford administration's political lexicon.

In my dealings with Ford, I always felt that if I could marshal the appropriate facts and form convincing arguments that the president would not hesitate to make decisions that cut across the grain of conventional wisdom. Despite the growing demands of his office, Ford rarely seemed distracted or uncomfortable with the matters under discussion. Knowing of Lyndon Johnson's infamous epithet that Ford had played football too long without a helmet, I waited to see if he would falter. He did not. He always maintained the air of a mild-mannered and gentlemanly chairman of the board; he was self-assured and never overbearing. I recall one meeting when Kissinger and Schlesinger, obviously geared for a knock-down-drag-out fight, began to raise their voices. Rather than let them continue, Ford said firmly, "I get the point; let's move on." I was always confident that the nation's security was uppermost in the president's mind.

THE AX FALLS

On the evening of November 1, 1975, I was in Secretary Schlesinger's office discussing how we might break the deadlock over the cruise missile and Backfire bomber. Schlesinger, with his shirttail out and stocking feet propped up on his desk, seemed preoccupied. Little did I realize that he had had a serious run-in with the president earlier that day over the proposed defense budget.

Trying to get his attention, I said, "You look worried, Mr. Secretary. Surely it can't be that bad."

"Oh, yes it is," said Schlesinger. "How would you feel if the president told you that you made him uncomfortable?"

"Come, come," I replied, trying to make light of the situation. "The president's joking; you make us all feel uncomfortable."

I had, in fact, become quite used to Schlesinger's rough manner and unorthodox style, although early on he had made me uncomfortable as well. At our very first meeting, he disagreed with a point I made. I expected him to ask me to explain why I felt the way I did, but instead, he simply said, "Rowny, you're full of shit." On another occasion, while I was briefing him, he got up, turned his back on me, and looked out the window.

Less than twenty-four hours after Schlesinger mentioned his run-in with the president, he was fired. I was stunned. Since I had spent much of my time overseas, I was not completely up to speed on Washington's bureaucratic battles. I asked my Washington-based friends for an explanation of what had happened. No one could give me a satisfactory answer. Several suspected that Ford thought Schlesinger had incurred the wrath of members of Congress by habitually being late for meetings and talking down to them. Others said Schlesinger spoke too freely with members of the press, and this annoyed Ford. Still others felt that Schlesinger was dismissed because he openly disagreed with Ford over the size of the military budget.

From the outset of his administration, Ford began to see for himself that Schlesinger was not a subordinate easily held in check. Shortly after Ford took office, disturbing reports appeared in the press suggesting that senior U.S. military commanders had been forewarned of President Nixon's resignation. The insinuation was that military officers, indebted to Nixon for his efforts to secure the release of U.S. prisoners of war, might seek to prevent his downfall.

Rumors continued to circulate in Washington that the source of those stories was Schlesinger. In an effort to clear up the matter, President Ford confronted the secretary of defense and demanded to know if he had, in fact, been the source of the erroneous reports. Schlesinger flatly denied that he was involved. Ford wrote in his autobiography, however, that he later determined that Schlesinger was indeed the culprit, and had it not been for his desire to maintain continuity within the administration, he would have fired him then.

When I saw the secretary later on the day of his dismissal, he said, wryly, "See, didn't I tell you I made the president uncomfortable?"

I am inclined to believe that Schlesinger's dismissal had a great deal to do with the sour relations between him and Kissinger over such matters as Schlesinger's desire to put greater emphasis on verification provisions that would give us more access to the improvements the Soviets were making in the accuracy of their ballistic missiles. The tension between the two was an acknowledged sore spot with the president. I am also convinced that the president had yet another reason for his move. Ford wanted to strip Kissinger of one of his bureaucratic hats—that of national security advisor. A major reshuffling of his cabinet provided the political cover that enabled him to do so. Some administration officials had complained to Ford that Kissinger had slanted matters for presidential decision to reflect his personal preferences. Ford was annoyed by the implication that he was not his own man in foreign policy.

Most people who are not familiar with the inner workings of an administration do not appreciate how powerful the national security advisor can be. By stripping Kissinger of his dual role in foreign policy, Ford neutralized Kissinger's advantages over the secretary of defense and other cabinet members. Although the White House bureaucratic structure that Kissinger had designed while working for Nixon remained virtually intact, the way that structure was used became entirely different once Lt. Gen. Brent Scowcroft became Ford's national security advisor.

President Ford said he wanted his national security advisor to be an honest broker, carefully taking into account the views of all the various agencies involved in foreign policy. No longer would Kissinger be allowed to deal from a stacked deck. Although Scowcroft had been Kissinger's military assistant, Ford made it clear to the general that he was working for him. Most of the subsequent publicity surrounding the "Halloween massacre" focused on the changes in other cabinet posts that occurred at the same time, for example, Ford's naming his chief of staff, Donald Rumsfeld, as Schlesinger's replacement at the Defense Department. As a result, Kissinger's demotion went largely unnoticed. Kissinger, of course, did not want to call attention to his own misfortune, but it was obvious that he felt the blow keenly. When Kissinger was the national security advisor he often kept silent at high-level meetings, secure in the knowledge that he could always write what he wanted in his reports to the president. Now, however, stripped of his national security advisor role, Kissinger felt that he had to defend his position in front of others, something he would have preferred not to do.

Some of my colleagues believed that the tales told about Kissinger losing favor with Ford were greatly exaggerated. They believed that Kissinger's enemies included politicians too cowardly to attack Ford head-on, who found a convenient scapegoat in the person of Henry

Kissinger. Regardless of whose analysis was correct, Kissinger was now out of the White House and relegated to Foggy Bottom to manage a State Department bureaucracy that he fundamentally distrusted.

Rumsfeld, his new counterpart at the Pentagon, was much smoother than Schlesinger in his dealings with Kissinger. Whereas Schlesinger often used blunt and rough language, Rumsfeld was very tactful and often flattered Kissinger on his extensive knowledge of U.S. and Soviet weapon systems. Kissinger, knowing that Rumsfeld was close to Ford, in turn tended to be restrained when dealing with the new secretary of defense. Kissinger was forced to compete with Rumsfeld as an equal in the National Security Council, which had become a more level playing field since Scowcroft's arrival. As one Ford speechwriter put it, "Kissinger no longer got to play God during his daily one-hour meeting with the president."

While a certain amount of tension existed between the two cabinet officers, it was kept under control and out of the press. At one NSC meeting, for example, Kissinger seized on a statement made by the chairman of the Joint Chiefs that the chiefs considered missile throw-weight a difficult quality to monitor. Kissinger argued that the chiefs, therefore, disagreed with Rumsfeld that strict limits should be placed on throw-weight. Rumsfeld, who was usually calm and collected, became animated and complained to the president that Kissinger was trying to drive a wedge between him and the chiefs. Rumsfeld need not have worried. The chairman of the Joint Chiefs of Staff spoke up that the chiefs and the secretary were together on the issue; they were simply trying to point out the difficulty in drawing up the treaty's verification provisions. The chiefs, having been burned by Kissinger's tactics in the past, were not about to be caught in the middle again.

At about the same time as the Halloween Massacre, Nelson Rockefeller withdrew his name as Ford's running mate. Press reports suggested that the vice president had acted because of his advanced age (he was 67) and his disinclination to play second fiddle for four more years. White House scuttlebutt, however, told a different story.

Ford was worried about the upcoming election. His relationship with Congress, particularly conservatives, was at an all-time low. Public opinion surveys indicated that Ford's popularity with the electorate was on the wane. One poll showed that only 25 percent of Republicans sampled would vote for Ford if Rockefeller were on the ticket. Disingenuously, Ford cited his dismay that Rockefeller would not be with him for the "last charge." But it was clear that Ford thought otherwise. In a way that only Washington politicians can, Ford let Rockefeller know that it was time to retire. The vice president got the message and announced his decision the following day.

FORD THE MAN

Throughout 1975, I felt that Ford received undue criticism from the media. His slow and deliberate manner in explaining issues made him easy prey for hostile reporters. They often attributed to him mistakes that were not of his making. An example was the temporary loss of the "football" during one of Ford's visits to Paris.

The "football" is the briefcase that contains the secret codes the president needs to arm U.S. nuclear weapons in the event of a surprise attack. It is carried by a military officer whose job it is to always remain close to the president. On this occasion, Ford disembarked from Air Force One at Orly Field and joined the motorcade for Paris, assuming that the officer and the football were in his party. It was soon discovered that the football had accidentally been left behind on the plane.

When the president's military aide realized his error, he radioed the aircraft and had the briefcase rushed to him in another car. For about an hour, President Ford would have been unable to send the coded signal to activate nuclear retaliation had the Soviets decided to attack. It was a grave blunder, but it was certainly not Ford's fault. Nevertheless, the press portrayed it as one more example of Ford's bungling.

The president's refusal to meet with Aleksandr Solzhenitsyn brought on more uncharitable treatment. It was leaked to the press that Ford had referred to Solzhenitsyn as "a goddamn horse's ass" at a staff meeting. The press reported that Ford was reluctant to meet with the dissident Russian author because he felt that Solzhenitsyn only wanted to visit the White House to publicize his book. Actually, much thought had been given to the matter, and the pros and cons of the visit had been thoroughly discussed. Kissinger and Scowcroft, among others, reportedly advised the president against seeing Solzhenitsyn because it might endanger upcoming negotiations with the Soviets in Helsinki. The press reports caused conservative Republicans to rise up in arms; they accused Ford of kowtowing to Brezhnev. Despite the president's offer to meet with Solzhenitsyn upon his return from Finland, the damage had been done.

Criticism of Ford by the media was partially offset by the good press he received following his prompt and competent handling of the *Mayaguez* incident. On May 12, 1975, the president was informed that the *Mayaguez,* a U.S.-flagged merchant ship, had been fired upon and boarded in international waters by Cambodian Khmer Rouge communists. Ford realized that the world was waiting to see how the United States would respond. He also knew that this was his first serious international test after the fall of Saigon, and his reputation as a decisive world leader was on the line. Ford immediately decided to rescue the *Mayaguez* crew. He ordered aircraft from the USS *Coral Sea* to bomb a Cambodian garrison. This, in tandem with an assault by the U.S. Marines, caused the Cambodians to free the hostages. The *Mayaguez* crew of thirty-nine was spared, even though forty-one Americans lost their lives in the incident. Ford had demonstrated that he was a decisive leader who was able to make tough decisions and accept the consequences. The Gallup poll in June showed Ford for the first time over the 50 percent approval threshold. His popularity, however, was short-lived and soon went into a decline.

FORD'S LAST STAND

Kissinger's change in status did not make him any less energetic. He continued to work hard at trying to reach an agreement with the Soviets. In January 1976 he made one more attempt to get Gromyko to compromise on the cruise missile and Backfire bomber. But, again, Kissinger got nowhere.

After this attempt, the administration put SALT II aside. Although we continued to meet with Soviet negotiators in Geneva, little or no progress was made. Dissension began to grow within the Ford administration over whether the United States should push aggressively for an agreement. Kissinger led a faction that believed that reaching an arms control agreement was critical for the Ford administration and that true strategic equality should be a long-term, and not a short-term, goal. Secretary of Defense Rumsfeld led a second faction that disagreed. He did not believe that the Soviets had any intention of accepting strategic equality with the United States. He felt that a treaty codifying the Soviets' right to more weapons than the United States would establish a dangerous precedent. The differences in opinion were aired with growing frequency at NSC meetings and in the press. Because Ford himself was not inclined to accept an agreement unless it was completely equitable and verifiable, the arms control lobby in Washington was stymied. SALT II was also put aside because President Ford, realizing that it was benefiting only the Soviets, decided against investing any more U.S. resources in the suspect policy of détente. From early 1976 on, the administration became preoccupied with the presidential campaign.

During the campaign, President Ford was roundly criticized for a remark made during a debate with Jimmy Carter. In the much publicized statement, the president asserted, "There is no Soviet domination of Eastern Europe, and there never will be under a Ford administration." Much of the press ridiculed Ford for what they saw as his naive understanding of international affairs; they labeled his comment a serious political blunder. Several of Ford's advisors tried to convince the president to admit that he had made a mistake and to retract the statement. Ford refused, insisting that he sincerely meant what he had said.

It was immensely interesting to me that my Soviet counterpart, General Trusov, understood what Ford had meant when others had not. He told me, "Your President understands the souls of the peoples of Eastern Europe. While we are dominating the East Europeans militarily, I don't think the Soviet Union can forever dominate their hearts and minds." It was reassuring and more than a bit ironic that a Soviet negotiator, particularly a general officer, would come to the defense of our president. Having made his remark to me in confidence, I felt that it would have hurt him personally and damaged my relationship with him if I had repeated it in public. But it was an encouraging sign that the Soviet Union might not always be such an implacable foe.

THE END GAME

After three-and-one-half years of negotiations, the SALT II Treaty was still not complete, but President Ford had done well during his short tenure. He recognized the potential pitfalls of linkage where Nixon had not, and he was careful not to overplay his hand. If the Soviets were ready for an evenhanded deal, then he was ready to meet them halfway. But the Soviets were unwilling to move toward an agreement except on their own terms, and in Ford they found a stalwart adversary.

President Ford's own assessment of his stewardship was in keeping with his character. His greatest achievement, he believed, was healing the wounds of Watergate and helping to dispel the aura of public distrust of government that had developed during the Nixon administration. In a discussion Ford had with some of my military colleagues in March 1977, he told them that he had inherited a country in an angry mood. He believed that by keeping cool and getting capable and honest people to join his administration, he overcame many, if not most, of the problems that he had inherited. It was the accomplishment of which he was most proud.

Ford helped the country recover from two of the most trying episodes in our history, Watergate and the Vietnam War. He lived up to his dictum that a president should mold, not follow, public opinion. That was no small task, given the nature of democratic government and the ascendancy of the fifteen-second TV sound bite. To be sure, I agreed with the intellectual thrusts of President Ford's policies. But more important, I felt that he led and governed with dignity and grace in an otherwise tragic setting.

Ford's approach to the Soviets was eminently sound and, in my opinion, successful. Had he become president in 1976, I am convinced that he would have reached an equitable SALT II Treaty with the Soviet Union. The Soviets respected Ford for his toughness. They sensed he was firm and patient but also fair. He understood their ambitions and kept his objectives clearly in mind. The same could not be said of the man who followed him to the White House, Jimmy Carter.

CHAPTER 4

The Carter Years: Averting Disaster

When Jimmy Carter arrived at the center stage of American politics, he was as much a mystery to the Soviets as he was to most Americans. The former Georgia governor's rural southern background, lack of experience in national and international politics, and born-again religious fundamentalism caused many in Washington and Moscow concern over the future direction of U.S.-Soviet relations.

I recall the searching questions put to me by my Soviet counterparts in Geneva during Carter's presidential campaign. Was Carter really, as the U.S. press described him, a "Southern-fried Kennedy"? Did he honestly believe his own campaign rhetoric that his moral example would be reciprocated by the Soviets? Carter often spoke of his personal conviction that arms control had not only strategic but also moral and spiritual implications. To the Soviets, this signaled that he lacked understanding of both their system and their objectives. They sensed from the outset his profound naiveté concerning their country.

Carter confirmed their initial suspicions by telegraphing his intention to move rapidly beyond simply limiting weapons. In his inaugural address on January 20, 1977, the president said, "We'll move this year a step closer toward the ultimate goal—elimination of all nuclear weapons from the face of the earth." The abolition of nuclear weapons has been a perennially popular presidential theme. Even Ronald Reagan, the most conservative president to deal with the Soviets, eventually got on the bandwagon. Carter not only was over-eager to achieve this goal but also was guilty of dangerous overstatement. He said he viewed the elimination of nuclear weapons as too important to be held hostage to American and Soviet ideological differences. In effect, Carter was telling the Soviets that his objective was to achieve an arms control agreement at almost any price. He had ignored Talleyrand's fundamental rule for negotiators: *"Mais surtout, pas trôp de zèle"* (But above all, not too much zeal).

Unlike Richard Nixon, Carter failed to appreciate the Soviets' deeply rooted respect for strength. Whenever they sensed weakness in an opponent, or, as in Carter's case, an overzealousness based on idealism, the Soviets looked for ways to turn negotiations to their advantage. So long as Carter remained the initiator, theirs was a no-lose situation. If a treaty emerged, the Soviets were confident they could make it come out on their terms. If not, the Soviets believed that they could foster the perception that the United States was responsible for the failure to agree.

President Carter brought to the White House boundless enthusiasm, honorable intentions, and great expectations, all laudable traits when tempered by realism. But Carter lacked the experience required to be practical in dealing with the worldly Soviets. He fell into the trap of projecting his own sense of fairness and rationality onto his adversaries. He incorrectly attributed to the Soviets the same Christian values, ethics, and beliefs that formed the core of his own thinking. He thereby obscured the key—and very real—differences that divided us. Despite overwhelming evidence to the contrary, Carter was convinced he could convert the Soviets.

Carter's approach made me question my role in his administration. Having studied the Soviet Union and its people for nearly three decades, I knew that the Soviets, like their currency, were simply not convertible. Their political system and way of life were fundamentally different from ours, and it was not about to change just because Carter willed it so. I believed that the manner in which the president was pursuing arms control was probably going to result in an agreement contrary to U.S. national interests.

Prior to the November 1976 elections, I had decided to leave the military. Although I took great pride in my service as a member of the negotiating team, I felt I had accomplished about as much as I was going to. I submitted the paperwork for my retirement and lined up a challenging job in the private sector.

Soon afterwards, I went to say goodbye to my boss, Gen. George Brown, chairman of the Joint Chiefs of Staff. Since our days as classmates at West Point, Brown and I had been good friends. I thought it only proper that I personally tell him of my decision. I was surprised that instead of wishing me luck and sending me on my way, Brown asked me to hold up my paperwork until after the election.

"You never know what might happen," Brown said. "You and I put on the uniform to serve our country, and this is no time to quit. The Soviets are continuing to build strategic weapons at a rapid pace, and we still face great challenges to our national security." He ended the conversation with a cryptic remark that intrigued me. "I might be in a position to make you an offer you can't refuse."

Several days after Carter won the election, Brown told me that Cyrus Vance would become the new secretary of state. The choice of Vance, a highly respected attorney and long-time Washington insider, was a surprise in light of Carter's campaign promise to bring to Washington fresh faces who would develop a new approach to foreign policy. Hamilton Jordan, Carter's closest confidant, had said in a *Playboy* magazine interview, "If after the inauguration, you find Cy Vance as secretary of state, . . . then I would say we failed."

I had worked for Vance in the early 1960s when, as secretary of the army and later as deputy secretary of defense, he supported the idea that armed helicopters be introduced into Vietnam. He was interested in ways the United States could most effectively conduct counterinsurgency operations. Vance was familiar with my work on the Army Howze Board that recommended the use of helicopters as weapons platforms. Helicopter pilots, unlike pilots of fast and high-flying, fixed-wing aircraft, could more easily distinguish friend from foe and thereby endanger fewer innocent civilians. Vance had sent me to Vietnam to test the concept. In doing so, he threw me into the middle of a bitter interservice confrontation, since the U.S. Air Force, and to a lesser extent the U.S. Navy, considered that delivering firepower from the air was solely within its province. Having placed me in this precarious situation, Vance then practically abandoned me through benign neglect when the issue became heated. Still, I chalked it up to his inability—or perhaps unwillingness—to knock heads together rather than to any lack of confidence in me or my ideas.

General Brown also told me that Harold Brown, with whom I had worked in various capacities, would become Carter's secretary of defense. "Cy Vance and Hal Brown both have a high regard for your knowledge of the Soviets and grasp of U.S. nuclear policy," he said. "They want you to remain on active service." Harold Brown, he added, appeared willing to make me sole representative of both the secretary of defense and the Joint Chiefs of Staff at the SALT II talks. I would thus represent the entire Department of Defense in arms control negotiations and play a key role in formulating policies.

George Brown went on to say that he needed me. "You understand the issues and the Soviets, and have my complete confidence. Where will I find another person with your background and experience? You have always placed duty and country ahead of your personal wishes, so why change now when you can make a real difference?" Having flattered me and appealed to my sense of patriotism, he said, "There will be ample time for you to launch a second career." Giving me the clincher almost as an afterthought, he added, "I talked to Scoop Jackson, and he agreed with me that you should stay on."

His last statement stunned me. Once again my career was being manipulated by Senator Jackson. In the back of my head, I could hear his appeal to my sense of duty, honor, country a decade earlier when he had persuaded me not to resist going to Vietnam to test armed helicopters in combat. He had more recently used the same arguments in the Nixon era when he insisted that I join the arms control team.

I went to see Jackson, hoping to convince him that I had paid my dues and deserved to be spared the agony of remaining at the negotiating table. But Jackson once again gave me a stern lecture on why I was duty-bound to remain on active service. He knew full well that he was the one person to whom I could never say "no." There was no point in resisting. I called my prospective employer and told him I had changed my mind.

THE NEW TEAM

In anticipation of being named secretary of defense, Harold Brown, after consulting with Carter, had developed a detailed plan for reaching a SALT II agreement. The new framework called for deep cuts by reducing the Vladivostok ceilings on overall weapons and MIRVed missile launchers by 10 percent. It would also reduce the Soviets' first-strike capability by cutting the number of their heavy missiles in half. In return, the United States would place range limits on its air-launched cruise missiles. George Brown had managed to get a bootleg copy of the proposal shortly after the election and asked me to give him a professional assessment. I told him I found it bold, reasonable, and fair. The chiefs had misgivings concerning the plan's recommendations. They wanted the Soviets to give up all, not simply half, of their heavy missiles and to include the Soviet Backfire heavy bomber in their weapons count. At the same time, they did not want to see us placing limits on our air-launched cruise missiles. My view was that getting the Soviets to cut the number of their heavy missiles in half would be a significant improvement over the Vladivostok framework. We would, of course, have to pay for it, but the price for doing so in terms of limiting our air-launched cruise missiles would not seriously affect our retaliatory capacity. I, too, believed the Backfire should be considered a heavy bomber, but the JCS would have to first convince the State Department on this issue, something I believed we could do later. I told Walter Slocombe, who had worked on the plan and was slated to become Brown's principal arms control advisor, that I would do my best to bring the chiefs on board.

Soon after Carter's inauguration, George Brown called me into his office. He told me that he was rescinding the offer to make me the arms control representative of both the civilian and military components of the Department of Defense. He went on to explain that since the secretary of state had two representatives (a State Department official and the director of the Arms Control and Disarmament Agency) on the arms control negotiating team, it would not be in the Pentagon's best interest to have only one. The defense community would be better served, he said, if Walt Slocombe and I were both at the table.

"The logic is fine," I said, "but what about your promise that if I stayed on I would represent both you and the secretary of defense?"

"I'm sorry," he said, "I guess we simply had not thought it through. But I still think you should stay. You told me you liked Hal Brown's proposal, and you and Walt Slocombe get along well. We'll talk to Cy Vance about taking you with him as a military advisor when he travels to Geneva and Moscow. If he agrees, you'll be the first military advisor to travel with the secretary of state."

My first inclination was to say no and resubmit my retirement papers. George Brown had reneged on his promise, and I was under no obligation to keep my end of the bargain. My civilian job was no longer available, but I was confident that it would take me no time at all to find another.

While I was still pondering my options, Secretary Vance called and confirmed that he was inviting me to accompany him to high-level arms control meetings. He added that since I had the support of both Browns and the ear of the military chiefs, I could be instrumental in bringing them aboard in support of the administration's new proposal. The opportunity was too attractive to pass up.

I knew that Vance had liberal leanings and, like his boss, was something of an idealist. I had learned from my Vietnam experience that Vance was weak in asserting his authority, not much of a manager, and often had difficulty seeing projects through to completion. Nonetheless, I thought that he respected my professionalism and felt that he would always give me a fair hearing. Whether I could convince him to adopt my ideas was another question. But if I didn't stand up to him, who would?

Ironically, many of the same factors underlying President Nixon's selection of Henry Kissinger as his national security advisor were at play in Carter's selection of Vance. Both presidents craved the prestige and respectability that an Eastern establishment intellectual with international experience would bring to his administration. By appointing a member of the famed Trilateral Commission and a trustee of the Rockefeller Foundation to serve as secretary of state, Carter hoped to establish his own foreign policy bona fides. The president may not have realized that Vance had certain shortcomings. Most glaringly, Vance did not take readily to building rapport with Congress and would not use his office as a pulpit for rallying public support behind the administration's ideas.

The selection of Harold Brown as secretary of defense was a good one. Brown was a child prodigy who, shortly after receiving his doctorate in physics at age twenty-two (at that age I was still a cadet at West Point), joined the Lawrence Livermore Laboratory. He became its director in 1960 and later was intimately involved in developing U.S. nuclear policy. In 1965 he was named secretary of the air force. I had come to know and respect him when I worked for Gen. Lyman Lemnitzer, the chairman of the Joint Chiefs of Staff. Brown was a brilliant scientist who also clearly recognized that common sense had to be applied to academic solutions. In this respect, he differed from his mentor, former Secretary of Defense Robert McNamara. For example, in 1963, Brown, the director of research and development, was opposed to McNamara's idea of installing an electronic fence in Vietnam to stop Vietcong infiltrators. The harebrained scheme called for dropping artificial palm trees containing sensitive detection devices along the demilitarized zone (DMZ). Any movement within twenty yards of the trees would cause a signal to register at an artillery battery, which would then automatically shell the area where the noise had been detected. An experiment conducted on a small version of this electronic fence was a complete failure. Deer and other animals triggered off the artillery; thousands of rounds were fired uselessly.

I had no concerns about Brown dreaming up such preposterous schemes. Like Vance, however, Brown did not appear comfortable with the idea of spending a great deal of time making informal contacts with members of Congress. Carter had campaigned as an outsider who was not part of the Washington bureaucracy. Now that he was president, he would have to work closely with the bureaucrats he had disdained. But he had selected a secretary of state and a secretary of defense who could not compensate for his inadequacies. It would prove to be a grave handicap to the administration.

The news that Zbigniew Brzezinski would join the Carter administration as national security advisor made my decision to join the new team somewhat easier. I had met Brzezinski the previous year while attending an Aspen Institute seminar. He showed a great deal of interest in a number of my ideas on arms control, and we talked about how they might best be implemented.

Brzezinski's career at Columbia University had in many ways paralleled Henry Kissinger's at Harvard. Both were of European origin, and both were thoroughly versed in history and America's vital role in shaping the postwar world. They had pursued similar academic careers, and both sought to influence national security policy through high-level government positions.

I knew that Brzezinski had a good feel for the critical role that military capabilities play in international relations. I was also aware that by dint of his background and training he had no illusions about Soviet goals and objectives. This made me confident that he would be sympathetic to the views of the secretary of defense and the Joint Chiefs of Staff.

I was not quite sure, however, how the conservative Brzezinski would fit in with liberals like Carter and Vance. Although he never confided in me his reasons for joining the Carter administration, my intuition that we would both become members of the loyal opposition proved correct. Brzezinski often took positions opposite to Vance's and generally supported the views of the Joint Chiefs of Staff.

From the outset, Brzezinski was a believer in linkage. He sensed the Soviets' desire to achieve respectability and superpower status and believed that they would use the arms control process to further those goals. Unlike Vance, who dealt with arms control on its own merits, Brzezinski habitually sought to tie arms control to other foreign policy issues. One notable example was the relationship he saw between Soviet policy in the Horn of Africa and SALT II. He believed that the failure of the United States to oppose the Soviets in this area was a mistake and gave rise to his celebrated observation: "SALT lies buried in the sands of Ogaden."

My role in formulating nuclear strategy became greater when, in addition to being General Brown's representative at the talks, I became his principal advisor on arms control. Brown did not like to immerse himself in the intricacies of arms control and had been taken to task by Senator Jackson for his lack of familiarity with the details of the negotiations. After one stormy session with Jackson, Brown said to me: "Ed, I haven't been worked over like that since I was a plebe. It will never happen again." Knowing of my friendship with Jackson, Brown was able to kill two birds with one stone. He got the powerful senator off his back and picked up a trusted friend to keep him informed. As a result of this appointment, I often went with Brown to National Security Council meetings. This put me in the unique position of being able to directly influence the policy-making process, while simultaneously being able to give my appraisals on which proposals would and would not pass muster in Geneva. I was the only member of the SALT II delegation who sat in on meetings of the NSC, something which greatly strengthened my position at the negotiating table. Moreover, knowing that I enjoyed the sympathetic ear of Brzezinski, I felt I could influence decisions in Washington.

Internal debates on arms control during the first several weeks of the new administration were relatively benign because Paul Warnke had not yet become the director of the Arms Control and Disarmament Agency (ACDA). Warnke, a former Defense Department general counsel and assistant secretary for international security affairs, faced serious opposition in Senate confirmation hearings because of his liberal leanings. He had written many articles about arms control over the years, and they had come back to haunt him. One notable example was his assertion that the Americans and Soviets were simply "apes on a treadmill" whose nuclear weapons were deployed only as a reaction to the other party. The implication that the United States had the same motives and goals in its acquisition of weapons as the Soviet Union was not lost on a number of senators who distrusted him.

Scoop Jackson led the opposition to Warnke. He and two members of his staff, Richard Perle and Dorothy Fosdick, contrasted Warnke's earlier liberal assessments of the U.S.-Soviet strategic competition with the more balanced view he presented to the Senate in his confirmation hearing. Warnke had even aroused the ire of Senator Hayakawa, an expert on English grammar, by inserting commas into one of his previous statements, thereby completely changing its meaning. To those who did not know their grammar, Hayakawa gave a simple example. "Suppose I should write: 'Carter said the Soviet leader was a fool.' But now let me insert two commas. 'Carter, said the Soviet leader, was a fool.' " The senators quickly got Hayakawa's point. After a long and acrimonious debate, Warnke was confirmed by a narrow margin. But the large number of votes cast against him was a clear message that any arms control treaty submitted to the Senate under his auspices would be subject to intense scrutiny.

In the meantime, only Leslie Gelb, a journalist turned government official; Walter Slocombe; and I were available to advise our principals when they attended NSC meetings on arms control issues. Since Gelb and Slocombe were new to the game, I initially enjoyed an advantage and was able to get a number of my views, such as rigid inspection proposals, incorporated into the U.S. SALT II positions.

I was able to maintain a good and close working relationship with Slocombe, but my relationship with Gelb was strained; I did not like his lone-wolf manner and his imperious way of doing business. Later, when Gelb became more at home with the State Department bureaucracy and Vance turned his attention to other matters, Gelb assumed an increasingly influential role in formulating the State Department's arms control positions. As a former *New York Times* defense and foreign policy reporter, I suspected that he was able to use his old boy network to garner support for the Vance-Warnke line among editorial writers at the *Times* and other influential newspapers.

THE MAN IN CHARGE

I formed my initial impressions of President Carter's character while we were preparing for Vance's first meeting with Gromyko in March 1977. It was clear to me that Carter was sincere and intelligent, and that he would energetically pursue arms control. He was an outspoken advocate of openness and honesty in foreign relations and was highly critical of Henry Kissinger's secret diplomacy. But his honest intentions were not enough to compensate for his lack of understanding of the Soviets. Within a week of assuming office, Carter sent a letter to Brezhnev stating that the United States would press for a quick SALT II accord that went far beyond what had been previously agreed. Brezhnev responded that he would only consider a treaty that was based on Vladivostok. Undaunted, Carter ignored Brezhnev's reply and continued to press ahead on a U.S. proposal based on deep cuts in weapons.

Carter had a technical approach to problem-solving. Having been trained as an engineer, I could understand this. At West Point, cadets who looked for technical solutions to problems were considered unimaginative and derisively called "wooden engineers." Similarly, while Carter (a graduate of the U.S. Naval Academy and a product of Adm. Hyman Rickover's nuclear Navy) understood the details of our strategic systems, he seemed to get so bogged down in particulars that he failed to grasp their larger purpose. I recall one occasion when the president got up at 5:00 A.M. so that he could study the technical specifications of a military system that we were to discuss with him later that morning. At the meeting, it was clear that, although Carter knew how the system worked, he had little or no understanding of how it fit into our overall deterrence strategy. I recently complained to Al Carnesale—at that time a consultant on arms control at the State Department and the White House who in 1991 became dean of the John F. Kennedy School of Government at Harvard—that Carter could not see the forest for the trees. Carnesale told me, "You understate the case. Carter couldn't see beyond a single leaf." Many other knowledgeable insiders held similar opinions.

As a result of such experiences, I found myself asking questions similar to those put to me by my Soviet counterparts prior to the election. Did the president have the strategic and political acumen required of a commander in chief? Was he a global thinker? Did he understand the Soviets' respect for strength and contempt for weakness? Did he truly believe that if he turned the other cheek they would follow his moral example? I was becoming increasingly worried that the president was in over his head.

I noticed that the president always seemed serious. He rarely smiled or laughed. His dress was more relaxed than his demeanor. He often came to official meetings in blue jeans and a sport shirt, seeming to equate informality with sincerity.

At these meetings, Carter was an attentive listener and often took notes, but I frequently had the impression that his mind was already made up. His comments and choice of words often left me with the feeling that the preacher in him was always present just below the surface. For example, when we were in the middle of a discussion at an NSC meeting about how to deal with heavy bombers, he asked if our relationship with the Soviet Union would be different if we had not dropped atomic weapons on Japan. If some detached historian had asked the question, it would have been understandable. But I found it strange for a president to be thinking out loud about a philosophical question while we were trying to solve a practical problem. It seemed that the president was trying to enlighten and inspire a government bureaucracy of which he was the head but not really a part.

SALT II TAKES SHAPE

My first concrete indication that arms control would take on an entirely different complexion in the Carter administration occurred at an NSC meeting in February 1977. In a departure from normal practice, Secretary Vance submitted for discussion a fallback position to the comprehensive proposal that he was going to present to Gromyko in March. The fallback position was primarily the work of his staff at the State Department. None of us in the Pentagon had been consulted. I expressed opposition to the idea on principle. To develop a fallback option without the benefit of the other side's objections to our initial offer would not only deny us knowledge of their objections, but it seemed a tacit acknowledgment that our opening position was without merit. Furthermore, I argued, since it is virtually impossible to keep a secret in Washington, the Soviets were certain to catch wind of the fallback position and simply ignore our primary offer. Secretary Vance insisted, however, that we develop our rock-bottom position and was able to get the president to sign off. I held my breath, hoping that I was wrong and all would come out well.

Vance's proposal for his March 1977 meeting with Gromyko was developed with the advice of Scoop Jackson. At that time, Jackson felt he could contribute to and cooperate with the Carter administration. The comprehensive proposal essentially limited both sides to between 1,800 and 2,000 strategic systems (down from the 2,400 agreed to at Vladivostok) and 1,100 to 1,200 launchers for MIRVed missiles (down from Vladivostok's 1,320). It called for a limit of 150 on heavy missiles (in 1977 the United States had 54 obsolete Titan heavy missiles, which were being phased out, compared with the Soviet Union's 308 modern heavy ICBMs). It also called for a ban on the deployment of cruise missiles with a range of more than 2,500 kilometers. The Backfire bomber would not be considered as part of the aggregate if the Soviets gave assurances that its strategic capabilities would not be improved. The Soviets, of course, did not want to discuss the Backfire at all. The proposal was historic in that for the first time in SALT, real cuts, not just caps, in the muscle of strategic weapons were contemplated. Brzezinski, in particular, favored such a comprehensive approach because he was anxious to test the intentions of the Soviet leadership. If they were not genuinely interested in arms reductions, as he suspected, he wanted to call their bluff early on in the game. He understood that this had to be demonstrated to the new team in Washington.

Vance's fallback position, known as the deferral option, proposed postponing discussions on both the cruise missiles and Backfire bombers. Vance was not certain that the Soviets would prefer his deferral option. He was certain that they did not want to discuss the Backfire at all, but he knew that they wanted to place limits on cruise missiles, where they were far behind the United States in technology.

At the March meeting in Geneva, Gromyko deferred to Vance and allowed him to speak first. I was astonished by what then took place. Apparently fearful that the Soviets would consider our comprehensive proposal too bold, Vance opened the negotiation by submitting our fallback position as the first of two alternatives. He immediately followed by proposing the more ambitious option, apparently believing that this sequence would induce the Soviets to come to an agreement if they knew in advance that we were willing to defer discussion of cruise missiles and the Backfire bomber.

Although Gromyko was as surprised as I that Vance would submit two alternative proposals, the foreign minister let him finish. Then, true to form, he lashed out against both options, calling them one-sided and asserting that they were designed to guarantee U.S. strategic superiority. Being inexperienced and courteous to a fault, Vance was stunned that the Soviet foreign minister would use such abusive language. Even though we had warned Vance, he could not believe that this was Gromyko's normal style, carefully calculated to intimidate his opponent.

I could not believe that Vance would sit and listen to Gromyko's invective without responding. It was bad enough that he served up our fallback position on a silver platter. Now it appeared that he was willing to be verbally assaulted for presenting such a gift. I passed the secretary a note suggesting that he diplomatically, but firmly, rebut Gromyko. Vance wrote back that he believed Gromyko was operating on explicit instructions from Moscow and that the foreign minister was obviously embarrassed by the excesses forced upon him by his superiors. It would not, in Vance's opinion, pay to "rub it in." I detected no such embarrassment on Gromyko's part. He always acted on the theory that the best defense was a good offense, and he routinely attacked new U.S. arms control proposals as one-sided. I had witnessed it all before.

The meeting collapsed when Gromyko learned that at a Washington press conference held while we were still negotiating, Brzezinski had criticized Gromyko's rejection of the U.S. proposals. The foreign minister stormed out, complaining bitterly to reporters that the U.S. proposals were "aimed at obtaining unilateral advantages for the United States, to the detriment of the Soviet Union."

My Soviet counterparts explained to me that Gromyko had rejected our proposals because Brezhnev had staked his domestic credibility on U.S. acceptance of the Vladivostok Accords. When the U.S. proposal leapfrogged on the Vladivostok framework, Brezhnev was fearful that going along would be perceived by the politburo as too accommodating to the West. It was not a very auspicious start for what Vance had hoped would be the beginning of an amicable relationship.

Two months later, Vance and Gromyko reconvened in Geneva with the hopes of jump-starting the talks. The United States proposed a blueprint for negotiations composed of elements of the Vladivostok Accords and Vance's two March proposals. The United States offered a new three-tier approach. The first tier called for an eight-year treaty based on a 10 percent reduction from the Vladivostok levels, while the second tier proposed a three-year protocol aimed at providing time to resolve the cruise missile and Backfire bomber issues. The final tier was a proposal for a joint statement of principles designed to act as guidelines for talks to follow SALT II. Discussions on the blueprint lasted for five months. By September, a refined three-tier approach effectively replaced the Vladivostok Accords as the basis for negotiations for the remainder of the Carter administration.

From this point, the negotiations proceeded steadily downhill. The Soviets pocketed one U.S. concession after another as we made successive and increasingly more generous proposals. The Soviets were engaging in what Viktor Karpov called "picking the raisins out of the cake." Karpov explained that when Soviet children get a piece of holiday cake "they pick out the raisins and leave the dough."

The Soviets interpreted our flexibility and overeagerness as signs of weakness and met U.S. calls for compromise with stiffer and more unreasonable demands that more often than not were met with acquiescence. The most egregious example involved Soviet heavy missiles.

The Carter administration's original proposal was to limit modern heavy missile deployments in the Soviet Union to no more than 150. The United States had no plans to produce or deploy heavy missiles, believing that such missiles were the most destabilizing of all weapon systems. Our new compromise proposal allowed the Soviets to complete their planned deployment of 308 SS-18 missiles. In return, the United States would be permitted to continue to develop—but not deploy—cruise missiles. It was an incredible idea, one that stood compromise on its head. In effect, the United States traded a prerogative it already had, that of developing cruise missiles, for the Soviet right to *deploy* its full complement of heavy ICBMs. Worse, it carried with it the implication that we would have to make further concessions for the right to eventually deploy cruise missiles.

The more concessions we offered, the more difficult the Soviets were to deal with. The negotiations became increasingly frustrating as the Soviets bombarded us with endless repetition of their "principled views." They consistently tried to get us to agree to broadly worded and ill-defined concepts and refused to discuss issues on their own merits. They routinely assigned self-serving definitions to their key arms control concepts and habitually sought advantageous loopholes for future exploitation. For example, they refused to accept our proposal that there be three categories of missiles—light, medium, and heavy—and insisted that there be only two categories: light and heavy. The United States possessed only light missiles, the Minuteman, and planned to develop a medium missile, the MX, with twice the destructive potential of the Minuteman. The Soviets possessed SS-11s (the equivalent of our Minuteman), SS-17s and SS-19s (equivalents of our planned MX), and SS-18s (with six times the potential of our Minuteman and three times that of the MX). They knew we had no plans to develop a heavy missile and therefore wanted to camouflage their SS-18 heavies by refusing to label their SS-17s, SS-18s, and our MX as medium missiles.

I complained to General Trusov that the Soviet argument was

illogical and contradictory. I told him I could not follow their reasoning.

"Don't waste your time trying to understand it," Trusov said. "It's a matter of dialectical materialism." He then gave me an example.

"A factory worker went to his political commissar with a dilemma. Two fellow workers, one with dirty and the other with clean hands, asked him for some water. There was only enough water for one to wash his hands.

" 'Which one do you think deserves the water?' asked the commissar.

" 'The one with dirty hands,' said the worker, 'because he has the greater need.'

" 'Wrong,' said the commissar, 'the one with clean hands should be rewarded for his habits of cleanliness.'

"Several days later the worker and the commissar met again. The worker said the problem had come up again, and proudly announced that he had given the water to the worker with clean hands.

" 'Wrong,' said the commissar. 'You should have given it to the worker with dirty hands; he had the greater need.'

"When the worker complained about inconsistency, the commissar said, 'You're now beginning to understand dialectical materialism.' "

QUESTIONS OF BALANCE

While the negotiations were stalemated, Secretary of Defense Brown initiated a major U.S. effort to redress the military imbalance. Brown realized that the maintenance of a credible military deterrent demanded that the United States respond in kind to major advances in the accuracy of the more numerous Soviet land-based missiles. He drew up plans to improve the accuracy and destructive effect of our Minuteman missiles. Brown also moved ahead with the MX mobile ICBM designed as the follow-on to the fixed-silo Minuteman. Determined to improve the sea-based leg of the strategic triad, Brown also pushed ahead with the Trident II submarine program. To his credit, President Carter approved these efforts. In fact, when the Reagan administration subsequently took office, it learned that the foundations for many of the needed improvements had already been laid.

There was, however, a downside to Brown's proposals. The secretary of defense recommended, and the president approved, the can-

cellation of the B-1 bomber program. The B-1 was slated to replace
our aging force of B-52 long-range bombers first deployed in the early
1950s. Technology advances so rapidly that aircraft become obsolete
in ten, and at most fifteen, years. But U.S. Air Force pilots complained
that the B-52s were older than they were. Brown believed that the future of the third leg of the triad centered around the development of
sophisticated ALCMs, but he did not feel that the U.S. defense budget
could support both an ALCM program and the B-1.

Brown's decision to scrap the B-1 came as a shock and a surprise to
those of us in Geneva. Not only were we not consulted on the decision,
but the first we learned about it was a story in the *International Herald
Tribune*. Perhaps Brown kept this decision from us because he realized
that we would object on grounds that it undermined our negotiating
leverage. He knew that the Joint Chiefs of Staff favored deploying the
B-1 and would join in opposing its cancellation.

At the Vladivostok summit, the United States had acquiesced to
the Soviet demand that long-range bombers be included in the count
of strategic delivery systems. The U.S. decision enabled us to approach the allowable level of 2,400 delivery vehicles, and thus we
came closer to the goal of essential equivalence. By canceling the B-1,
we were signaling to the Soviets that we really did not put as much
stock in heavy bombers as we had earlier claimed. This, in turn,
made transparent our shift in emphasis to cruise missiles and caused
the Soviets to redouble their already aggressive efforts to thwart our
cruise missile development program.

On my staff in Geneva, the senior Air Force delegate was Col.
Gerald Werbel, a fine officer and former B-1 test pilot. Werbel was so
incensed over the cancellation of the B-1 that he immediately quit
and asked to be retired from the Air Force. Later, he must have been
pleased that one of President Reagan's first decisions upon assuming
office was to reinstate the B-1.

There were other disturbing signs that President Carter was at a loss
on how to deal with the Soviets. The most notable and widely publicized was his handling of the Enhanced Radiation Weapon (ERW)
program, popularly known as the neutron bomb. Studies showed that
in order for NATO's doctrine of flexible response to be effective in
countering the Warsaw Pact's large advantage in conventional forces,
we would have to use tactical nuclear weapons (TNWs) to stop advancing waves of Soviet armor and infantry. The use of TNWs would
inevitably result in numerous civilian casualties and wide-scale destruction on German territory. To avoid such damage, the United

States developed the neutron bomb, which would stop Soviet tanks with deadly radiation rather than by devastating blasts of TNWs. Civilian casualties would thus be minimized because the radiation of ERWs dissipated rapidly and could be confined to a limited area. Neutron weapons were an attractive and technologically feasible option for making flexible response a more credible military doctrine.

The Soviets launched a disinformation and propaganda campaign to mobilize U.S public opinion against neutron weapons. Georgi Arbatov, the head of the United States and Canada Institute in the Soviet Union, embarked on a speaking tour in the United States. He appeared on television talk shows and wrote op-ed pieces that were published in our newspapers. Members of the Soviet embassy in Washington buttonholed reporters and members of Congress. It was a full-court press. President Carter, succumbing to pressure from the media, announced on April 4, 1978, that he was voluntarily deferring production of neutron weapons. He left open the option of future deployment, but he implicitly linked continued U.S. restraint to unilateral Soviet efforts to reduce their conventional and nuclear advantage in Europe. Brezhnev's reaction was swift and predictable: "We resolutely reject any attempt by the United States to impose unacceptable terms on the Soviet Union."

Over the course of the next several months, U.S. public opinion against neutron weapons continued to mount. Despite the fact that such weapons were actually more humane and less destructive than TNWs, the issue of deployment became moot when the president condemned neutron weapons on moral grounds, stating that a weapon system expressly designed to destroy people and spare real estate was ethically unacceptable. The net effect was that Carter surrendered neutron weapons and received nothing in return. His decision undermined the confidence of our German allies, who had initially yielded to U.S. pressure and had, at considerable political risk, supported Carter's plan to deploy neutron weapons in Europe.

STAYING ON

During this time, I had renewed doubts about remaining on the negotiating team. As I once again considered retiring, I realized that I could not in good conscience abandon a ship that was now in serious danger of sinking. There were other reasons to stay also. I learned that my good friend George Brown had terminal cancer. In my long talks with him during the weeks prior to the end of his tour,

Brown implored me to remain on the job. He felt it imperative that the next chairman of the Joint Chiefs of Staff have the benefit of my experience and institutional memory. In June 1978, Brown was replaced as chairman of the JCS by U.S. Air Force Gen. David Jones. George Brown died on December 5, 1978. He had served his country well. While my relationship with Jones was not as intimate as the one I had enjoyed with Brown, it turned out to be solid.

I also stayed because Paul Warnke decided not to play an active role as chief negotiator, which strengthened my influence. When appointed director of ACDA, Warnke let it be known that, contrary to my recommendations, with which several members of the negotiating team agreed, he also intended to be chief arms control negotiator. It soon became obvious that he could not do justice to both jobs. At first, Warnke tried to attend the first and last few meetings of each negotiating round, leaving the management of the intervening weeks to his deputy, Ralph Earle. Warnke was obviously bored by the few sessions that he did attend. The pace of negotiations was too slow for him; he had come to the negotiating table to "deal." By contrast, his counterpart Vladimir Semenov acknowledged that his major function was to lay down Moscow's line.

Semenov disliked negotiating with the able and knowledgeable Earle because he considered Earle a second-string player. He only wanted to negotiate with Warnke, the team captain. Warnke's attempted solution was to elevate his deputy to the rank of ambassador, with the title of acting chief negotiator. But this did little to smooth Semenov's feathers. He felt that he was being denigrated by being forced to deal for weeks on end with our number-two man.

Oddly enough, this enhanced my position because by dint of seniority I became the number-two man when Warnke was not in Geneva. As a result, I did most of my active negotiating with the Soviet number-two, Viktor Karpov. Semenov finally resolved his dilemma by getting himself reassigned to the prestigious post of Soviet ambassador to Bonn and having Karpov designated as his successor. I had learned from my extensive discussions with Karpov that he knew more about U.S. and Soviet weapons than any member of the Soviet team. Unlike most of his colleagues, Karpov quickly tired of repeating the same old arguments. He would race through his notes, allowing him to report to Moscow that he had discharged his obligations. Explaining his behavior, Karpov would—when he was out of earshot of his notetaker—apologize for having repeatedly subjected me to Moscow's party line. Karpov would then occasionally lay out a position that actually made sense. He gave me the feeling that, unlike the others, he realized that the complete avoidance of dialogue with Americans would turn us off and ultimately work to the Soviets' disadvantage. It was fortunate that we developed a working relationship because he and I later became the chiefs of our respective START negotiating teams.

Karpov showed evidence of having good connections in high political circles in Moscow and enjoyed the full confidence of Foreign Minister Gromyko. The six years he had spent in Washington as a junior officer in the Soviet embassy not only gave him a good command of English but also an understanding of politics inside the Washington beltway. And having come up through the ranks, Karpov had none of Semenov's inhibitions about dealing with Earle.

At about the time Karpov replaced Semenov, Leslie Gelb, who headed the State Department's Political-Military Division, became more involved in the arms control process, in part probably because of Vance's waning interest in the negotiations. It often appeared, in fact, that Gelb was single-handedly running the arms control process at State. This became evident at NSC meetings on arms control where each principal was allowed to bring along a second person. Vance invariably brought Gelb. When Vance was called upon to give the State Department's position, he often called on Gelb to present it. Obviously better versed than Vance on the details of State Department positions, Gelb would respond to points brought up by the secretary of defense and chairman of the Joint Chiefs of Staff.

I learned that Gelb was giving background briefings to the press. Several newsmen called me and asked whether I agreed with what Gelb had told them. They interpreted the rule of not quoting their sources to mean only that they would not publish their names, but it did not inhibit them from quoting Gelb when they tried to elicit more information from me. On one occasion a reporter told me that Gelb had said that the Soviets intended to phase out their heavy missiles. He asked me if I had any evidence to support Gelb's statement. I had none, and in fact I was not certain that Gelb had said it. This was one of the many games reporters liked to play.

THE AMY FACTOR

Everyone who worked for Carter seemed to have a pet story about his daughter Amy. My most notable experience occurred in Geneva in the summer of 1978 when the president and his family came to visit the negotiating team. During a reception in his honor, Carter approached me with ten-year-old Amy in tow.

"General," he said, "I'd like Amy to learn about nuclear weapons and arms control. Would you sit down and explain these things to her?"

I was floored by the request. Amy came and sat down next to me on the sofa, swinging her white-stockinged legs and chewing a large wad of gum. She was obviously totally bored and uninterested.

"Amy," I said, "you don't want to know anything about nuclear weapons or arms control, do you?"

"Naw," she said, chewing her gum furiously.

"Wouldn't you rather go upstairs and watch television?" I asked.

"Yea-ah!" she said enthusiastically.

I was much relieved and sought out her governess. I told her that Amy and I had finished our discussion and that she wanted to watch television. Amy bounded off happily, and I returned to the reception, being careful for the next half hour to keep my distance from the president and the First Lady. As he was leaving, President Carter said, "Thank you for educating Amy. It's so important that she learn about nuclear war." I could only hope that Amy would not let on how short her lesson had been. I now wonder if I planted the seed of one of Carter's major gaffes during an election-year debate with candidate Ronald Reagan when the president noted that he consulted Amy on the subject of nuclear war.

Increasingly, the Soviets were troubled by what they saw as Carter's religious fundamentalism. Academician Alexandr Shchukin once asked me the branch of Christianity to which the president belonged. When I told him that Carter was a Baptist, I was startled by his blunt and callous retort: "Every Soviet knows you can't trust a Baptist." When I probed further into what was behind this outburst of bigotry, Shchukin told me that Baptist missionaries had tried so hard to convert Soviet citizens that a strong backlash had resulted.

I soon discovered that missionaries come in many forms. One of the members of my military staff, convinced that our Soviet counterparts would appreciate Russian-language Bibles, asked if I would mind his offering some to guests at a cocktail party at my apartment. I said that I *did* mind; I did not want my guests to feel that I had invited them to my place to save their souls. Quite disappointed, he came up with an alternative plan. He asked if I would allow him to place six Bibles on the table in my foyer. He planned to tell my guests that there was some reading material on the table to which they were welcome. Reluctantly, I agreed.

What I did not know was that another officer on my staff caught wind of the plan. He procured six copies of *Playboy* magazine and placed them on the table alongside the Bibles. The Soviets, having been offered some reading material as they left, eagerly availed themselves of the opportunity. To the deep chagrin of my military missionary, they took all six *Playboys* and left the Bibles behind.

On several occasions, I engaged the Soviets in discussions on religion. General Trusov, knowing I was Catholic, asked how many missiles my pope had. Having once seen General Trusov's wife coming out of a Russian Orthodox church in Geneva, I asked him if she was a member. "No, no," Trusov replied nervously. "No Communist official or member of his family can practice a religion. It is forbidden. My wife goes to church because she admires the icons and enjoys the chanting and the smell of incense. She goes for aesthetic reasons only."

The next Sunday I stopped by the Russian Orthodox church on the way home from my own church service. There was Mrs. Trusov, fervently crossing herself with two fingers in the Orthodox tradition. Unfortunately, she saw me and became noticeably upset. She immediately left the church, studiously avoiding me. I always regretted that I probably prevented her from ever again attending church in Geneva.

WAR OF WORDS

Throughout 1978 the Soviets waged a highly effective propaganda campaign, blaming the United States for the failure to conclude a SALT II treaty. It began with a *Pravda* editorial on February 11, 1978, which was reprinted widely in the Western press. The editorial claimed that the Soviet Union was engaged in "constructive negotiations" but that the United States consistently presented "one-sided proposals." It warned that the "many attempts at intimidating the Soviet Union were futile." In March, a *Pravda* editorial, signed by Georgi Arbatov, repeated the earlier claims. Arbatov followed up his editorial with a visit to the United States during which he charged that various "opponents of détente" were becoming "more bitter" as prospects for a SALT II agreement became "more real." This well-coordinated and extensive public relations campaign had its intended effect on the U.S. public. The domestic pressure to conclude an arms control agreement was palpable. One could hardly pick up a newspaper without reading a stinging editorial lambasting Carter for the delay.

By the end of September, Carter's domestic and international prestige had risen dramatically as a result of the successful conclusion of the Egyptian-Israeli Camp David peace accords. Buoyed by a new sense of diplomatic optimism and feeling the pressure of public opinion, President Carter embarked on an aggressive public relations campaign of his own. He declared that the final round of SALT II was at hand. Administration spokesmen, dubbed by their opponents as "SALT sellers," spoke around the country hoping to pressure senators into favoring the still unfinished treaty. The campaign backfired, however, and senatorial resistance stiffened to the administration's arguments. Something had to give, and that something was Paul Warnke.

Citing personal reasons, Warnke resigned in October 1978 as chief negotiator and director of ACDA. His departure was widely perceived as an attempt to pave the way for Senate approval of the emerging SALT II agreement and especially to placate Senator Scoop Jackson, Warnke's most vocal opponent. Warnke was replaced at ACDA by retired Army Lt. Gen. George Seignious. The appointment of a career military officer as the new ACDA director was widely interpreted as an effort to garner conservative support for SALT II. When Warnke left, his deputy, Ralph Earle, was named chief U.S. negotiator of SALT II.

THE LAST LAP

By late November 1978, after numerous unilateral U.S. concessions, hopes were high in the Carter administration that an agreement could be reached by Christmas. Secretary Vance and Foreign Minister Gromyko were scheduled to arrive in Geneva on December 21. It was anticipated that the remaining issues could be quickly resolved and a treaty signed at a summit in 1979. To the Soviets, however, near-term deadlines and high U.S. expectations offered an opportunity for mischief-making. Knowing that the Americans wanted to get home for Christmas with the issues resolved, they stalled from the very outset, hoping that we would become impatient and grant additional concessions.

The negotiations were complicated by a development on the international scene. A week before Vance arrived in Geneva, President Carter dropped a bombshell by announcing that the United States and the PRC would establish diplomatic relations on January 1, 1979. The notion that the United States might establish formal ties with the PRC had long been a sensitive issue with the Soviets. The matter had taken on an added element of volatility in the Carter administration because Brzezinski and Vance had divergent views on the timing of such a move. Vance favored postponing any announcement until after a SALT agreement was signed. He also suggested that economic enticements be offered to the Soviets to cushion what he believed would be a serious blow to Russian sensibilities. Brzezinski, who was generally credited with convincing the president on the timing, felt that the Soviets might renege on a SALT deal when they learned about the new U.S.-China ties. He believed that the announcement should coincide with Vance's meetings in Geneva.

The Soviets were caught by surprise when the United States played the China card. In characteristic fashion, they did not react to the matter directly. Instead, they showed their displeasure by introducing a new issue into the SALT negotiations. The one they chose was remotely piloted vehicles (RPVs). It was clear from the beginning that this was a diversionary ploy. The Soviet claim that RPVs were the equivalent of manned bombers was as ludicrous as it was bogus. RPVs—miniature, unmanned aircraft used largely for reconnaissance and communications—were much smaller than fighter aircraft. The idea that they could be armed with nuclear weapons and therefore should be counted as U.S. weapon systems was nothing short of fantasy. Vance attempted to play down the significance of the RPV issue and moved to accommodate Soviet concerns. The Soviets suddenly shifted ground and raised another issue: missile telemetry. This was not the first time I had seen the Soviets use bait-and-switch tactics.

The U.S. and Soviet positions on the encryption of telemetry—coding of data relayed from missiles to ground stations during flight testing—were far apart. Secretary Vance, realizing that it was unlikely that the issue could be settled quickly, had hoped to postpone consideration of this thorny problem. The Soviets, however, insisted that the matter be discussed then and there.

The United States did not hide its data by encrypting missile telemetry and wanted the Soviet Union to do the same. Being able to monitor what the Soviets were up to during their missile tests was one of the few ways we had of determining how many warheads a missile could carry. It also provided data for estimates of the missile's yield and accuracy. Academician Alexandr Shchukin, trying to appeal to our penchant for abiding by Marquis of Queensberry rules, made light of the situation. "Gentlemen don't read each other's mail," he said, alluding to Secretary of State Henry Stimson's famous statement about the unseemliness of espionage.

Anxious to have a treaty in hand, Secretary Vance was ready to cut a deal. Knowing that the Joint Chiefs felt strongly on the matter, I was not willing to give in. I was convinced that missile telemetry was essential for accurate assessments of Soviet military capabilities. I voiced my objections to Secretary Vance, careful to make it clear that I was speaking on behalf of the Joint Chiefs and not simply giving a personal opinion. Not wishing to be blamed for making a decision on the spot, Vance referred the matter to Washington. The National Security Council's response was a masterpiece of bureaucratic fence-straddling. It decided that the Soviets could not encrypt telemetry pertaining to an agreed-upon list of missile performance character-istics contained in the text of the treaty. The catch-22 was that the Soviets were under no obligation to accede to our demands that specific missile properties be included in the text. Consequently, of the ten performance indicators that we specified should not be en-crypted, the Soviets only accepted the five that we could already ascertain by other means. The remaining five, all critical elements in technical assessments of missile capability, could be encrypted.

THE SLIPPERY SLOPE

Because the Soviets had introduced new issues, U.S. and Soviet ne-gotiators left Geneva on Christmas Eve farther apart than we had been a week earlier. Upon returning to Washington, I told the Joint Chiefs of Staff that I could not support ratification of the emerging treaty, that Secretary Vance had made too many concessions, and that the treaty would undercut our security. I said that under the circumstances I thought it best that I leave the negotiating team and retire from the Army. The chiefs agreed with my assessment and expressed concern that the treaty would not serve our best interests, but they felt it would prove embarrassing to the president if I were to leave the delegation at such a critical juncture. They asked me to remain in place until the treaty was completed and said I could resign then if I was still dissatisfied with the final product. "Besides," they added, "you know the issues and know where the skeletons are buried. We need you to continue your mission of damage limitation."

I then went to see Secretary Vance, feeling that it was only fair that I tell him what I had told the chiefs. If he disagreed with them and felt it more appropriate that I resign before the treaty was completed, I would do so. Vance and I talked for several hours. He was cordial and polite throughout, as ever the perfect gentleman. He expressed disappointment that I could not see my way clear to support the treaty. He argued that we were getting the best agreement possible given our lack of leverage at the negotiating table. I still felt that he failed to understand that a bad arms control agreement was worse than no agreement at all.

Vance said that it would be up to the JCS to make the final determination on whether the treaty was an acceptable risk to the nation's security. He reiterated his belief that signing an agreement was better than coming up empty-handed after six years of negotiations and suggested that the treaty was a good first step. I told the secretary that a first step is only good if it leads to a second step on firm ground. This step was into a chasm. By signing the agreement under consideration, we would be allowing the Soviets to pocket our mistakes and set the terms for SALT III. I told Vance that if I resigned after the treaty was initialed I would undoubtedly be called upon to testify against it when it came up for ratification. It was a civil meeting; we parted with a businesslike, but not overly warm, handshake.

Two interesting events occurred in the spring of 1979 while I was still part of the delegation. While visiting Moscow during a break in the Geneva negotiations—I traveled to the Soviet Union as often as possible to learn more about the Soviet people and to maintain my language proficiency—I thought it might be a good idea to pay a social call on my military counterparts who were on home leave. When I phoned their offices, however, I was told that they were out of town. I knew this was untrue because I had spotted one of them the previous evening at the Bolshoi Theater. After several more unsuccessful phone calls, I tried to visit them at their offices but was stopped by a guard inside the front door. I asked to speak by phone to General Trusov. A secretary answered in Russian, asking who I was and what I wanted to speak to Trusov about. I gave her my name and said that I had some new information to pass on to the general. For the next five minutes I could overhear an animated conversation going on at the other end. Finally the secretary came back on the line, saying that General Trusov was not there. I asked to talk to General

Beletsky but was told that he was also not there. Exasperated, I asked her if she would come to the front desk for a note to give to General Trusov when he returned. Again there was a long delay and some conversation on the other end. Finally, she said she would come down and pick up my note. I wrote that I very much wanted to see Generals Trusov and Beletsky and had some new information to impart.

The next day I received a message through the U.S. Embassy that Generals Trusov and Beletsky would meet me at 8:00 P.M. that evening at the Russian military liaison office. When I arrived, the generals were obviously ill at ease and greeted me nervously. It was the first time I had seen them in uniform. Under Swiss law, foreign nationals were forbidden from wearing military uniforms in Switzerland. We had a short and strained conversation under the watchful eye of a KGB officer. I decided to keep the conversation light and did not say anything about my new information.

As I was leaving, I told the generals that I would be happy to put them up at my home when they made their next trip to Washington. They both became quite agitated at my offer and beat a hasty retreat. I asked their interpreter why they were so irritated. "Because you insulted them," he said. "You should know that they are not allowed to invite you to their apartments, and by inviting them to your home you upstaged them." I knew that the Soviets were secretive and xenophobic, but I had no idea they carried such matters so far.

At a dinner party the following evening, hosted by the U.S. consular officer in Leningrad, I received a telephone call from Washington. There would be a critical meeting of the NSC the following day at noon; would I be able to attend? I said I did not think I could make it but that I would try. An hour later, I received an urgent message from the chairman of the JCS telling me that I should try my best to get back to Washington. There were no scheduled U.S. flights from Leningrad to Washington, and even if I took an overnight train to Moscow and caught the first commercial flight out in the morning, I would arrive too late.

My host took getting me back to Washington for the meeting as a personal challenge. He proposed that we drive to Helsinki (about 200 miles) where I could catch an 8:00 A.M. flight to London and from there take an 11:00 A.M. Concorde to Washington. Factoring in time differentials, I would arrive an hour before the meeting. We had to depart immediately because the bridges over the Neva River were raised at midnight to allow ships passage into the port of Leningrad.

We made it over the river with fifteen minutes to spare and soon arrived at the Russo-Finnish border. The Russian guard let us pass into the three-kilometer zone separating the two countries. But when we reached the gate leading into Finland, it was already closed for the night. My host returned to the Russian gatehouse and after much discussion and the passage of several silver dollars, the guard let us use his phone. After numerous calls pleading our case on the grounds that national security interests were at stake, we were able to convince the Finns to drive twenty kilometers from the nearest town and let us through. At 2:00 A.M., a disgruntled and sleepy guard opened the gate and let us pass after I eased his inconvenience with a twenty-dollar bill. We then began a wild night ride to Helsinki.

It started to snow. After several near accidents on icy bridges, we arrived at Helsinki airport at 7:55 A.M., five minutes before takeoff. Realizing that we were about to miss the plane, and much to the amazement of the Finnish authorities, my host drove out on the tarmac to intercept the plane as it taxied for takeoff. Fortunately, the pilot stopped, turned off one of his engines, and allowed me to board. I was inclined to believe my friend's good-natured boasting that as a former U.S. Army Ranger nothing could stop him. I took the Concorde from London to Dulles International Airport, where a helicopter was waiting for me, and by 11:30 A.M. I was at the Pentagon's helipad. Fifteen minutes later I was in the situation room at the White House. Promptly at noon Brzezinski and my boss, General Jones, arrived. They were startled to see me and asked how I had managed to get back in time. I told them it was a long story and muttered something about a crazy ex-Army Ranger.

The meeting turned out to be an important one, because Secretary Vance proposed that the United States should make further concessions to assure that a treaty would be ready for signature by June 15 at the planned summit. The question before us was whether the Soviets would sign the agreement on the basis of the concessions already made or if new ones would be required. Because I was the most experienced person to have negotiated with the Soviets, the chiefs and Brzezinski wanted my opinion. I told the NSC that I had no doubts about the Soviets signing the treaty, but we had to expect them to play their eleventh-hour tactics to the fullest. I added that we had already made too many concessions and that the Senate might not ratify the treaty even if we stood firm on what had already been agreed upon in Geneva. The chiefs and Secretary Vance knew, of course, of my desire to quit the delegation. Vance withdrew his pro-

posal that we make further concessions. The trip had been worth the
mad dash.

As the weeks passed, there was considerable turmoil and intrigue
within the Washington bureaucracy. Even Ralph Earle, Warnke's
successor, was worried. He confided in me that he saw a mounting
danger that the Senate would not ratify the emerging treaty unless the
United States took a tougher stand.

In May I returned to Washington in a last-ditch effort to get the
chiefs to try to turn things around and get a better treaty. But they
told me that they were being pressured by the president to wind up
the treaty. The depth of the crisis was brought home to me when
Bernard Rogers, the Army chief of staff, reversed his earlier stand
that the military could not support the treaty. He now said that he
thought SALT II would be a "modest but useful step." It was a bad
omen.

As I often did when troubled, I went to see Scoop Jackson. I told
him that I was very unhappy over the deal about to be signed and
once again found myself agonizing over whether I should retire. He
told me that the treaty had a poor chance of passing the Senate and
that I could best help defeat it by staying at the negotiating table. He
advised me to wait until the treaty was initialed and then retire.

Secretary Vance and Foreign Minister Gromyko agreed to return
to Geneva at the end of May to work out the remaining differences.
Because the agreement was scheduled to be signed by President Carter
and General Secretary Brezhnev on June 15 in Vienna, most of the
U.S. negotiators thought that this last round of negotiations would
be conducted in a spirit of cooperation and wrapped up rapidly. Not
so. The Soviets once again resorted to stalling. They brought up
issues we considered long settled. The sessions were interminable and
often acrimonious. Vance and Gromyko were not able to resolve
several sticky issues and turned them over to Earle and Karpov.
Karpov characteristically dug in his heels, and Earle, not wanting to
be blamed for negotiating a flawed treaty, was in no mood to make
further concessions. The sessions degenerated into a protracted tug-
of-war.

At six o'clock on the evening of June 14, 1979, Karpov and Earle
finally hammered out the last of the remaining details. Earle quickly
initialed his copy. Karpov, however, notified Earle that he had some
problems with it and asked to meet with Earle at 9:00 P.M. When
they met, Earle remained firm on the major issues but agreed to

several minor modifications. Shortly before midnight, Earle and Karpov agreed to agree, and Karpov finally initialed the treaty.

THE SIGNING

Soon thereafter, the delegations assembled in the U.S. conference room for a glass of champagne to celebrate the completion of the agreement. I excused myself from the festivities and went to my office where I cabled my resignation from the SALT team to the chairman of the JCS. My message was short and to the point. I stated that I could not, in good conscience, support the treaty being submitted for the president's signature, and I therefore felt it my duty to resign from the delegation. I also requested that I be excused from traveling to Vienna for the signing ceremony and that I be put on the Army's retired list effective July 31.

The next morning, a scant eight hours after I had sent my cable, I received a reply. I was excused from going to Vienna, but my retirement would be effective on June 30 and not, as I had requested, July 31. It was Washington's way of expressing displeasure. I was given two weeks to bring to a close a U.S. Army career of thirty-eight years.

When President Carter arrived in Vienna, he thought he would quickly sign the SALT II Treaty and engage Brezhnev on other matters. But the General Secretary pushed back the clock and began another round of eleventh-hour negotiations.

Brezhnev introduced a new and unrelated subject, mobile land-based missiles. Brezhnev said that the mobile version of the MX could not be verified by national technical means (NTMs) and therefore should be prohibited. It was a red herring; the United States had never agreed that weapon systems could be verified by national technical means alone. We felt that on-site inspection would be required.

Not satisfied with the havoc he was raising, Brezhnev introduced a second diversionary tactic. He insisted that any future agreement would have to include intermediate-range missiles and forward-based systems. SALT III, as far as the United States was concerned, was something to be considered later and had no business being discussed in Vienna.

A more serious stumbling block to the signing of SALT II was the Backfire bomber. Secretary of State Vance told President Carter that he had received verbal assurance from Gromyko that the Soviets would not produce more than thirty Backfires per year. In a surprisingly prudent move, Carter demanded that those assurances be put in writing. Brezhnev refused, but Carter held his ground. To break the impasse, Brezhnev promised to provide the president with a letter specifying Backfire production rates. On the strength of that promise the president signed the agreement. But when Carter received Brezhnev's letter, it made no mention of the thirty-planes-per-year guarantee. It simply said that the Soviets would not increase their current rate of production. Up to the very end, the Soviets repeatedly demonstrated that they were cunning, if not outright devious, negotiators.

SALT II was finally signed on June 18, 1979. Splashed across the front pages of almost every newspaper in the world was a picture of Carter and Brezhnev with raised champagne glasses, toasting their success. "In signing this treaty," an ebullient Brezhnev said, "we have helped to defend the most sacred right of every individual—the right to live." Not to be outdone, Carter said that without SALT II, ". . . an unrestrained competition would tempt fate in the future, insult our intelligence, and threaten the very existence of humanity." He concluded, "If we cannot control the power to destroy, we can neither guide our fate, nor preserve our own future."

Carter returned to the United States on the crest of a wave of optimism, satisfied by the terms of the treaty and confident that he could convince the Senate to ratify it. He was mistaken. Scoop Jackson publicly condemned the treaty, bringing congressional opponents of the agreement out into the open. They criticized Carter and Vance for their excessive zeal and lack of toughness. More than forty senators initially said they were against the treaty, half because they felt that we had appeased the Soviets on the Backfire and heavy-missile issues and half because they believed that the treaty was unverifiable.

THE DEMISE OF SALT II

Shortly after I left the Army, I joined the fight to defeat SALT II, a battle conducted on several levels. While I was confident that the Senate would not ratify the treaty, I did not want to leave it to chance. I believed that there should be a tangible record of the treaty's flaws and how they had come about. I felt that the more lessons I could impart to future negotiators, the better I could assure that any agreement reached would be a good one.

The best organized and most effective opposition group was the

Committee on the Present Danger, founded in 1976 by several concerned persons, among them David Packard, CEO of the Hewlett-Packard Company; Lane Kirkland, president of the AFL-CIO; and Richard Allen, who later became President Reagan's national security advisor. Originally established to point out the growing military imbalance between the Soviet Union and the United States and to strengthen our military posture, the group, which I joined in August of 1979, soon propelled itself into the forefront of the opposition to SALT II. It was very effective, both because it included many influential people and because they and others contributed sizeable sums of money to back its work.

A second, more informal organization was the Madison Group. The name was derived from our meeting place, the Madison Hotel, where we gathered several times a week to plan and coordinate our efforts. This "Council of Cardinals," as we thought of ourselves (after Cardinal Richelieu who had masterminded Louis XIII's policies), was made up largely of Senate staffers who formulated and promoted their bosses' policies.

The chief guru of the group was Sven Kraemer (Fritz Kraemer's son), who had formerly served three presidents as a staff member at NSC and was now working for Senator John Tower's Republican Policy Committee. Another half-dozen key members came from the offices of conservative senators. Richard Perle and Frank Gaffney were two of Senator Henry Jackson's foreign policy assistants, Dave Sullivan worked for Senator Gordon Humphrey of New Hampshire, and Jim Lucier and John Carbaugh were on North Carolina Republican Senator Jesse Helms's staff. The Madison Group was a formidable collection of movers and shakers, knowledgeable about weapon systems and the inner workings of the Senate.

Sven Kraemer's strategy was to highlight a set of issues around which we could all rally. These were the same issues I had raised with the Joint Chiefs of Staff concerning the inequities of SALT II. In the past, I had been careful not to divulge what had taken place in my meetings with the chiefs to anyone outside the administration, but now that the treaty had been sent to the Senate, I felt free to discuss publicly its shortcomings. Kraemer had me make up a list of issues on which the Joint Chiefs of Staff had been overruled by the White House. He used this to argue against the chiefs' contention, once the treaty was signed, that it was a "modest but useful step."

Kraemer had a two-part plan: to get the Senate Armed Services Committee (SASC) involved in the ratification process and to devise conditions to the treaty that senators could turn into killer amendments. Senator Jackson was most anxious to involve the Armed Services panel in the hearings. He was the most powerful man on the committee; its chairman, Mississippi Senator John Stennis, took a back seat and let Jackson practically run the show.

Jurisdiction over the treaty's ratification was a very touchy subject with the Senate Foreign Relations Committee (SFRC). Senator Frank Church, the panel's chairman, felt that the SFRC had an exclusive mandate, by Senate rules and precedent, to deal with ratification. One of his committee members, Senator Jesse Helms, disagreed and sided with Jackson, whose announced reason for getting the Armed Services panel into the act was that SALT II dealt with weapons and defense policies, matters that, at least in part, fell under SASC's purview. Jackson's real reason, however, was more practical: SASC had a conservative bent, while the SFRC was liberal. SASC could, therefore, be expected to call more witnesses opposed to the treaty and have them highlight its flaws. Jackson knew more about arms control than any other senator and was substantively and emotionally involved with SALT II. He chafed at the thought that the SFRC, which he considered soft on the Soviets, had primacy in the Senate's consideration. He felt that Senators Claiborne Pell, Edmund Muskie, and Frank Church were under the influence of George McGovern, whom he viewed as the most intelligent and the most misguided individual on the SFRC. Jackson considered McGovern lacking in any understanding of the Soviets and their objectives. Jackson felt that if he could get a number of senators to debate the conditions he wanted to attach to the treaty, then the treaty's flaws would be exposed. Our objective in the Madison Group was to draw up these conditions and turn them into matters the administration would have to renegotiate with the Soviets before the Senate would give its consent. Since the Soviets could be expected to oppose reopening issues they considered settled, these conditions would, in effect, kill this fatally flawed treaty.

One of the most influential and certainly the most mysterious person to fight against SALT II was Bill Casey, who later was chosen by Ronald Reagan to head the Central Intelligence Agency (CIA). I had had chance encounters with Casey before, but until he asked me to meet him in his law office I had not realized that he enjoyed such a powerful position in the inner circles of Republican Party policymakers. I learned quickly that Casey was a superlative organizer. He kept a file of three-by-five-inch cards with the names of people who had special knowledge on a large variety of issues. He would assign them tasks, usually asking for a written report that he would integrate with other information and then act upon. He was a loner who preferred to deal with people separately, either in private meetings or over the phone.

Casey's list was made up of a variety of highly placed individuals in government, think tanks, industry, and academia. His list included very few media personnel; Arnaud de Borchgrave and Patrick Buchanan were the only journalists whose names I spotted. Casey preferred to work unobtrusively behind the scenes; he shunned publicity. I once told Casey that he was losing potential support from reporters and television commentators by refusing to talk to them, but Casey seemed not to mind. He believed that cultivating a public image was not very important; in fact, he told me that being in the spotlight would only make his job harder. Knowing of his background as a member of "Wild Bill" Donovan's wartime intelligence group, I thought of him as a master spy. He operated in such a low-key and laid-back manner that I was amazed he ever got anything done. But he was a speed-reader who soon after I gave him a report would return it filled with comments. The memos he asked me to write for him were generally of two types. The first was on some fundamental issue in SALT II, such as the Soviets' unilateral right to heavy missiles. Casey would invariably come up with an idea on how such an arcane matter could be explained more clearly or succinctly. The second category included things that he had heard from a senator or member of his staff. Casey was always looking for ways to exert pressure on senators, whether through their colleagues or through influential constituents. Although I was never certain what Casey did with the information I furnished, I was frequently called by influential senators, like Paul Laxalt of Nevada, or wealthy businessmen, like Joseph Coors, president of the Coors Brewing Company, to elaborate on a topic Casey had discussed with them. I also knew that he was in close touch with Ronald Reagan. I became convinced that Casey was operating effectively at a high level and with a select group of contacts to scuttle SALT II. The intriguing question, to which I never learned the answer, was whether Casey was asked to help kill SALT II or whether he did it on his own initiative.

During the summer and fall of 1979 I worked to provide grist for the mills of Casey, the Committee on the Present Danger, and the Madison Group. Several members of this latter body sought to target Paul Warnke as the perpetrator of all of SALT II's shortcomings, but

I opposed this tactic. Warnke had been out of the SALT II process for more than a year, and President Carter and Secretary Vance had more to do with setting U.S. policies than Warnke. Advocates of making Warnke the fall guy sought to take advantage of the hostility to him in the Senate, thereby picking up additional votes against the treaty. While I had disagreed with Warnke on most substantive issues, I preferred not to engage in mud-slinging because he had never attacked me personally.

Our efforts to defeat the treaty were made easier because the administration spent considerable time and effort having its large group of "SALT sellers" speak to public groups, which had little direct influence. The administration did not devote much time and effort to senators, especially those in the undecided column. The administration mistakenly believed that it enjoyed the support of the majority of the Senate and had the undecided senators in the bag. For example, no one in the Carter administration seemed to know that Tennessee Republican Howard Baker had serious problems with SALT II. The administration likewise failed to pay any attention to Ohio Democrat John Glenn's early statements that he had misgivings about the treaty's verification provisions. The administration also was apparently not aware that Georgia Senator Sam Nunn had his own agenda, namely, to force the administration to spend more money on defense programs Nunn considered important. The Committee on the Present Danger, the Madison Group, and Bill Casey outmaneuvered the administration at almost every turn.

The Madison Group asked me to personally call upon as many as possible of the 100 members of the U.S. Senate. The group also saw to it that I was invited to appear before the Foreign Relations, Armed Services, and Intelligence committees of the Senate, which were taking testimony on the treaty.

Talking with the senators was a taxing and time-consuming task. During the summer and fall of 1979, I had one-on-one sessions with sixty-two senators, our meetings lasting anywhere from fifteen minutes to four hours. Perhaps twenty or so of my visits were courtesy calls to senators whose positions were well known and unlikely to change. The other forty or so calls were substantive ones at which I presented my case against SALT II. My first contacts were with conservative Republican senators opposed to the treaty, such as Jake Garn of Utah, John Danforth of Missouri, and Jesse Helms of North Carolina. But I moved quickly to speak to others I had come to know over the years. I went to see Charles Mathias, my senator from Maryland. Although he and I held opposing views on arms control, Mathias was very friendly. An astute observer of the personalities of his colleagues, he gave me good tips on how to approach them. He told me that Rhode Island Democrat Claiborne Pell was very protective of the interests of the U.S. Navy, which had a large presence in his state. If I could show Pell how SALT II might harm the Navy, it would cool his ardor for the treaty. He also told me that New Jersey Democrat Bill Bradley was one of the most influential senators because of the high respect his colleagues had for him. Although Bradley paid little attention to arms control, Mathias thought it would be worth trying to get him involved. Mathias also thought that I should capitalize on Jake Garn's opposition to SALT II by providing him with additional arguments to help him convince others.

This extremely valuable advice reinforced an insight I had formed earlier about how Washington in general, and the Senate in particular, works. Relationships are more important than ideology. Mathias said he admired me for the long years of study I had devoted to nuclear strategy and understanding the Soviets. Although he did not share my views, he was ready to help me by explaining the leanings and idiosyncrasies of his colleagues.

I next went to see Senator Daniel Patrick Moynihan of New York. Moynihan disagreed with me philosophically, but during his visits to Geneva I had enjoyed long discussions with him on the role of arms control in foreign policy. I then went to talk to three other liberal senators: George McGovern, Republican Mark Hatfield of Oregon, and Democrat William Proxmire of Wisconsin. These senators were unhappy with the treaty because it permitted the United States to test and deploy the M-X. They seemed less concerned that the treaty allowed the Soviets to deploy new missiles than that it permitted us to deploy similar missiles. To me, this was convoluted reasoning, but I saw no advantage in straightening out their thinking. I was more disposed to muster opposition to SALT II wherever I could find it.

Opponents of SALT II received an unexpected windfall from Foreign Relations Committee Chairman Frank Church. Up for reelection in Idaho and fearful of being perceived as too soft on the Russians, Church announced in August the presence of a Soviet combat brigade in Cuba. He said that the Senate should not consider ratifying SALT II until the Soviet troops were removed. Although Church was correct about the combat brigade, it had nothing to do with SALT II. Still, Church's disclosure helped turn a large segment of public opinion against the Soviets and eventually resulted in several senatorial votes against the treaty.

Moderate senators who were in the undecided column were crucial to the outcome. One of these was John Glenn, a former marine and astronaut, who had special knowledge of satellite and overhead photography and knew that it was insufficient to detect Soviet cheating. He told me he would not only vote against SALT II because of his concerns but would urge some of the other undecideds to join him.

Perhaps the most influential of the undecideds I talked to was Republican Senate Minority Leader Howard Baker, who had voted for SALT I and was favorably impressed by the Vladivostok Accord. Apparently worried that he would be attacked by conservatives in 1980 when he ran for the Republican Party's presidential nomination and dissatisfied with the way the United States had negotiated, Baker began to lean against ratification of SALT II. His objections had to do with the heavy missiles, the Backfire bomber, and verification issues.

When I first went to see Baker, I sensed he might oppose ratification, but I was not certain he knew enough about the details of the treaty to stand up to liberal colleagues. I went back to see him several times, and each time I felt he gained greater confidence that he could defend his stance. I also sensed that Baker was disappointed that the Carter administration had taken him for granted and did not seek his support. It proved to be one of the administration's biggest mistakes. Supporting Baker in his misgivings and getting Casey to prevail on others to do the same helped fill the void. I felt I had succeeded in getting an important senator to oppose SALT II.

Another important undecided was Sam Nunn. A recognized expert, Nunn had more credibility on defense matters than any other senator except Jackson. Jackson had tutored Nunn in his early days in the Senate and at one time thought of Nunn as his successor. Later, Jackson apparently felt that Nunn was not tough enough with the Soviets, and the Jackson-Nunn relationship cooled. President Carter had sent his fellow Georgian a confidential note soon after he was elected asking Nunn to support his efforts. However, I knew something was developing when at a Madison Group breakfast I learned that Nunn had asked the Committee on the Present Danger to do some research for him. When I spoke to Nunn, he said he was worried about the treaty's inequities and its verification provisions. But it became clear to me from our first conversation that Nunn's primary worry was not that SALT II was a bad treaty, but that its passage would negatively affect our defense programs.

To gain Nunn's support, the president accelerated the Navy's Trident program and ordered improvements to our land-based intercontinental ballistic missiles. After Nunn saw that the president was strengthening U.S. defenses, he backed off his opposition and said he could support the treaty. President Carter later admitted that Nunn had used SALT II as a vehicle to extract from the administration a higher level of defense expenditures.

During the fall of 1979 I concentrated on preparing to testify before the Senate Foreign Relations Committee. I explained to the panel why the treaty was inequitable, unverifiable, and did not contribute to deterrence or stability. Most of the senators were favorably disposed toward ratification and avoided asking detailed questions. Instead, they raised peripheral issues and questioned my motives. For example, Senator Pell wanted to know why I had stayed on the SALT team after I had expressed my doubts to the Joint Chiefs. I told him my philosophy was "hope springs eternal" and had concluded that my continued presence at the table might limit the damage.

Indiana Republican Richard Lugar asked if I thought the treaty should be amended. Even though Lugar had told me he would vote against the treaty, I felt it best that I not openly advocate amending it because to do so might have exposed the Madison Group's plan to seek killer amendments. I told Lugar that SALT II was fatally flawed, but whether it should be amended was up to the committee to decide.

Senator McGovern told me that he did not agree that parity was important and failed to understand why the side with more weapons should be more emboldened to strike first. The answer seemed so obvious to me that I did not know where to begin to try to turn his thinking around. After all, the bully scares the weakling and not the other way around. I simply told him that I disagreed with him and left it at that.

Florida Democrat Richard Stone said that he was interested in why we had "given away the store" during the negotiations and asked detailed questions about what had happened at the Vance-Gromyko meeting in March 1977. He said he had read a statement by Brzezinski that the March 1977 plan was a good one, and wanted to know what had gone wrong. But before I had time to answer, Maine Democrat Edmund Muskie interrupted and asked me what I thought about what Brzezinski had said. I answered that I agreed with Brzezinski and that even though he and I were of Polish origin, we were not Poles apart. This got a laugh from the senators; they knew that Muskie was also of Polish origin.

New York Republican Jacob Javits struck a nerve by asking if my opposition to SALT II did not amount to second-guessing the Joint Chiefs of Staff. I had to handle this one carefully in view of the strong opposition to SALT II the chiefs had registered to me privately prior to their turnabout. I simply told Javits that I thought he should read their statements and make up his own mind.

I tried to be measured in my responses and looked for opportunities to dispel the notion, gained largely from the media, that I was an inflexible hawk. Although the atmosphere was tense—the senators trying to attack my credibility and I trying to highlight the flaws of SALT II—I was, on the whole, satisfied with what I had accomplished during my testimony.

Because the committee had not given me sufficient opportunity to outline in detail the fatal flaws of SALT II, I developed a list of some forty questions I thought they should have asked me. John Carbaugh had his boss, Senator Helms, submit these questions to the chairman, Senator Church, asking that I respond in writing. Several committee members, notably Pell and McGovern, objected; but Helms, the acknowledged master of Senate procedural rules, prevailed. He knew that if a committee member wanted to ask a question of a witness it was difficult, if not impossible, for the chairman to refuse. The questions were designed to reveal some of the weakest parts of SALT II. One asked: "Why does the Soviets' sole possession of heavy missiles give them a unilateral advantage?" Another asked why the United States had been outmaneuvered at the negotiating table into addressing intentions rather than capabilities of the Backfire bomber. This technique of answering my own questions allowed me to highlight the loopholes the Soviets had built into the treaty's verification provisions. I worked hard to explain complex technical matters in language that nonexperts could understand. Senator Helms inserted the questions and answers into the *Congressional Record*.

The Madison Group later saw to it that the Foreign Relations Committee drew up thirty-six "conditions" to the treaty. Most of these conditions, like the forty questions, were suggested by me and introduced into the hearings by Senator Helms. I was asked by the Foreign Relations panel in early October to submit in writing my views on each of the thirty-six conditions. My comments were subsequently printed in the record of the "mark-up" of the committee proceedings. Of the thirty-six, twenty-three were subsequently adopted, and two of these, because they mandated reopening negotiations with the Soviets, were killer amendments.

The Senate Armed Services Committee, to the consternation of the Senate Foreign Relations Committee, held parallel hearings. Senators Jackson and Tower used the opportunity to have me testify; they asked me many of the questions the SFRC had tried to sweep under the rug. Jackson used every trick he could to bring SALT II's flaws to the fore. He saw to it that reporters with conservative leanings were given briefing papers explaining what was at stake. A number of influential conservatives were prevailed upon to write articles and make speeches condemning SALT II. Jackson, Tower, Stone, Glenn, Helms, and others made statements on the Senate floor that were inserted into the *Congressional Record*. The Committee on the Present Danger then reprinted many of these remarks and sent them to a large mailing list. In addition, Sven Kraemer had the American Security Council reprint the entire record of the testimony before the SASC and mail it to its members. Such maneuvers did not just overtake the administration's "SALT sellers"—they left them far behind.

On December 20, 1979, after much arm-twisting by Senator Jackson, the SASC formally stated that the treaty was "not in the national security interests of the United States." Senator Church, intent on protecting the turf of the SFRC, prevailed upon Majority Leader Robert Byrd to prevent the SASC statement from being filed officially. But Jackson had accomplished his basic objective through the publicity that had surrounded the Armed Services panel's hearings.

In fact, by the time the Senate hearings were over in November, the treaty was effectively dead. At the time, we counted forty senators who said they would oppose the treaty if it came to a vote, six more than the thirty-four needed to defeat it.

President Carter faced up to the facts. After the Soviets invaded Afghanistan in December 1979, he withdrew the treaty from Senate consideration. He made the astonishing statement that he had learned more about the Soviets in the preceding two weeks than he had in his entire life. The statement showed just how naive he had been.

ART IMITATING LIFE

Shortly after I retired, I received a phone call from playwright Arthur Kopit. He had received a generous commission from a wealthy businessman to write a play explaining the rudiments of nuclear deterrence. Kopit was asked to interpret deterrence in the universal language of drama. The hoped-for objective was to reduce the risk of nuclear war. Kopit wanted me to be his real-world tutor. I tried to convey to him the nuts and bolts of deterrence theory to put into his play. Kopit found comprehending it all extremely difficult. He could not explain deterrence theory because he himself was unable to understand it.

Kopit wrote a play within a play to try to highlight his frustration at trying to grasp the complexities. On the invitations to the opening performance, the title of the play *End of the World* was followed by the captivating statement: "Symposium to Follow." The three lead characters were himself and thinly veiled portrayals of Harvard historian Richard Pipes and me. But the actors playing Pipes and me could not explain deterrence theory to the actor playing Kopit.

My favorite lines in the play had to do with a reference to one of the prints I collected by artist M. C. Escher. I had always been fascinated with the illusions that Escher could create in his art, but in no way did I think it had anything to do with my views on deterrence. In the course of the play the Kopit character looked at an Escher print and asked the actor playing me, "Is that water really running uphill?"

"No," was the reply, "it's an illusion."

"Just like your God-damned theory of deterrence," the actor playing Kopit said. The audience roared.

The play had its tryouts at Washington's Kennedy Center. To insiders, it was interesting and humorous, but its arcane philosophy and scholarly overtones were lost on most of the audience.

It opened on Broadway several weeks later but closed after only a week. The play was simply too esoteric and complicated for most theatergoers to appreciate. Ironically, it is still performed at the University of Moscow as well as on campuses in the United States.

THE FORTUNES OF FAILURE

Carter's lack of understanding of the Soviet Union and its goals made it impossible for him to conclude an acceptable SALT II agreement. Fortunately, the system of checks and balances in the U.S. government prevented the ratification of a disastrous treaty that would have established the precedent that the Soviet Union was entitled to a more powerful strategic arsenal than the United States.

Carter's overzealousness and his naive approach to world politics were compounded by serious divisions within his own administration. Divergent factions developed opposing ideas on how to deal with the Soviet Union. One faction favored SALT II and accommodation with the Soviets, while another faction favored a tougher approach. In the end, Congress was forced to make the tough decisions.

Had President Carter not withdrawn the treaty from Senate consideration, there is no doubt in my mind that the mandated amendments to the draft treaty would have resulted in another year or two of difficult negotiations. And in the end, the amendments would have lived up to their name and killed the treaty.

Even staunch Democrats readily admitted that Carter's foreign policy record was an unmitigated disaster. During his term in office the Soviets were allowed to solidify their positions in Ethiopia, South Yemen, and Mozambique; their surrogates were in Angola and Nicaragua; and their own troops had invaded and occupied Afghanistan.

As a negotiator and a user of power, Carter was simply no match for Brezhnev. He was unable to translate his effusive rhetoric into viable policies. His well-meaning, idealistic, and enthusiastic nature was met with reproach and even disdain. Aware that Carter had assumed the role of *demandeur,* Brezhnev was unwilling to enter into an agreement except on Soviet terms. Fortunately, SALT II crumbled under the weight of its own weaknesses. It was a disaster averted but only after the efforts of many people.

The man who was to follow Carter could not have been more different in perspective. Ronald Reagan had no illusions about the Soviets and, as a consequence, was far more successful in dealing with them.

CHAPTER 5

Reagan's First Term: Turnabout

Of all post–World War II presidents, Ronald Reagan best understood Soviet negotiating objectives. He instinctively knew something that I had been forced to learn through long and painful experience; namely, the Soviets, as a way of furthering their foreign policy goals, wanted simply to keep the negotiating process going. Reagan realized that he could not abandon negotiations—public sentiment would not allow it. But he decided that an arms control agreement for its own sake would not do; it would have to be equitable and verifiable. The challenge was to reach that goal while keeping the process from working for the Soviets.

Reagan was not a man to deal with nuts and bolts; details bored him. Unlike Carter, he was a big-picture man who did not feel compelled to provide lengthy or complicated arguments to support his policies. Yet, he had an innate sense, an intuitive feel, for the right thing to do. His grasp of issues seemed to emanate from a deepseated set of values. He also had a stubborn way of sticking to his convictions; he lived up to his nickname, Dutch.

As soon as he became president, Reagan embarked on a threepronged course of action. First, he planned to rebuild our defense forces and strengthen our military posture. This would not only enhance our security but give us greater leverage at the negotiating table. Second, he wanted to break with the tradition of merely limiting delivery systems, as called for in SALT II, and opt for reducing the total number of weapons themselves. Third, he planned to broaden the overall U.S. approach to the Soviet Union, going beyond the notion of arms control as the centerpiece of U.S.-Soviet relations. He was determined to engage the Soviets on other fundamental issues that divided us, such as human rights and regional differences.

But I am getting ahead of my story. Having retired from the Army in protest over SALT II, how did I get back into the negotiating business? The chain of events that led me back to the table began just before Christmas of 1979, after my Senate testimony had helped defeat the SALT II treaty. I received a phone call from Ronald Reagan. He said that he admired me for having resigned from the SALT II delegation in protest over the treaty, that he had been following my testimony before the Senate, and that he agreed with me. He asked if I would meet with him early in January. I wondered how Reagan had learned so much about my testimony. When I told Scoop Jackson about Reagan's call he said, "Oh, yes, I talked to Reagan and told him the three of us were on the same wavelength. I suggested he call you." It was entirely in keeping with Jackson's bipartisanship that he, a Democrat, would pass on ideas to a Republican presidential candidate.

I worried about our meeting. The media had characterized Reagan as a wild cowboy. Although I shared his conservatism, I did not want to give comfort to those who had branded me an inflexible hawk. But I was curious about this actor turned politician who had, early on, joined the Committee on the Present Danger.

At our meeting, held in a suite at the Washington Hilton, I was pleasantly surprised. Reagan's views appeared sound and his manner reasonable. I formed three immediate impressions. First, he had a good grasp of fundamentals underlying the issues. Second, he possessed great charm. And, finally, he had an exceptional ability to communicate.

Reagan recited the fatal flaws of SALT II, agreeing with me that the exclusive right of the Soviets to possess heavy missiles—that is, missiles more than three times the size and capability of our largest ballistic missiles—gave them a huge advantage and provided them with a first-strike capability. He also agreed that the Soviets' Backfire was a strategic bomber and should have been included in their weapons count. Finally, he supported my judgment that the verification provisions of the agreement were weak and easy to circumvent.

Toward the end of our meeting, Reagan asked me to head a group of campaign advisors on defense and arms control issues. I hesitated. I told him that before accepting I had to be assured that he favored reaching an arms agreement.

"Of course I do," he said. "I would support an agreement but only if it were fair and verifiable."

It was a good answer, one I would have given myself, but I told him that I was still leery about working for a candidate who was characterized in the press as something of a wild man.

Reagan smiled and said, "Well, General, they describe you as being to the right of Attila the Hun, and I don't believe that either." Touché. He won me over. I said that I would be delighted to be an advisor and to campaign for him.

At our get-together, Reagan asked what I thought of the theory of deterrence called MAD, an apt acronym for mutual assured destruction. "Isn't there a better way to deter a potential enemy from firing his missiles at you than to threaten to fire your missiles back at him?" he asked. "If he has a pistol at your head, isn't there a better way to deter him than holding a pistol at his head?"

"Yes," I said, "you could put on a helmet."

"Then why not do so?" he asked.

"Because," I said, "our scientists haven't been able to develop a system to protect us."

"I have faith in our scientists," he said. "I believe that if I challenge them they can design a protective shield."

In 1981, and again in 1982, Reagan asked his advisors if U.S. scientists could develop such a defensive system. "No, not yet," they answered. When he asked again in 1983, they answered, "Yes, provided we have your strong support." Accordingly, in March of that year, Reagan asked U.S. scientists to assign a high priority to designing strategic defenses against Soviet missiles. My conversation with Reagan in 1980 had been the first indication of how strongly he felt about what we came to call the strategic defense initiative, dubbed "Star Wars" by the press. I later learned that Reagan had been sold on the possibilities of strategic defense by the brilliant Hungarian-born scientist Edward Teller.

Throughout 1980 I became increasingly convinced that America needed Reagan in the White House. I was happy that the American people were coming around to the impression that I had formed after our first meeting, namely, that Reagan was a completely responsible person.

While campaigning in New York, I ran into a Soviet negotiator I had come to know in Geneva. I asked him what the Soviets thought about Reagan as president.

"We hope he wins," he said. "We don't want four more years of Carter. He was weak—we respect strength. Carter didn't understand us and made us nervous. We prefer resolute leaders. In fact," he said, "we generally prefer Republicans over Democrats." So, too, did the American public that year.

Several days after Reagan's overwhelming victory, I received an urgent call from the White House. The head of the transition team for the CIA, Lawrence Silberman, had broken his ankle and had to resign. Would I go to Langley and take over the CIA transition? Ambassador William Middendorf would be its nominal head, but I would have to do the work.

Several quick phone calls to Scoop Jackson and Al Haig convinced me to accept. I got along well with Stansfield Turner, the outgoing CIA director; I knew Frank Carlucci, his deputy; and moreover, I felt that the CIA's work was vital to the nation's security.

Bill Casey, whom I had worked with during efforts to scuttle SALT II, had been designated by Reagan to head the CIA. While Casey was knowledgeable and had many influential friends, he was difficult to work with. For one thing, he had a dour manner and wore an expression that made him look perplexed. For another, he mumbled, which earned him the title "Mumbling Bill." I often could not understand what he said. But I soon learned that Casey had sound and strongly held views on how to turn the CIA around. He wanted to increase the number of intelligence satellites the United States put up over the Soviet Union and to revert to the CIA's former emphasis on human intelligence (HUMINT), or intelligence collected through firsthand observation and contacts.

I soon learned that Casey had a big advantage on his side. He was probably closer to the president than any person other than Reagan's wife, Nancy. Casey had been an early Reagan supporter and had raised a great deal of money for the campaign. Reagan called Casey frequently to get his opinions on people Reagan had in mind for key jobs and often took Casey's recommendations over those of his White House advisors. For example, I told Casey that I heard that Senator John Tower was approached by a member of the Defense Department transition team about becoming Reagan's secretary of defense. "It's not going to happen," said Casey. "Weinberger did a good job for Reagan in California, has had high-level Washington experience, and knows the defense issues. Reagan would be more at ease with him than with Tower. I know that Reagan owes John Tower a lot for having campaigned for him. I also appreciate that Tower has a lot of friends on Capitol Hill and would pick up strong congressional support for our defense programs. But then Weinberger doesn't bring with him Tower's liabilities." Casey did not spell out what those were, but, knowing Tower, I could well guess. I suspected that Casey had provided the same views to Reagan and was not surprised when I heard the next day that Weinberger was offered, and had accepted, the bid to become Reagan's secretary of defense.

Reagan confessed that he also had difficulty understanding Casey's mumblings, but it did not seem to prevent him from asking Casey's advice and following it. Casey was the first to suggest to Reagan that the United States supply Stinger antiaircraft missles to the mujaheddin in Afghanistan. He also advised Reagan on whom we could trust to help us in Iran and Nicaragua. I was not in a position to know the extent of Casey's involvement in the Iran-Contra affair, but I do know that Casey traveled frequently to Central America, where he had many contacts, especially in El Salvador. Casey also traveled often to Algeria to meet with persons knowledgeable about what was going on in Iran. I recall Casey telling me at a dinner party several years earlier that he had been to Teheran and met with the shah. "The Shah," he said, "is finished. He's a sick man and has lost his nerve. He'll be out within a year." That was six months before the shah fell, and he seemed at that time to be firmly in power and enjoying complete U.S. support.

Casey was part of a trio that had been close to Reagan for many years. The others were Caspar Weinberger and beer magnate Joseph Coors, an important financial backer. Coors also supplied funds for influential think tanks like the Heritage Foundation. Lists of prospective nominees to administration positions, including the second and third tiers, were sent to Coors to see if they passed the litmus test of being "Reaganauts."

Another crucial group of advisors consisted of people Reagan had met after he became a candidate. This group, which included Alexander Haig, David Stockman, and Donald Regan, was not especially cohesive. They were simply individuals who provided advice on matters in their fields of expertise. A third group was less concerned with substance than with image. Its members included Texas businessman James Baker, image-maker Michael Deaver, and veteran of the bureaucratic wars Richard Darman. The three moved into offices close to Reagan's shortly after the election and monitored issues across the board. Their primary objective, from the outset, was to enhance Reagan's image with the public.

The first and second groups were in constant conflict with the image men. But Baker, Deaver, and Darman often won out because they worked as a team and appeared frequently to have the last word with the president-elect. The one person whose advice to Reagan they did not contest was Casey.

Between Reagan's election and inauguration, Casey came up with an idea that paid great dividends. He suggested that Reagan ask thirty "wise men" (actually twenty-seven men and three women) to write position papers on key foreign policy issues. These persons included such luminaries as Henry Kissinger, John McCloy, Henry Jackson, Jeane Kirkpatrick, John Tower, Caspar Weinberger, Don Rumsfeld, and Edward Bennett Williams. They covered the entire spectrum of foreign policy issues, including our relationship with the Soviet Union, our policy in the Middle East, our stance in Central America, and the release of U.S. hostages in Iran.

Each of the "wise" men gave Reagan and other aides a ten-minute oral summary of his or her paper, after which there was a freewheeling discussion of the subject and other ideas. Among the ideas presented was a recommendation that Reagan press for dismantling the Berlin Wall and the unification of Germany. Scoop Jackson said that the United States was not paying sufficient attention to Mexico and recommended that one of Reagan's first acts as president be a visit to the president of Mexico. I discussed the future of arms control and recommended that Reagan press for freeing Poland from the Communist grasp by backing Lech Walesa and the Solidarity labor union. Casey introduced a concept for the release of U.S. hostages from Iran. He said that President Carter had been too predictable and recommended that Reagan exploit his media image by acting in an unpredictable manner. This made President Reagan's advisors nervous. They wanted to play down Reagan's wild cowboy image. Casey said, "You need to send signals to Ayatollah Khomeini that he will suffer the consequences of U.S. political and military might if he doesn't release the hostages." I do not know what signals were sent, but I was not surprised when the hostages were released.

Participating in Casey's idea of discussions by the thirty wise men was one of my most fascinating times in government. Reagan was not only brought up to speed on foreign policy issues but had an opportunity to size up several of the participants for possible administration jobs. Soon after the discussions took place, hints were dropped at Blair House that Alexander Haig might become secretary of state and Jeane Kirkpatrick, ambassador to the United Nations.

Several weeks later, when the CIA transition was coming to a close, Bill Casey asked me to be his deputy.

"No," I said, "what you need is a specialist, a real expert in intelligence. You should not choose an amateur to be your deputy."

"Who do you suggest?" asked Casey.

"Admiral Bobby Inman," I replied.

"I've spoken to one of his friends about him," said Casey, "and was told that Inman is intent on retiring and wants to take a job in civilian life."

"Why don't you talk to Inman yourself?" I said. "Tell him he's uniquely suited for the job and appeal to his sense of duty. He's spent his entire career in the military and has a strong sense of patriotism."

Casey took my advice and persuaded Inman to become his deputy.

Shortly after his inauguration, Reagan offered me the job of director of ACDA. I said I would accept but only if, as director of ACDA, I would not also be required to be the chief arms negotiator. I said I felt that Carter's naming Paul Warnke director of ACDA as well as chief negotiator had been a mistake. Reagan agreed.

Several weeks later, in fact the day after Senator Charles Percy of Illinois told me his Foreign Relations Committee would unanimously support my nomination, I read in the *Washington Post* that I had been dropped and that the job had been offered to Prof. Eugene Rostow of Yale. I was stunned, especially since I had met with Rostow following Percy's call. I had gone to see Rostow to get his advice on whom to ask to be my deputy and what my priority tasks should be. Rostow gave me no indication that he was in the running. When I asked him about this several days later, he said he had sworn not to disclose that he had been offered the job.

Reagan's closest aides reportedly advised him that he already had Republican support and needed a prominent Democrat to head ACDA to help his image. That was not, of course, the reason they gave me. They said that after the president selected Alexander Haig as secretary of state he could not risk naming another military officer to a high administration post. It was the first, but not the last, time that I observed the clout that Baker, Deaver, and Darman exercised over Reagan.

As a peace offering, I was offered the job of chief arms control negotiator. I demurred, not certain that I wanted to be associated with the same Reagan aides who had treated me so haughtily and callously. I went to see Jackson and Haig for advice. They reminded me that Washington was a jungle. They thought that despite what had happened I could contribute to Reagan's goals and urged that I accept. I did and was confirmed by the Senate without difficulty.

In retrospect, I was better suited for the job as chief arms control negotiator than I was for director of ACDA because I had close to seven years' experience negotiating with the Soviets, knew the players and the issues, and could speak Russian. Still, the imperiousness of Reagan's close advisors preyed on my mind and left me apprehensive. These suspicions proved well founded.

Despite pressure from the media to resume arms control negotiations with the Soviets, Reagan was in no hurry to do so. He wanted first to develop a five-year defense plan, feeling that once the administration decided those systems it needed the question of which ones to limit would become clear.

Rebuilding our military strength after ten years of neglect was not easy. It called for great leadership and uncommon courage. I can recall the pressure put on Reagan at several high-level meetings. Donald Regan, secretary of the treasury, said at one such meeting, "Mr. President, the country is experiencing double-digit unemployment and double-digit inflation. You simply cannot spend so much on the military. You need to spend more on social programs."

Reagan answered with conviction, "Our biggest social program is the defense of our country. Without it we risk losing our freedom. Providing for our security is my number-one priority. Under the Constitution, I'm the commander in chief and I will not jeopardize our liberty." Though Reagan acted to beef up defense spending despite contrary advice from most of his cabinet, he did have the strong support of Weinberger, Haig, and Casey.

Immediately following the inauguration, I began pressing for a new approach to arms control. My main idea was that we should reduce the number of weapons that could do damage, not simply reduce the number of launchers that could carry the weapons. President Reagan had previously indicated his clear preference for the reduction of weapons in contrast to SALT II's limitations on launchers, limits which could be easily circumvented. To dramatize the policy shift, he decided to call the new negotiations Strategic Arms Reductions Talks (START), with the emphasis on reductions. However, negotiations on limiting intermediate-range nuclear forces (INF) were assigned first priority.

In 1979 the NATO Council had called upon the United States to embark upon a two-track approach to respond to the Soviet Union's massive buildup of ballistic missiles aimed at Europe. On one track, we were asked to negotiate with the Soviets on INF. On the second track, the United States was called upon to deploy land-based ballistic and cruise missiles in Europe. It was important to NATO's well-being that Reagan respond to the Council's request and as soon as possible begin negotiating INF with the Soviets. We did so in May of 1981, with Paul Nitze heading the U.S. team. This decision to concentrate on INF put my START negotiations on the back burner. The administration at that stage could only handle one negotiation at a time. Moreover, President Reagan wanted us to develop a good set of proposals to take to START, proposals that the Soviets were likely to accept.

I thought President Reagan was doing the right thing in moving ahead slowly. His deliberate approach reminded me of the Russian saying: *"Tische yedesh, dalshe budesch."* (The more deliberately you proceed the farther you'll get.) Once he had his ducks in a row, the president outlined his comprehensive plan for strategic arms reductions at Eureka College in May 1982. He called for deep cuts— approximately one-third of the warheads of each side—and for on-site verification.

I threw myself wholeheartedly into the negotiations, which commenced shortly thereafter in Geneva. I took with me a good set of proposals that I had helped develop. Despite my earlier brush with Baker, Deaver, and Darman, I felt that I enjoyed the full support of the president. Unlike Carter, who had pressed his chief negotiator to move rapidly toward an agreement, Reagan put me under no such pressure.

I assembled, on the whole, a good team, six of whom spoke Russian. And, unlike SALT II, where I was simply a member of the team, I was now the boss.

Viktor Karpov, with whom I had negotiated during SALT II, was appointed to head the Soviet START team. With the exception of Gen. Konstantin Trusov, who had died, and Gen. Ivan Beletsky, who had retired, Karpov brought the same experienced Soviet negotiators from the SALT talks back to the table. Trusov was replaced by Viktor Starodubov, a protégé of Marshal Nikolai Ogarkhov. Starodubov was nonpolemical, more reasonable, and less of a hard-liner than Trusov. General Beletsky was replaced by Gen. Nikolai Detinov, who was also more flexible and broadminded. The military members of the Soviet team, who had caused us the most difficulty in the past, were now a more amenable lot.

I looked forward to negotiating with Karpov. I had come to know him quite well and believed that if any two persons could conclude a good agreement we could. Viktor Pavlovich Karpov came from a middle-class family; his father had been a competent and sought-after dentist. Karpov had made top grades at the University of Moscow studying diplomacy and had impressed his instructors with his grasp of international affairs. He was assigned, at an early age, to the foreign ministry and married the daughter of a highly placed member of the Communist party. Karpov, who was heavyset and had a sallow, jaundiced complexion, once boasted to me that his only exercise was lifting a glass. I came to know that it seldom contained water.

Karpov was a quick study who always did his homework. He had a phenomenal memory and was an excellent debater. He had served for several years in the Soviet embassy in Washington and spoke colloquial English. In Moscow, he continued to read the *New York Times* and the *Washington Post*. He told me that he originally followed the comic strip *Blondie* but had switched to *Doonesbury* so that he could keep up with American slang.

During SALT II, Karpov and I had often paired off. He had become the number-two man on the Soviet negotiating team, the same position I had achieved by virtue of seniority. Minister Vladimir Semenov, the Soviet chief negotiator of SALT, had relied heavily on Karpov. Either because he respected Karpov's ability, or perhaps because he knew Karpov had highly placed supporters in Moscow, Semenov tolerated Karpov's rude interruptions at the negotiating table.

It had become obvious to us early in SALT II that Karpov had a serious drinking problem. When there was a party, he was always the first to arrive and the last to leave, and he managed to consume at least two drinks to my one. He often came to meetings with a hangover, and sometimes even intoxicated. Alcohol had the opposite effect on Karpov that it had on me. A third drink caused me to slur my words and let down my guard, the reason I never went beyond a two-drink limit. Four or five drinks seemed to sharpen Karpov's wits;

he became more articulate and aggressive. Except when he was completely intoxicated, which was seldom, several drinks made him a more formidable negotiator.

When START was about to begin, several members of my team recommended that we serve alcoholic beverages during the informal sessions following the formal meetings. They argued that the Soviets were naturally rigid and inflexible and that several drinks would cause them to unwind and show more flexibility. However, having watched the behavior of both sides at social functions where alcohol was served and recalling the reports I had heard about the effects of alcohol on the informal sessions of SALT I, as Alexis Johnson had done at SALT II, I decided against it. My observations were that the Soviets drank more heavily than the Americans, yet it was the Americans who revealed more information than they received. Knowing that Harold Nicholson had written about "the idle diplomatic lubricities" of Alexander I and Metternich, I decided that alcohol would be served only at social functions.

During SALT II, I had tried to find out who Karpov's supporters were in Moscow. One Soviet negotiator told me that Karpov had good connections with Yuri Andropov, the KGB chief who later became Brezhnev's successor. I was never able to confirm this, but it was obvious Karpov had a highly placed guardian angel in Moscow. On one occasion, Karpov became intoxicated and openly involved with a Geneva bar girl, who was a Czech refugee. It was an embarrassment to the Soviet team, and he was sent back to Moscow. I thought we would never see him again. But several weeks later, Karpov, dried out and apparently forgiven for his amorous escapade, returned to Geneva. He said he had been in a sanitorium with a stomach ailment. I suspect it was liver trouble. It was several months before he began drinking again.

I had a good working relationship with Karpov; he called me Ed and I called him, in the familiar Russian style, Viktor Pavlovich. After a while, I was able to detect when Karpov was ready to display some flexibility and when he was simply mouthing the Soviet party line. In these latter instances, his body language was to cross his arms and avoid eye contact.

I had looked forward to the time when the two of us could negotiate as heads of our respective teams. But at the first official meeting of START, in Geneva in May 1982, Karpov launched an hour-long, vituperative, almost vicious attack against the U.S. position I had just laid out. He had spoken in tough terms before but never with so much venom. I was stunned and disappointed.

Later, in our private sessions, I found a more relaxed, even amiable Karpov, a man not at all offensive.

"What gives, Viktor Pavlovich?" I asked.

"Ed," he said, "you have to realize that I'm now the head of our team. No more mister nice guy. I've got to show the team, and have them report back to Moscow, that I can be tough with you. It'll be different from now on. I have to act in the old Russian tradition—the tyrant in charge. I have to imitate my boss, Andrei Gromyko.

"However," he added, "don't take how I act officially too much to heart. We can still be the same Ed and Viktor Pavlovich when we meet informally." But after that it was never quite the same. Karpov's change in style caused me to wonder whether I, too, was undergoing any changes in my new position. Whereas I had previously been a special pleader for the military point of view, I now felt obliged to represent all points of view.

Despite my status as head of the negotiating team, I was never able to make the American delegation as disciplined as the Soviets. It seemed impossible to impress on our people the need to keep the subject matter of our negotiations confidential. Used to speaking openly in their daily lives, our representatives often found it hard to refrain from speaking freely to reporters. This at times got us into difficulty with the Soviet negotiators because of the confidentiality pledge both sides had taken at the beginning of the negotiations.

We had convinced the Soviets that we could make greater progress in Geneva if there were no press briefings and nothing said publicly about what went on at the negotiating table. When someone on our side transgressed, which unfortunately happened quite often, Viktor Karpov was quick to take me to task. Ironically, the Soviets also leaked details of the negotiations, but they did so by talking to Western reporters in Moscow. When I complained about this, Karpov said he had no control over what happened in Moscow and that the confidentiality rule did not apply to his superiors. He was right, and, theoretically, we were free to do the same. However, our leaks in Washington differed from theirs in Moscow. Ours usually served to air the competing viewpoints of U.S. agencies in developing negotiating positions. Soviet leaks, by contrast, were on matters that had been brought up at the negotiating table, usually some difference of opinion between Karpov and me, which, in actuality, were differences between Moscow and Washington. Our leaks often revealed classified matters or gave the Soviets our bottom line. Providing such information, of course, played directly into Soviet hands.

As chief START negotiator, I had direct access to President Reagan. I found that he did not seem overly bound by precedents and did not worry about what had gone on in previous negotiations. Therefore, he did not feel it necessary to follow a traditional or set pattern. This permitted him to be innovative and to come forth with bold ideas. For example, even though the United States had rejected the limitations imposed by SALT II, Reagan announced that we would not exceed the limits if the Soviets showed similar restraint.

The president had a quiet, gentle, laid-back way about him. I attended dozens of meetings where I marveled at Reagan's detached, almost disinterested, manner. While I never saw him fall asleep, as others have reported, he often appeared bored, especially when details were discussed. On such occasions he would doodle on his scratch pad. He particularly liked to draw horses' heads. Once, when someone began lobbying for a pet project not on the agenda, I looked over at Reagan's notepad. He was drawing a horse's rear end. Seeing that I had caught him, he turned over the pad and grinned.

The president and I seemed to hit it off. He loved to talk about his experiences as an Army lieutenant during World War II, when he acted in training films. He told me that he had never met a general until he became governor of California. "What shall I call you, general or ambassador?" he asked.

I told him it had taken me twenty years to get to be a general and only twenty minutes to become an ambassador.

Reagan laughed and from then on he always addressed me as "General."

Reagan loved to tell stories. Sometimes he did this to break the tension when his subordinates' arguments became heated. He often recounted his experiences as a negotiator when he headed the Actors Equity Guild, repeating the same stories many times over.

I told Reagan that labor leader George Meany had advised me never to sit down at the negotiating table if I was not prepared to get up and walk away. Reagan said that he agreed and had learned that to be a good negotiator one had to have patience and simply sit at the table longer than his opponent. He said he learned to fake drinking coffee; when no one was looking he would empty his cup into a potted plant. "I never had to get up from the table before my opponent did," he boasted. "However, you can't sit there forever," he said. "You need to look for an opening." One of his favorite stories was how he followed his counterpart to the bathroom, where he said, "In here you and I are the only ones who know exactly what we're doing." They were able to strike a deal, away from the constraining influence of their advisors. He later used the technique of getting his negotiating partner into a one-on-one session in his meetings with Gorbachev.

Watching Reagan, I wondered if there was any correlation between acting ability and successful negotiating. I had worked for Douglas MacArthur, a man given to using histrionics successfully in negotiating. I had also observed Gen. George Patton, who inspired men to fight through his theatrical appeals. President Nixon has recounted the success of Chou En-lai as a negotiator, something he attributes to Chou's acting ability. Pope John Paul II, whom I observed to be a good negotiator, had studied acting.

I believe Reagan's training as an actor served him well. He learned to read from cue cards that contained short, well-thought-out, grammatical sentences. We dreaded unrehearsed press conferences and other situations where Reagan had to ad-lib responses to tough questions. We simply could not anticipate all the questions that might be asked him and feared he would stumble. We need not have worried; he seldom misspoke. His poise when appearing before a crowd was magnificent and his timing impeccable. Long after his presidential campaign debate with Carter, most people remember only Reagan's seemingly impromptu words, "There you go again."

Whatever the correlation between acting and negotiating skill, the president left no doubt about the approach he wanted to pursue. He said that we should not be *demandeurs,* pressing for results simply to give the appearance of making progress. He told me that if the Soviets showed flexibility, or had a good counteroffer, I was to reciprocate. But if they did not, he wanted me to know that I was under no pressure to seek an agreement.

Reagan was highly influenced by Secretary of Defense Caspar Weinberger, a long-time friend and trusted lieutenant, who could be counted upon to carefully guard the nation's security interests. He and Casey were invariably together on the issues.

Weinberger did not hesitate to use Casey's influence with Reagan when it suited his purpose. For example, Weinberger learned in 1983 that the Soviets had, for several years, been building a major radar site at Krasnoyarsk. If true, this would be a blatant violation of the ABM Treaty. Casey was undoubtedly aware of the same evidence but did not have Weinberger's sense of going for the jugular. The matter would not have been brought immediately and forcefully to Reagan's attention if Weinberger had not urged Casey to do so.

Weinberger, a short, wiry man, had a Napoleon-like personality. He talked fast and arrived at decisions quickly—at times I thought almost too rapidly. For example, Weinberger advised Reagan to declare the ABM Treaty null and void because the Soviets had violated its terms on several occasions—notably with respect to the Krasnoyarsk radar. What Weinberger failed to take into account was the strong public support for the ABM Treaty. Serious though the violation was, and even though Foreign Minister Shevardnadze subsequently acknowledged the transgression, the public insisted on more egregious grounds than Krasnoyarsk for walking away from the ABM Treaty.

Weinberger was tireless when it came to building up our military forces. Knowledgeable on the details of weapon systems, he also knew how the procurement process worked. During Reagan's first term, "Cap" Weinberger courted members of Congress and pretty much got his own way. But after several years, Weinberger became overworked and frustrated; he began avoiding members of Congress. Budget deficits grew; as a consequence, he started to lose the congressional members' support.

Weinberger relied a great deal on members of his staff but was not dominated by them. He picked his subordinates carefully, making certain that they were on his philosophical wavelength. The Defense Department did not have careerists in its top posts, as did the State Department. Hence, in-house opposition by the bureaucracy at Defense was not as strong as at State. Weinberger's subordinates were appointed because they supported Reagan's views, whereas many of Haig's and later Shultz's advisors were holdovers from former administrations, who, more often than not, opposed Reagan.

In my opinion, Alexander Haig's performance has been underrated. I had known Haig well since the Korean War when I was a member of the staff of Gen. Edward ("Ned") Almond, Douglas MacArthur's chief of staff. Haig was Almond's aide-de-camp. He was a captain, and I a lieutenant colonel. After the Korean conflict, we often saw one another both officially and socially.

Haig was an intelligent, highly energetic officer. I considered him ambitious, but no more so than many of his West Point contemporaries. He always stood out in a crowd as being the best groomed, a characteristic he carried over into civilian life after he retired. He had his suits tailored in London and liked to look trim and fit. He played tennis regularly and always somehow managed to have a good tan.

Until Kissinger brought him into the White House in 1969, Haig methodically climbed the Army career ladder. At the White House, however, Haig found his element and rose rapidly. He was loyal to Kissinger but did not hesitate to let him know when he disagreed. I think no one else could have held the office of the president together as well as he did during Nixon's last days in the White House.

When I was appointed chief negotiator, Haig phoned to tell me that his deputy, Under Secretary of State Walter Stoessel, would swear me in.

"I don't want to be sworn in by Stoessel," I said. "I want to be sworn in by you."

"Oh, come on, Ed," he said, "I can't spend my time swearing in ambassadors. There's an ambassador sworn in almost every day, and I'd have no time for anything else."

"Then let's skip the ceremonies and have me sworn in at my desk," I said.

"No," Haig said, "that won't do." When I persisted, Haig told me that for old time's sake he would make an exception. After swearing me in, Haig made a few remarks.

"Ed's not a first-class ambassador," he said. "These we reserve for countries like France and England. But we have to call him ambassador because the title goes with the job." Then he told a story.

"When Eva Peron was planning her grand tour of Europe she had difficulty getting accepted. Rome, London, Paris, and Madrid all turned her down. But Lisbon agreed to host a visit. As is customary, the visiting dignitary had to be given an award.

"But they didn't feel Eva deserved a first-class award," said Haig. "Instead they gave her a lesser award: 'The Award of Chastity, second-class.'"

"I now know exactly what you think about arms control," I told Haig.

So long as Haig was secretary of state, I was able to get most of my views accepted at the State Department. Haig often relied more on my advice than on that of his own bureaucrats. But it was obvious to me from the outset that Haig would not last long. He simply did not fit in well with the advisors Reagan had brought into the White House.

His first clash with the palace guard took place the day after inauguration. Haig simply did what all of us in the military are trained to do. A newly appointed officer shows his boss he's on top of the situation by volunteering a plan of action. If the boss likes it, the new man knows he's off on the right foot. If he does not like it, the boss says so and in this way provides valuable guidance to the new subordinate. This normal procedure in the military was looked upon with suspicion and fear by the president's advisors. They felt that Haig was moving in too fast, coming on too strong. Haig made things worse by announcing that henceforth he would be the president's vicar for foreign policy. This remark was aimed more at State Department bureaucrats than at the White House. Haig wanted to let his new staff know he would not be dominated by them. But someone told the press, on background, that Haig was out to upstage Reagan in the formulation of foreign policy.

On Saturday mornings, Haig did not follow his weekday dentist schedule of an appointment every thirty minutes. He often had me come to his office for long discussions about arms control. During several such sessions, we were interrupted by calls from the White House. They were usually from underlings, nitpicking some minor matters. Yet Haig took the bait. He would argue with the person at the other end of the line who was badgering him, all the while lighting one cigarette after another. His face would become flushed, and he would hyperventilate, his cheeks puffing in and out.

"Give in, Uncle Al," I said. "They're trying to get your goat and you're letting them do it. You're dealing with barnyard hens; soar over them like an eagle. These are small matters; give in on them and hold fast on the bigger ones. Since they don't know enough to challenge you on the big ones, you have little to lose."

"I won't do it," snapped Haig. "Small or big, these are matters in my province and they don't seem to realize it."

One Saturday, Haig was called on the phone three times, each time on something trivial. And each time Haig hotly contested the issue. Around noon, his wife, Pat, called, reminding him that he had promised to come home and relax.

"Dammit, Pat," said Haig, "are you going to haze me, too?"

"Let up, Uncle Al," I said. "That's not some White House weenie you're talking to. That's your wife, and she's on your side."

Haig called his wife, apologized, and soon left for home. Whether his recent heart bypass surgery had anything to do with his conduct, as the press had speculated, I do not know. But it was clear that Haig was not the calm and composed officer I had once known. He was not dealing with Reagan's staff as coolly as he had dealt with Nixon's during Watergate.

Then came the day the president was shot. I happened to be in the White House. The impression going out to the world was that things were in disarray. Behind the scenes, there had been an argument between Weinberger and Haig over the order of succession. I was told that they both had finally agreed that something needed to be done to reassure the public. So I was not surprised when Haig came to the White House briefing room. But I was surprised when he made remarks that heightened, rather than reduced, public anxiety. His flustered appearance and nervous demeanor were hardly reassuring.

I am certain Haig had the best of intentions. But it was not his finest hour. His blustery and overpowering two-minute "I'm in charge" speech was played over and over on the television networks. It was the beginning of the end for Haig as secretary of state.

Soon after the president returned from the hospital, I was in Haig's office going over evidence that the Soviets had deployed a new submarine without having retired an old one and, therefore, were exceeding SALT II limits. Although the treaty had never been ratified, Reagan had declared that the United States would not exceed SALT II limits if the Soviets did the same. But I had advised Haig that we should notify the Soviets that because they had exceeded SALT II limits we would no longer consider ourselves bound by them. Haig took my advice. I was invited to attend a cabinet luncheon the next day at which the issue was discussed. The luncheon went well, so well in fact that I was suspicious because there had been so little opposition to Haig's position.

After lunch, Haig and several of the president's closest advisors went into the Oval Office. I went home to finish packing for our departure that evening for Geneva.

I was called at home by my secretary. "Turn on your TV," she said. "Haig's reading his letter of resignation." The ax had fallen. I was stunned, especially since the lunch had been so relaxed and easygoing. But then I realized Haig's resignation might have come earlier had it not been for the president's hospitalization. The Baker, Darman, and Deaver trio had had their way. Characteristically, they said that Haig was not fired but had simply turned in his resignation. That is probably correct; it was not Reagan's style to fire anyone. But my guess is that Haig had been told that it was time to go. To this day, I continue to believe that it was not Reagan who felt Haig was

overbearing but the White House insiders who viewed him as a
threat. Haig had also not helped himself with his flustered public
performance when Reagan was shot.

When George Shultz succeeded Haig, he brought a significant
change of style to the job. For one thing, he relied heavily on the
advice of State's bureaucracy. Career State Department officials in
the main felt that compromising with the Soviets did not expose us to
serious risks.

I never felt that Shultz had a comprehensive plan to bring the
Soviets around to our thinking. His approach seemed to be simply to
put out fires as they flared up. He apparently felt that if he did so, the
Soviet Union would collapse due to its inherent weaknesses. While in
retrospect Shultz was right, I felt that the Soviet collapse would be
hastened if we kept the pressure on them to reform. Being an activist,
I was uncomfortable with Shultz's laid-back approach.

Shultz and Weinberger had worked together in the same engineering firm, Bechtel. There they had a friendly but competitive relationship. When they became members of Reagan's cabinet, this rivalry
intensified. Shultz invariably took positions opposed to Weinberger's. Although he was reserved and often played his cards close to his
chest, Shultz was more articulate and generally the better organized
of the two. Weinberger was direct and blunt, often shooting from the
hip. Shultz would invariably say something like, "There are three
possible courses of action we can take. Let me give you the pros and
cons of each." In contrast, Weinberger would say, "There is only one
course of action open to us." Weinberger, however, usually won the
tough decisions, probably because he shared Reagan's conservative
leanings. More important, I think Weinberger triumphed because he
was closer to Reagan personally.

An even keener rivalry took place at the next level between Richard Perle and Richard ("Rick") Burt. Perle had become Weinberger's
arms control guru and Burt had risen to a similar position on Shultz's
staff. The press corps, more in tune with Burt than with Perle, called
Burt the Prince of Light and Perle the Prince of Darkness.

I had known Perle during the years he had worked for Scoop
Jackson. He was an archconservative. Like Jackson, he did not trust
the Soviets and was suspicious of State Department bureaucrats.
Perle was generally perceived as being highly intelligent and very
tough; his opponents accused him of being mean. When pleading his
case, Perle adopted a low-key, charming, and almost pixieish ap-

proach. He marshaled his facts carefully, selected those that best supported his view, and convincingly laid them out. But Perle was no respecter of rank. He would take on anyone who opposed him; the higher the person's position the more he savored the challenge. For example, Perle was scheduled to give a talk in London in March 1985. The day before, Sir Geoffrey Howe, foreign minister of the United Kingdom, had made a lengthy speech criticizing the United States's stand on the Strategic Defense Initiative (SDI). Perle changed his talk, reportedly not bothering to clear it with the White House, and sharply criticized Howe. In referring to the foreign minister's long speech, Perle sarcastically said, "Length is no substitute for depth."

I knew Burt less well, but I had observed him carefully during the years he reported for the *New York Times*. Burt was extremely clever, hard-charging, and ambitious; some said devious and manipulative. Like Perle, Burt could exude charm and argue his case persuasively. I was told he habitually fed tidbits of information to his old friends in the press corps in order to gain their support.

I had originally opposed Burt's joining Haig's staff, largely because he had, when he worked for the *New York Times,* reported the confidential positions of rival U.S. government agencies. I felt this gave Soviet negotiators an opportunity to play one part of our negotiating team off against another. During his confirmation hearings, Burt asked me to talk to Senator Helms. He said that his *New York Times* articles had been written when he was an investigative reporter and that once in office he would treat interagency splits as confidential matters. Burt was confirmed, and after Shultz took over as secretary of state, Burt quickly marshaled his bureaucratic skills. He moved from head of the Policy Planning Staff to become director of the State Department's powerful European Bureau.

It was fascinating to observe the skirmishes between the Prince of Darkness and the Prince of Light at subcabinet meetings. Perle was, of course, drafting Weinberger's position papers, while Burt was doing the same for Shultz. Each probed for the weak points in the other's position and tried to draw the other out. It was also fascinating to watch how they tried to outmaneuver each other bureaucratically. For example, Perle arranged to have the State Department legal officers join those at the Defense Department to study whether the negotiating record supported a broad or narrow interpretation of the ABM Treaty. When they all agreed that the negotiating record supported the broad interpretation, it cut the ground out from under those in the State Department who wanted Secretary Shultz to back the narrow interpretation.

In retrospect, although the press saw the two as simply bickering, the debates of the two Richards (Perle hated to be called Dick) served a useful purpose. They helped bring out all sides of difficult policy issues facing the president. Because of the close analyses each made of the problem, the decisions reached were better than they might otherwise have been.

While all this was going on behind the scenes, the president began speaking out vigorously on foreign policy issues. A little more than two years into his administration, on March 8, 1983, he delivered the never to be forgotten "Evil Empire" speech to the National Association of Evangelicals. It was not a fire-and-brimstone oration but a soft-pedaled talk to a group of church leaders who were interested in praising virtue and damning evil. Reagan said that America was a country founded upon and devoted to morality. He reminded them that Alexis de Tocqueville had written that America is good and that if America ever ceases to be good it will cease to be great. Toward the end of the speech, he implored the church leaders, who were holding the United States and the Soviet Union equally at fault on the nuclear freeze issue, not "to ignore the facts of history and the aggressive impulses of an evil empire."

The speech was made before Peggy Noonan's time as White House speechwriter. She, being sensitive to rhetorical traps, would, I am sure, have spotted and excised the potentially troublesome "evil empire" reference. The phrase was immediately and sharply assailed by the American press as an insult to the Soviet Union. The Soviets at first ignored it. One of the Soviet negotiators told me in Geneva that it was, after all, no worse than the "evil capitalists" pronouncements the Soviet leaders habitually made in reference to us. But the U.S. media replayed the thirty-second TV bite steadily for months afterwards, giving the impression that the one-time utterance was being repeated by the president. Finally, the Soviet leaders, recognizing the value of playing it up, joined the drumbeat and exploited the "evil empire" theme by referring to it in interviews and articles written for Western consumption. The speech had little effect on our negotiations, but once the media took Reagan to task, the Soviet negotiators could not resist bringing it up and making us listen to their feigned indignation.

Meeting with reporters on New Year's Day almost nine months

later, Reagan confessed he had made a mistake. Calling the Soviet Union an evil empire, he admitted candidly, was not the best way to characterize a nation with which he was trying to conclude an arms control agreement. It was as close to a public apology as one could get. Yet the media did not let up. One by-product of the incident was that it heightened the degree of scrutiny paid to drafts of the president's speeches. Subsequently, the texts prepared for Reagan's final visit to Moscow in 1988 were carefully edited. Words such as *dictatorship* and *totalitarianism,* thought to be offensive to the Soviets, were taken out. Speechwriters became acutely sensitive to the power of the press to exploit some obscure remark.

In March 1983, during negotiations in Geneva, a severe jolt to my delegation occurred when a so-called hit list appeared in the *Washington Post.* The list was an appraisal of eighteen members of the START delegation, which had been prepared without my knowledge by my Washington liaison office for Kenneth Adelman, the nominee to replace Rostow as head of ACDA. Believing that such an appraisal would be helpful to Adelman, one of my staff officers dropped it off at Adelman's office shortly after I had left for Geneva. Although it was in a sealed envelope and marked "personal and confidential," a disgruntled secretary in the ACDA director's office made a photocopy and gave it to the press. The appraisal gave high marks to four of the delegation, passing marks to ten, and low marks to four others. Among the four at the bottom of the list were the State Department and Joint Chiefs of Staff representatives. The first I knew about the memorandum was when I read about it in the *International Herald Tribune.* I immediately called my Washington office. My staff officer admitted that he had written the memorandum on his own initiative, but because I had left town, he did not have the opportunity to show it to me. I called my team together and apologized for the memorandum. I told them that while I had not seen the appraisal, I accepted responsibility for it, since it had been written by a member of my staff. Most of my delegation, especially those who had been rated highly, accepted my apology. Others, and especially those who had been rated poorly, were understandably upset. My biggest problem with them was one of credibility; they found it hard to accept that I was not the instigator of the report, let alone that I had not seen it. Fortunately, wounds, in time, healed. Still, the unfortunate incident caused me considerable personal anguish and was an unwelcome blow to the morale of my delegation.

By the summer of 1983 the Soviets had one central objective. They were determined to prevent the United States from deploying ground-launched cruise missiles (GLCMs) and Pershing II intermediate-range ballistic missiles (PIIs) in Europe. General Secretary Yuri Andropov, the former KGB chief who succeeded Brezhnev, launched an all-out effort to block their deployment. He openly criticized Helmut Kohl's Christian Democratic Party (CDP) and threatened to walk out of the INF negotiations if we deployed the missiles in Europe.

Paul Nitze, our chief negotiator of INF, believed that Kohl could not overcome the pressures against deployment. Nitze felt that if the CDP accepted missiles on German soil it would fail to win the elections. This, he believed, would seriously jeopardize the future of NATO. As a result, Nitze took his celebrated "walk in the woods" with Yuli Kvitsinsky, his Soviet counterpart. He proposed that the United States would give up deploying Pershing II missiles while going ahead with the GLCMs if the Soviets would limit their SS-20 missile deployments. It would have resulted in a bad deal because the Pershings threatened vital Soviet command-and-control installations, and the Soviets had a respectful fear of them. They had no similar fear of our slow-flying GLCMs, against which they could defend themselves. Several members of Nitze's team came to me to learn more about the plan he had offered to the Soviets but had kept from them. They wanted me to dissuade Nitze from pursuing it; I agreed that the proposal was ill-advised. Unfortunately, whereas I had previously met with Nitze several times a week to coordinate our efforts, once the story broke, I could not get in to see him.

Luckily, the Soviets turned down Nitze's proposal in Moscow even before the Reagan administration got around to disowning it. The Germans, displaying great courage, accepted U.S. missiles on their soil, the CDP won the election, and Kohl became chancellor. It was a close call; Nitze's lack of faith in the steadfastness and will of the German people almost cost us dearly.

Nitze's walk in the woods reminded me of the talks in the park I had with members of the Soviet delegation during SALT II. Some of my most candid exchanges were with academician Alexandr Shchukin, the only Soviet negotiator permitted to accept invitations to dinner without having an interpreter present. Invariably, such interpreters were "tails," KGB agents; fully one-third of the Soviets supporting the negotiating team were intelligence officers. Shchukin told me that only an academician, the title given members of the prestigious Soviet Academy of Sciences, was afforded the privilege of private conversations with foreigners. Shchukin was quite proud of his status. He boasted that he was elected to the Academy of Sciences by secret ballot, the "only secret elections to take place in the Soviet Union." Since Shchukin spoke little English, we would converse in French or in Russian, while our wives carried on their conversations in German. A dinner party with the Shchukins was a veritable Tower of Babel.

Shchukin, in fact, was the only Soviet with whom I could carry on a rational conversation about the different approaches to deterrence theory of the United States and the Soviet Union. Shchukin had read *The Absolute Weapon,* the annual reports of U.S. secretaries of defense, and many other U.S. writings. He told me candidly that military officers dominated Soviet strategic planning and that their thinking was rudimentary, if not crude. To the Soviet military, deterrence was simple: more and bigger weapons. Shchukin thought that only Marshal Nikolai Ogarkhov had a good grasp of deterrence theory, but he was not powerful enough to carry the day.

Shchukin did not personally believe that a Soviet leader would ever launch a first strike, but he said that U.S. fears that it might happen served Soviet political ends. The "cutting edge—the usable forces," he said, were conventional forces. This was the main reason why the Soviets maintained such large numbers of troops and such a preponderance of tanks and artillery pieces. Shchukin predicted, however, that the Soviet Union's economy could not indefinitely maintain such large forces, which he said accounted for 25 percent of the Soviet Union's gross national product (GNP). I passed this information on to Washington, recommending that they revise upward their estimates that the Soviets were spending 12 to 14 percent of their GNP for military forces. My reports were not taken seriously or acted upon. Once our intelligence community forms a mind-set on an issue, it is very difficult to get it to act on new information that differs from the conventional wisdom. Shortly after Mikhail Gorbachev came to power in 1985, he admitted that the Soviet Union spent 35 percent of its GNP for military forces. This was in contrast to the 6 percent of GNP the United States was spending.

At the START talks, meanwhile, we were making steady progress and I thought that prospects for reaching an agreement were bright. Yet Moscow continued to focus on preventing U.S. missiles from being stationed in Europe. When we deployed the first Pershings in November 1983, the Soviets walked out of the INF negotiations. Shortly thereafter, when we were preparing to go home for the Christmas break, Karpov told me the Soviets would not resume

START the following year unless we took steps to redress the strategic situation in Europe. This was a euphemism; they were holding both the INF and START talks hostage to our deployment of missiles.

The Soviets stayed away from both sets of talks for over a year. Ostensibly, it was because they felt that they could get us to reverse our stand on the missile deployments. But there were other factors at work. For one, the Soviet Union was undergoing still another leadership change. Konstantin Chernenko had succeeded Yuri Andropov. As Reagan remarked, "I can't get down to business with the Soviet leaders; they keep dying on me." Another factor was that the U.S. defense modernization program was still in its early stages, and there was as yet no clear indication of how much the negotiations would be affected by new technology. Finally, the United States had begun research and development of SDI—something that worried the Soviets and that they wanted to stop. But so long as we were negotiating only offensive systems they could not get at SDI. Accordingly, they broke off the negotiations until they could figure out a way to address defensive systems.

In the fall of 1984, the Soviets began to make overtures about returning to the negotiating table. As our missile deployments continued in Europe, the Soviets realized that they had failed in their attempt to hold negotiations hostage to the deployments. They showed increasing signs of worry over SDI and said that they were ready to negotiate "offensive weapons in space." We told them that we had no plans to put weapons in space, only nonlethal devices that would destroy any weapons launched at us simply by making physical contact with them. We explained that we would be ready to resume negotiations about defenses designed to counter offensive weapons, provided "space" was excluded. Unable to make progress, we proposed a compromise. We would return to Geneva to negotiate START and INF but would be willing to add a third area of negotiations, defense and space (D&S).

A meeting in January 1985 in Geneva between Gromyko and Shultz, which I attended, drew up a mandate for resuming negotiations and proposed that they begin in March. The Soviets made broad hints that more progress would be made if we returned to the table with new faces. I did not take these suggestions seriously. I felt the Soviets were up to their old trick of getting us to change our negotiators while they continued with the same ones. I recommended to the White House that they approach Max Kampelman about heading the new Defense and Space forum. I had known Kampelman for a number of years and was impressed with the way he had handled human rights negotiations during the previous administration. Although Kampelman had been appointed by President Carter, I felt that he would serve Reagan equally well.

I had heard rumors that former Texas Senator John Tower had been sounded out to take a job as a negotiator; and I knew the president felt that he owed Tower a political favor. I also had heard that Tower's wife wanted to taste the social life of Geneva as an ambassador's spouse. I thought the offer was to have Tower head up either the D&S or INF negotiations. I was caught completely by surprise when Secretary Shultz summoned me to his office one day late in January and told me that "it had been decided" that there would be a new lineup in Geneva. Mike Glitman, Nitze's deputy, would replace his boss at the INF talks. Nitze had decided to step down because of his wife's poor health. Kampelman would head the U.S. delegation and the D&S team. So far, so good. Then came the shocker. I would be replaced by Tower. The president, Shultz said, wanted more ready access to Nitze's and my advice; he wanted us to remain in Washington as special advisors. I told Shultz the news came as a stunning blow. I had heard the Soviets talk about a new team, but I never imagined that we would fall for their ploy. I was convinced that they would not change their negotiators.

Shultz denied that the Soviets played any role in the change. When I asked him the real reason for the shift, he simply stared in silence. He asked me not to deny my expertise and advice to the president. I said I would need to hear this from the president himself. Shultz immediately phoned President Reagan and arranged for me to see him an hour later.

We rode to the White House together in Shultz's car. During the ride I once again tried to extract from him why I had been replaced. Shultz gave me no answers. He said only that the decision had been made and was irrevocable.

The payoff to Tower did not seem to be the main reason. Otherwise, Tower could have simply replaced Nitze. I searched my memory for any possible affronts I might have directed at Shultz. Was it possible he felt I was a threat to his position and undermined his authority? From what I had observed, he may simply have decided I was a thorn in his side. Or was there some third party or some other factor—unknown to me—that brought about the change? To this day I do not know the answer.

As we approached the southwest gate of the White House, Shultz told me he would not be joining me when I met with the president. He repeated that the president would ask me to stay on as his advisor and he hoped I would not let the president down. It was not enough; I decided it was time to quit.

When I met with the president alone in the Oval Office, he greeted me warmly and asked what I thought about my new assignment. I was obviously upset and my hands shook. I told him that the change, and particularly the stealthlike way in which it had been done, had seriously shaken me. I said I was disappointed that we would fall for the Soviet trick of changing negotiators. The president told me this was not the reason for the shift. When I asked him what the reason was, he simply said that he valued my advice and hoped I would stay on.

"I'm a big boy," I said. "You don't have to sugarcoat the pill. I'm a soldier and can take it."

"No, no," Reagan insisted. "I want you to stay on."

Twice more, with variations on the same theme, I told President Reagan that since I did not know why I had been sacked as chief START negotiator it would be best if I simply faded away quietly. President Reagan then pushed the right button. "General, you're a soldier, and I'm your commander in chief. If I gave you a direct order to stay on to advise me, would you refuse?"

I told the president that I had not expected him to play his hole card. By training and temperament, I obeyed orders and he knew it. If I was being ordered to stay on, I said I would give it a try. Several days later, I was given the title of "Special Advisor to the President and Secretary of State for Arms Control Matters."

Just as I had predicted, the Soviets returned to Geneva with their teams essentially intact. Karpov doubled in brass as head of the Soviet delegation and head of their START team. Yuli Kvitsinsky moved from INF to Defense and Space. Alexandr Obukhov, Karpov's deputy, took over INF. I always knew the Soviets valued continuity highly and now had my proof. They had gotten us to perform major surgery on our staffs, while leaving their scalpels unused.

It was a replay of my having been dumped as director of ACDA. Now, as then, I was originally dismayed and disappointed. But often things that look bad at the time come out better in the long run. Removed from the day-to-day business of negotiating, I was freed to advise the president and gained greater influence over the formulation of our policies.

Moreover, as working relationships evolved, I found myself in a unique position to speak my own mind. Paul Nitze and I, having been given identical titles, theoretically had equal positions. However, Shultz relied more on Nitze's advice than mine. Nitze was moved into an office on the seventh floor of the State Department, close to Shultz's, while I remained in my fourth-floor office. Nitze and I both contributed to the development of Secretary Shultz's positions, but we operated differently. After a State Department position was decided, Nitze lined up behind it, even though he may have earlier recommended otherwise. As for myself, if I agreed with the State Department position, I supported it. If I disagreed, I reviewed the matter once more to determine if my original disagreement had been mistaken. If so, I reversed course and supported the State Department. If, however, I still felt that my original position was in the best interests of the United States, I stuck to it and did not throw my support behind the secretary.

Whenever I decided not to line up with Secretary Shultz, I wrote a memo to the president, stating my reasons. I sent copies of such memos to Shultz so that he knew my positions and why I had adopted them. Secretary Shultz obviously did not like this, but he did not block me from taking my contrary views to the president. As a result, Nitze was advisor to the secretary of state, while I was, at times, an independent advisor to the president. This did not endear me to the State Department bureaucrats, but it did leave me with a feeling that I was giving the president my best shot.

My differences with Secretary Shultz were largely over matters where I clashed philosophically with Paul Nitze. For example, we felt differently about how to treat research for strategic defenses. Nitze recommended that there be a permitted-prohibited list of tests that we would negotiate with the Soviets. I felt that the Soviets had no incentive for agreeing to tests that might lead to the development of strategic defenses. Consequently, we would be better off not giving them an opportunity to prohibit tests we wanted to conduct.

Nitze and I also disagreed on verification. He felt that it was enough if verification provisions were "adequate," while I wanted them to be "effective." There was more than a nuance involved. Nitze believed that we should make an issue over Soviet noncompliance only if the United States could not take steps to counter violations that seriously affected our security. I, on the other hand, maintained that we should, as a matter of principle, hold the Soviets accountable for all violations. This difference in philosophy put me on the side of pressing for stricter, more intrusive verification provisions, such as on-site inspection.

A crucial player in my dealings with the president was Robert ("Bud") McFarlane, Reagan's national security advisor. A former Marine Corps officer, McFarlane was serious and intense. He orchestrated the president's cabinet sessions on arms control matters but took no sides at the meetings. He would open a meeting with a brief summary of the issue and the relevant facts. He would then invite the cabinet officer he felt was furthest from the president's view to make the first argument. This meant that Shultz would usually go first. Reagan often joked that McFarlane was giving Shultz an advantage because they were both former Marines. Weinberger would then give his views, followed by others around the table. McFarlane always called on Nitze, who would speak in support of Shultz. I was given the privilege of speaking last, a great advantage since it gave me an opportunity to hear all the arguments. At times I was worried that time would run out without my having had a say. But even when the meetings ran overtime, the president would stay late and hear me out.

I attended all of Reagan's cabinet meetings in which arms control was discussed. We talked about everything from how many air-launched cruise missiles would be permitted on bombers to whether spare ballistic missiles could be stored and if so where and in what amounts. We even speculated on how we could give each missile its unique identifying "fingerprint."

On about half of these issues, I disagreed with the Shultz-Nitze position. I was careful not to disagree for the sake of disagreement and would give my reasons, always trying to be objective and non-polemic. The president sided with me whenever I recommended strict verification provisions. He often repeated the Soviet saying: *"Doveraj no proveriaj"* (Trust but verify). Although we had heard him say it dozens of times, he would add: "That means 'Deal, but cut the cards.' " The president also sided with me on the prohibited-permitted issue; he did not want to constrain SDI in any way.

After one particularly difficult session at which Nitze and I had disagreed, Casey pulled me aside and said, "What are you trying to do, upset the President and get him to call you ambassador instead of general?" I complained to Casey that the president had sided with me on only half the issues where I disagreed with Shultz and Nitze. "In baseball," he said, "a .500 batting average would put you in the Hall of Fame."

On several occasions, I was surprised that James Baker, who seldom spoke up at these meetings, came to my support. I suspected that Baker knew I was in close touch with conservative senators such as Malcolm Wallop, Paul Laxalt, Jake Garn, and Jesse Helms. Baker knew that I had swayed a number of votes during the debate over SALT II and may have had in mind the difficulties of getting a treaty ratified that did not have the backing of these influential senators. Over the years, I had learned that each of them could be helpful in different ways. Wallop, for example, was well versed on the issues and could be counted upon to influence a number of his colleagues. Laxalt was not interested in details, but if convinced that an issue was important, he was a good conduit to the president, who respected his judgment and would often act on his advice. Garn was a loner but a very thoughtful person. It was always profitable to try an idea out on him first. If he did not accept it immediately, it meant either that the idea needed rethinking or required a better rationale. "Cousin Jesse," as Helms asked me to address him, could always be counted upon for support but was an asset best used sparingly, because several members of his staff were inclined to overkill and to air issues publicly.

At the conclusion of the cabinet meetings, the president never announced his decision, if, indeed, he had at that time reached one. Rather, McFarlane would write up the arguments, undoubtedly adding his own recommendations, and submit them to the president. A day or two later we would read the decision in an NSDM signed by the president. I never knew whether Shultz and Weinberger were given advance notice of decisions or an opportunity to rebut them. To my recollection, there was never a reversal of an NSDM once it had been issued.

Throughout his first term, Reagan strengthened our military posture. To be able to negotiate better and succeed at improving U.S.-Soviet relations, he needed only a more flexible, more amenable leader at the head of the Soviet Union. Fortunately, this came to pass in Reagan's second term. Mikhail Gorbachev rose to power and introduced *perestroika* and *glasnost*. This turned things around. Containment and a policy of strength were—at long last—to prove themselves.

CHAPTER 6

Reagan's Second Term: Results at Last

After President Reagan's 1984 landslide reelection victory, I sensed a marked change in his approach to the Soviet Union. While he still maintained conservative and pragmatic leanings, he began to reveal a mellowness and a sense of idealism not present in his first term. At our meetings, he would make statements like "We have to work with the Soviet leaders to achieve a stable relationship." There was, of course, nothing new about our desire to achieve such a relationship; it had always been a primary goal of U.S. policy. But the fact that Reagan repeatedly brought it up suggested that he no longer felt it was up to the Soviets to change their ways. There was a danger that he might come to believe that it was up to the United States to accommodate a still dangerous Soviet Union. When Reagan suggested the possibility of ridding the world of nuclear weapons altogether, I became quite nervous.

I had given the matter much thought, and I was convinced that abolishing all nuclear weapons was both unrealistic and a threat to our national security. If such an agreement were reached, the likelihood that the Soviets would hide some of their weapons, or clandestinely produce new ones, was a great risk. At first, I tried to shrug off

Reagan's remarks. I took comfort in the hope that perhaps he was speaking in a general sense about a long-term vision for a better world and did not have anything specific in mind. Still, the perceptible change taking place in what Reagan was saying concerned me.

Reagan may have felt that with the restoration of U.S. military power and the emergence of a new breed of Soviet leader in the person of Mikhail Gorbachev, the time was ripe to negotiate with the Soviets on fundamental issues. Or, perhaps he thought about what he might accomplish in his unique role as leader of the world's most powerful state.

Several of us in frequent contact with the president talked among ourselves about whether there was any substance to the White House gossip that his wife, Nancy, was encouraging him to etch his place in history. Reagan had already mentioned to us that she had urged him to "remove the scourge of nuclear weapons from the face of the earth," and none of us doubted the strong influence the First Lady had on her husband's thinking. But we liked to believe that her entreaties were confined to such minor matters as choosing dates picked by her astrologer to meet with world leaders. We could see that dates for high-level meetings were being jockeyed around for no apparent reason and believed the rumors that there was a celestial element at work.

Reagan's first summit with Mikhail Gorbachev was scheduled for Geneva early in his second term. It was billed in Washington as a "get to know one another" encounter. As the date of the summit grew nearer, Reagan made increasingly frequent references to the opportunities it presented for a new start in U.S.-Soviet relations. He did not repeat his earlier hints about accommodating the Soviets, but only reiterated a general desire to get East-West relations on a more solid footing. I was pleased that he often repeated the view that reaching an arms control agreement would not be enough to bring about fundamental changes in Soviet behavior and restated his sound conviction that the possession of nuclear weapons was only the symptom, and not the cause, of poor relations. He insisted to his advisors that he wanted to engage the new Soviet leader in wide-ranging discussions on the major sources of tension between the United States and the Soviet Union.

The good news was that Reagan appeared to be promoting the idea, which I had long been urging on him, that arms control should be moved away from the center of our relationship with the Soviet Union. The bad news was that Reagan was acting like a president in his second term, increasingly thinking out loud about the legacy he wished to leave. He began to talk to us about reaching new, sweeping agreements on arms control. I feared that if the thoughts he was expressing in private were conveyed to the Soviets, it would play into their hands. It would give them reasons for continuing to concentrate on arms control, derailing the possibilities of making progress on a broad agenda. Worse, it might encourage the Soviets to place Reagan in the position of being the *demandeur* on arms control and cause us to enter into an agreement that would not be in our strategic interest. As the president's advisor on these issues, I felt it was important to stick to the fundamentals that had made his presidency so effective internationally. I decided to concentrate on reinforcing the idea that he focus on human rights and regional issues and not introduce any new or far-reaching proposals on arms control. To assist me, I enlisted the help of those who were close to Reagan, especially William Casey and Senator Paul Laxalt. Whenever I felt strongly about an issue and was not certain I could convince Reagan on my own, I would ask close friends of the president to help get the message across. I felt that they, better than I, could disabuse the president of any notions he might entertain that the Soviets, because they had a new leader, would automatically abandon their long-held positions and suddenly become more reasonable. I tried to reinforce his basic pragmatic instincts in the face of evidence that his dream, possibly reinforced by his wife's desire to see him go down in history as a peacemaker, was turning him into an "ivory tower" idealist.

With the help of those close to Reagan, I tried to convince him that Gorbachev would join him in a broad dialogue. After all, I pointed out, the Soviet leader had done a great deal of talking about *glasnost,* and perhaps he was ready to extend this new spirit of openness to East-West relations. The president seemed to buy this argument and tried, through diplomatic channels, to get the Soviets to agree to a broad agenda. The Soviets, however, rebuffed these efforts and countered by proposing an agenda confined to arms control. Under the circumstances, the president decided to go to the Geneva summit meeting without a fixed agenda and to simply look for opportunities to broaden the discussions whenever he could.

Several weeks before the summit was scheduled to take place, the rather bizarre ritual of drafting the summit's final communiqué began. The idea, which had been around since the days of Nixon and Brezhnev, was that it would help structure the discussions if the sides could agree, in advance, on the meeting's final outcome. In theory, it was not a bad idea, but in practice it had several serious drawbacks. In the first place, it played into the Soviets' hands because they always tried to control the agenda. Second, it tended to put a damper on spontaneous discussion during the meetings because that would be ruled out by the Soviets, who would claim that it did not contribute to the final outcome. And, finally, it put the State Department in the driver's seat, because its people drafted the communiqué.

It was this last point that caused a row prior to the Geneva summit. Rozanne Ridgway, the head of State's European Bureau, had been working in great secrecy on the final communiqué with Oleg Sokolov, the deputy to the Soviet ambassador in Washington. But the copy that was given to the Soviets was leaked and it came to the attention of Defense Secretary Weinberger. Not having been a party to its drafting, Weinberger was furious. He was especially incensed that it contained the words "serious differences can only be overcome by sustained dialogue." Weinberger believed that saying this was a mistake, that such differences could only be overcome if the Soviet Union stopped being aggressive. When he complained to Reagan, the president ordered Shultz not to agree to a prenegotiated communiqué. He told Shultz, quite correctly, that such a communiqué would inhibit his discussions with Gorbachev. For the remaining Reagan-Gorbachev summits, the communiqués were hammered out during the meetings themselves. Because the Soviets often negotiated harder on the communiqués than they did on the issues, it resulted in communiqués becoming bland compromises or, on occasion, not being issued at all.

THE GENEVA SUMMIT, NOVEMBER 19–21, 1985

At the summit's first plenary session, Gorbachev deferred to Reagan as the senior leader and asked him to speak first. When Reagan obliged, I was relieved that my entreaties—or perhaps those of Casey and Laxalt—had prevailed. Reagan did not advance any new arms control proposals but rather tried to get Gorbachev to warm up to him. He reminded the Soviet leader that they both came from humble backgrounds and were now sitting together as the world's two most powerful leaders.

Reagan took to the offense and charged the Soviets with complicity in regional disputes such as Afghanistan, Angola, Cambodia, Ethiopia, and Nicaragua. He spent most of his time on the Soviet invasion of Afghanistan, telling Gorbachev that the United States was particularly concerned by this act of direct Soviet military intervention. I began to breathe easier; Reagan was on what I considered the right track.

Instead of engaging Reagan on these issues, as we would have wished, Gorbachev launched into a harangue on arms control. It was obvious that being new to the game, Gorbachev was simply following in the footsteps of his predecessors and taking the advice of Andrei Gromyko, whom he had retained as foreign minister. Arms control was a safe subject on which the Soviets had a well-developed party line. Soviet leaders had always avoided discussions of regional issues at summits, believing that doing so would only legitimize linkage with arms control. Accordingly, they tried to relegate regional issues to diplomatic channels.

When it was Reagan's turn to speak again, he took a page from Gorbachev's book and did not respond to the matters the other had raised. Instead, Reagan told Gorbachev that the United States was deeply concerned over the state of human rights in the Soviet Union. He emphasized that relations would continue to be strained so long as the Soviets' record did not improve. Gorbachev responded that human rights had no place in their talks—that humanitarian issues (as the Soviets called them) were internal problems. He was blunt: "Don't interfere in our internal affairs, and we won't interfere in yours." Gorbachev then quickly returned to his original theme: the necessity to reach an arms control agreement. As though speaking for the record and not to Reagan, he talked about the responsibility the two leaders had to seek world peace, repeating the standard Soviet line that the peace-loving peoples of socialist countries wanted, above all, to avoid the risk of nuclear war. It was predictable rhetoric, devoted more to posturing than to addressing issues.

When it was again Reagan's turn to speak, he told Gorbachev that the United States considered human rights not an internal problem but a universal one. "We cannot trust the leader of another country," he said, "who is not trusted by his own people." He dwelled on this theme at some length, making certain that Gorbachev understood that human rights was of great concern not only to him but to the people of the United States. Satisfied that he had made his point, Reagan then responded to Gorbachev's overtures on arms control. He said that it was not enough to speak in generalities, it was necessary to address particulars. Reagan said that the two sides should cut the number of nuclear warheads in half and that it was absolutely essential to be able to verify that the weapons eliminated were destroyed. Gorbachev surprised Reagan by saying that he, too, was interested in sizeable reductions of strategic weapons and that the two of them should discuss how large those reductions should be. Gorbachev added that he would like to accelerate negotiations on INF.

Detailed discussions on reductions did not take place, however. By the time the first plenary session was over, it was obvious that the two leaders had, for the most part, talked past one another. Gorbachev had made it clear that he wanted to discuss only arms control, while Reagan succeeded in getting Gorbachev to hear him out on his broad agenda.

Prior to lunch, the press was allowed to come into the meeting room for a photo opportunity. While the photos were being taken, both leaders dodged reporters' questions and simply smiled for the cameras. The photo session was made more lively by the entrance of the president's son, Ron, who had managed to get himself accredited to the press corps as a correspondent for *Playboy* magazine. He came into the room dressed in a red gym suit and wearing Reebok sneakers. When the president introduced him to Gorbachev, the general secretary was astonished to learn who he was. He looked around uneasily for help in the awkward situation. Gorbachev seemed relieved when the president's son, rather than ask Gorbachev any questions, simply asked if he could get a picture of the two of them shaking hands.

An hour or so after the afternoon session had begun, Reagan suggested that Gorbachev join him for a walk around the estate, which the Swiss government had made available for the meeting. Gorbachev was impressed that the Swiss had gone to the trouble of planting tall trees in front of the chain-link fence so as to conceal the large number of security guards who stood practically shoulder to shoulder. Gorbachev quipped that Switzerland was a bigger police state than the Soviet Union. He said that he would speak to the KGB about learning from the Swiss how to perform their duties discreetly. In fact, planting the trees had been the idea of the mayor of Geneva. He did so because the citizens of Geneva were uncomfortable that the Soviet compound was enclosed by a high barbed-wire fence. They considered it an affront to the beauty of their city and the openness of their society. They recognized that tight security for the summit was necessary, but they wanted it camouflaged as much as possible.

Reagan steered Gorbachev off to a boat house at the edge of Lake

Geneva. He must have been confident that he would succeed in getting Gorbachev alone for an informal discussion, because he had arranged to have two large overstuffed chairs set before a roaring fire. It was a warm and cozy setting, a very welcome counter to the dreariness of the cold and windy day. The two leaders talked informally for an hour and a half with only their interpreters present. Reagan had often said that he believed he could bring Gorbachev around to his way of thinking if he could confront him alone, away from his advisors.

Later, I went to the boat house and talked to the caretaker. He showed me the elaborate steps that had been taken to get the location ready for the meeting. It was not a spur-of-the-moment occurrence, as some of the press corps suggested. Hot tea and coffee were available, and electric heaters had been placed in the bathrooms. The caretaker showed me a sign that someone had put up on a low overhanging beam. It read: "Low bridge. Former Presidents: Duck!" (The prankster obviously had Gerald Ford in mind. Ford had, on several occasions, bumped his head when alighting from his helicopter.) Fortunately, no reporters were present, and a picture of the sign did not show up in the press.

Later, Reagan told us what had transpired during their fireside chat. Obviously concerned, the president first spoke about what happened when they parted. He said that he had suggested to Gorbachev when they were leaving the boat house that they both look for additional opportunities to get away from their aides and speak together informally. Reagan told us that the suggestion seemed to make Gorbachev uneasy; he gave a noncommittal answer. Reagan said that Gorbachev had spent a great deal of time in the boat house explaining his policies of *perestroika* and *glasnost* and talked freely about the economic troubles he was having at home. It was clear, Reagan reported, that Gorbachev was determined to make socialism work. The president was struck by the deep-seated nature of Gorbachev's indoctrination and training. Because of this, and perhaps because he was trying to get even for Reagan's "evil empire" remarks, Gorbachev spoke at length about the "evils of the capitalist system" and of "man's exploitation of man." Reagan said he replied that capitalism was not perfect, but that, as Churchill had said of democracy, it was better than any other system. Probably thinking about Nixon, Reagan noted, "The people can even throw me out."

At this point, Gorbachev said that if he was not careful, the Soviet people would throw him out as a consequence of his policies of *perestroika* and *glasnost*. He was determined to use *perestroika* to make socialism and the economy work together. Still, Reagan explained, Gorbachev was vague about what changes he would introduce. He rejected out-of-hand Reagan's suggestion that he establish a free-market economy, saying it was outside the realm of Lenin's ideals. Reagan was disappointed to see how rigid and doctrinaire Gorbachev was in his economic philosophy and said Gorbachev seemed unwilling, or unable, to believe that a Soviet free-market economy was proper or even workable. It looked to him as though Gorbachev seemed content to introduce a large number of random changes and see what came out at the end.

I asked Reagan if the two had discussed anything about arms control. "Yes," said the president, "Gorbachev asked me to give the rationale for SDI in layman's terms. I told him that the American people look at the sky and think what might happen if missiles suddenly appeared to blow up our country." "And what was Gorbachev's reply?" I asked. He said that Gorbachev answered, "The missiles are not yet flying, and whether they will ever fly depends on how we conduct our respective policies. But if SDI is implemented, only God himself knows where it would lead." "The SDI discussion got nowhere," said Reagan, "but I at least found out that Gorbachev, when he doesn't know the answer to a problem, calls on God."

We took the opportunity to ask Reagan about his first impressions of the Gorbachevs, especially what he thought about Gorbachev's wife, Raisa. Reagan said she was very strong-willed; he was certain that she had a dominating influence on her husband's thinking. "She's one tough customer," he said. "She has a mind of her own." But Reagan couldn't resist joking and quipped, with a twinkle in his eye, "You know, Raisa is the first wife of a Soviet leader who weighs less than her husband."

Later, several persons who had overheard Nancy Reagan's conversation with Raisa Gorbachev confirmed to me Reagan's assessment of Raisa. She, like her husband, was steeped in Communist ideology and had badgered Nancy even more severely than her husband had lectured Reagan. She told Mrs. Reagan that, unlike the United States, the Soviet Union had no unemployed, no poverty class, and no homeless people. "In the Soviet Union we do not exploit the labor of a large segment of our population," she said, "as you have exploited your Negroes for over 300 years. And we didn't take land away from original settlers and push them into concentration camps, the way you treated your Indians." It was not very gracious talk to pour out at their first meeting. Nancy apparently took in all of Raisa's railings without responding in kind. The First Lady maintained a dignified silence and turned the conversation to something less inflammatory as soon as she could.

Later in the day I had a good opportunity to observe Gorbachev at close range. He was shorter and heavier in real life than he appeared in his photos. His birthmark, so prominent on television, was hardly noticeable. He was well-dressed and sported a Western-cut suit of Italian silk, a tailored white shirt with French cuffs, and an Oleg Cassini necktie. He was alert and attentive and did not appear at all nervous. I had seen previously that he was open and affable with large groups; he liked to work the crowd in the manner of a Western politician. In a smaller group and away from the cameras, he shifted gears and became quite formal and reserved. Although he did not use Gromyko's vituperative and insulting language, he was firm and at times blunt. He spoke in long, involved sentences and was somewhat repetitive. My overall impression was that he was a very tough negotiator. He lived up to Gromyko's well-known description: "Gorbachev has a nice smile but teeth of iron."

As for the substance of the later meeting, it quickly brushed by human rights and moved to SDI. Reagan explained that SDI was a defensive shield, its missiles were not weapons, and it would harm no one. Gorbachev became vehement and asked, "Why don't you believe me when I say that the Soviet Union will never attack?" Before Reagan could answer, an excited Gorbachev said, "I want an answer from you. Why don't you believe me?" An astonished Reagan answered, "Look, no individual can say to the American people that they should rely on personal faith rather than sound defense." Gorbachev retorted, "I don't agree with you, but I can see you really mean it."

The remainder of the meeting was a desultory rehash of old positions which got nowhere. There was a long and stormy session on what to put in the final communiqué. It wound up stating that the United States and the Soviet Union "have agreed that a nuclear war cannot be won and should never be fought." As for SDI, and the ABM Treaty, which had taken up most of the time, they were not even mentioned.

After the meetings, Reagan conducted a critique of what had transpired. Secretary Shultz told the president that Gorbachev was stopping off in Prague on his way home to debrief the Warsaw Pact foreign ministers.

"I wonder if they would like to hear our side of the story?" Reagan asked. I reflexively nodded yes, and to my surprise, Reagan said, "Let's phone them and ask."

About an hour later, we heard from Jay Niemczyk, our ambassador in Prague, that the Czechoslovakian foreign minister would, indeed, like to hear our version of the summit. Not wanting to slight the foreign ministers of the other major Soviet bloc countries, we phoned our ambassadors in Warsaw, Budapest, and East Berlin. They, too, said that their foreign ministers would appreciate a debriefing.

The next day I was dispatched to Czechoslovakia, Poland, Hungary, and East Germany. I was cordially received in all four countries where the officials, for the most part, listened attentively and asked reasonable questions. The one exception was East Germany, where the foreign minister toed the Soviet line and wanted to debate U.S. policies with me. Policy differences aside, however, he and the other foreign ministers told me that what I told them had happened in Geneva coincided with what they had heard from Gorbachev.

A year later I received an invitation from the Jakes Communist government in Czechoslovakia to bring them up-to-date on arms control. I said that I would do so if I could also speak to the members of the dissident group, Charter 77, provided, of course, that they wished to speak to me. I was informed that the leaders of Charter 77 welcomed the chance to meet with me and that the Czechoslovakian government had no objections. On my second visit to Prague I talked to, among others, Vaclav Havel, Jiri Dienstbier, and Rita Klimova. This was remarkable, considering that Charter 77 was an illegal organization and that many of its members had spent several years in prison. Using the Czechoslovakian experience as leverage, I asked the Polish government if they wanted a briefing under the same terms. General Jaruzelski agreed, and I was able to meet with Lech Walesa and a dozen members of the then-illegal workers' union, Solidarity. They were highly appreciative of President Reagan's support. It also gave me an opportunity to raise with Walesa my long-held goal of arranging the return of the remains of Ignacy Jan Paderewski, the famous pianist, composer, and statesman, to Poland. Paderewski died in the United States in 1941, and all presidents since John F. Kennedy had pledged to return his body to his native land "when Poland shall be free," an event I said was rapidly approaching.

As a result of these and subsequent meetings, I was able to keep in close touch with opposition leaders in Poland and Czechoslovakia.

All in all, I made five trips to Czechoslovakia and Poland, allowing me, over the next several years, to convey President Reagan's strong support of the dissidents. The trips led to understanding of and backing for U.S. policies. My visits to Poland also allowed me to fulfill a lifelong goal; Paderewski's remains were returned to Poland on June 29, 1992.

In view of my success in Eastern Europe, President Reagan sent me on similar missions to Asia. After each summit and after most meetings with foreign ministers, I traveled to Tokyo, Seoul, Canberra, and Beijing. These visits also were of benefit to the United States. My consultations with the Japanese, as I shall describe later, were especially fruitful.

As for the aftermath of the Geneva summit, President Reagan, as soon as he got home, reported to the American people on national television. He said while he could promise them hope of progress, he could not guarantee it. To learn what lasting achievements had been made, he said, we would have to await "the final report card." He explained that his subsequent reports would deal "with all four of the elements of the East-West relationship: regional issues, human rights, bilateral matters, and arms control." I was pleased—and somewhat relieved—that Reagan was once again promoting a broad agenda. At least for the time being, he had pushed his "dream" into the background.

PROPAGANDA OR PEACE?

In the first days of January 1987, Gorbachev made a dramatic move in an attempt to seize the initiative on arms control. In a private letter to Reagan, he called for the elimination of all nuclear weapons in both countries by the year 2000. In view of Reagan's discussions with us a year earlier about his dream of eliminating all nuclear weapons, Gorbachev's proposal worried me. I could not see how we could give up all nuclear weapons and still preserve our national security. Our original reason for deploying nuclear weapons was to deter a conventional or nuclear attack upon ourselves and our allies. The Soviets still possessed an overwhelming superiority in conventional arms, and they alone had the capability of a first-strike nuclear attack. If we entered into an agreement to scrap all nuclear weapons, our open society precluded any possibility that we could hide any weapons. Given their closed society, however, the Soviets could easily hide such weapons. Besides, the Soviets could, in time of crisis, quickly produce nuclear weapons clandestinely, an impossibility in the United States. I was convinced that Gorbachev had made the offer as a propaganda ploy.

That propaganda was his objective became obvious when, several days later, Gorbachev made public the contents of his letter to President Reagan. Had it been a serious proposal, Gorbachev would have followed his offer with some quiet diplomacy. But by making his proposal public, he posed a dilemma for Reagan. Should it be considered nothing more than a bold ploy and dismissed out of hand, or would it be better to counter it with a concrete and serious proposal of our own? In view of the widespread attention the world press paid to Gorbachev's offer, I recommended to the president that he choose the latter course and treat Gorbachev's proposal as though it were a serious one.

Over the next several weeks, the administration developed with great care a reply designed to smoke out whether the Soviets were indeed serious about eliminating all nuclear weapons. Even if they were, the United States had to devise a counterproposal that would avoid premature destruction of our nuclear arsenal until we could be absolutely certain our future security would be preserved. The plan we developed was not to do away with all nuclear weapons, as the Soviets had proposed, but to offer to eliminate all strategic ballistic missiles. Caspar Weinberger, the secretary of defense, thought this was a safe proposal because he believed the Soviets would never accept it. Besides, he argued, if the Soviets were to accept it, we would still come out ahead because they would be giving up more ballistic missiles than we. Weinberger was confident that our superiority in cruise missiles and aircraft bombs would give us an edge. Ken Adelman, the director of ACDA, was worried about the Weinberger proposal. He believed it was a slippery slope that would lead to an agreement eliminating all nuclear weapons. Adelman understood clearly the risk to our security if that happened and on several occasions had tried, unsuccessfully, to get the president and the National Security Council to focus on the issue. I, too, was concerned about our counteroffer, but given President Reagan's strong desire not to permit Gorbachev a propaganda victory, I felt it best to back the plan. My biggest worry was that the president's dream of eliminating all nuclear weapons might reappear.

Gorbachev's letter also contained a proposal that intermediate-range nuclear missiles in Europe be reduced to equal levels on both sides. We were delighted that the Soviets seemed willing to reduce the number of such weapons, provided, of course, that the missiles removed from the Soviet inventory would be verifiably destroyed.

After sending a generally worded but nevertheless affirmative reply to Gorbachev, President Reagan dispatched me on a round of consultations to major Asian capitals to explain our counteroffer. This trip turned out to be a mixture of both good news and bad. The good news was that the Asian leaders appreciated being consulted. The bad news was that they felt they were being put at a strategic disadvantage by the Soviets' offer to reduce intermediate-range missiles in Europe but not in Asia. I assured them that the United States would follow up its acceptance of the Soviet proposal with another designed to get them to reduce their missiles in Asia.

The Japanese, in particular, feared that the United States would paint itself into a corner and allow the Soviets to retain SS-20s in Asia. Fortunately, I had a good personal relationship with a number of Japanese officials. Before my first visit to Tokyo, the Japanese government had looked into my background. They found the memorandum I had written in 1949 when I was on General MacArthur's staff recommending that the United States pull its occupation troops out of the cities and villages of Japan. This, and my subsequent recommendation that the Japanese be allowed to develop a self-defense force, made me very popular. Because the Japanese, unlike the Soviets, rely heavily on trust developed through personal relationships, I counted on being able to assure the Japanese that we would not let them down. I told them that the United States would not allow any Soviet SS-20s from Europe to be redeployed to Asia and that the Soviets would have to scrap the SS-20s in Europe that were over an agreed limit. I reminded them that we had Pershing II ballistic missiles and GLCMs in Europe but none in Asia, and therefore we had no negotiating leverage to get the Soviets to reduce the number of SS-20s in the Pacific region. The Japanese, while remaining polite throughout, said that nothing less than "proportionate and concurrent reductions" of Soviet SS-20s in Asia would be satisfactory.

State Department officials were annoyed with the Japanese position. After all, they argued, the Soviets would be reducing their total number of weapons and to object to the way the Soviet Union was proposing to do so would upset the negotiations. But President Reagan was sympathetic to the Japanese. He wrote Prime Minister Nakasone that the United States would insist that the Soviets reduce their SS-20s in Asia as well as in Europe. Reagan seemed to be indicating that he was more interested in promoting good relations with the Japanese than in reaching an arms control agreement with the Soviets. But Reagan was having it both ways. By standing firm, Reagan was able to preserve our friendship with our Asian allies, confident all along that he could achieve his goal of ultimately reaching agreement with the Soviets. This was most welcome and gratifying. I had always favored arms control agreements with the Soviets providing they were equitable ones, but I believed that we should not pay for such agreements by sacrificing valuable allies.

START AGAIN

In July 1985, Gorbachev changed foreign ministers. He replaced the experienced, dour, and inflexible Andrei Gromyko with Eduard Shevardnadze, who, though inexperienced in foreign affairs, had for over a decade impressed Gorbachev with his intelligence and versatility. Shevardnadze picked as his deputy Alexandr Bessmertnykh, an able and experienced diplomat who had served for several years as an assistant to Anatoly Dobrinin, the long-time Soviet ambassador to the United States. I had come to know Bessmertnykh quite well and found him a tough but reasonable advocate of the Soviet Union's arms control policies. In the summer of 1986, Shevardnadze proposed that experts from the United States and the Soviet Union get together for a freewheeling, informal session to try to break the logjam on START. The main issues were acceptable levels of bomber weapons and sea-launched cruise missiles (SLCMs). U.S. and Soviet experts met informally in Moscow August 11–12 and again in Washington September 5–6, 1986.

During our meeting, I had long and detailed discussions with Col. Gen. Nikolai Chervov of the Soviet Defense Ministry. He had an unusually open mind for a senior Soviet military officer and displayed an uncharacteristic willingness to narrow our remaining differences. I told Chervov that the United States would not accept any deal that would count individual bomber weapons in an agreed ceiling of strategic weapons. Chervov surprised me by saying that I should not be overly concerned: "A way around this stumbling block was possible." In view of the rigidity of other Soviet officers on this issue, it was indeed good news. I also told Chervov that SLCMs could not be included within a combined aggregate of weapon systems because it was impossible to determine whether they were armed with conventional or nuclear warheads. Chervov again surprised me, saying that it might be possible to work out a "side deal" in which SLCMs were limited but not counted in the aggregate. Both of these matters, because of Soviet intransigence, had been long-standing obstacles to progress. But if Chervov could convince Moscow to be flexible, I felt it would be possible to move toward a satisfactory START agreement.

Deciding to push my luck, I told Chervov that the United States wanted to see Soviet SS-20s reduced in Asia. I mentioned my consultations in Tokyo, stressing that the Japanese were adamant on this point. Chervov said he knew all about my discussions with the Japanese. He proceeded to prove it by relating details of our conversations, making me wonder if they had been bugged. But on this issue he gave me no solace. He said bluntly that the Soviets would not reduce their SS-20s in Asia.

REYKJAVÍK

Shortly after our START meeting in Washington, Gorbachev proposed to Reagan on September 19, 1986, that they get together at a neutral location midway between the two countries. This caused some difficulty for Reagan, since he had announced publicly that he would not meet with Gorbachev until after the November congressional elections. But anticipating that he would receive widespread criticism from the media if he did not accept Gorbachev's offer, Reagan agreed to meet for a weekend in Iceland. Reagan insisted that he was not going to a summit but simply to an informal meeting to see how East-West relations might be improved.

The planned meeting was nearly derailed when the Soviets jailed American journalist Nicholas Daniloff on trumped-up espionage charges. The Soviets offered to release Daniloff if the United States reciprocated by releasing an accused Soviet spy. I thought this was outrageous and said so, drawing a rebuke from one of White House Chief of Staff Don Regan's senior assistants. He also learned that I had told UN Ambassador Jeane Kirkpatrick how I felt about the trade, and she had spoken out publicly against it. I was told to stick to my knitting and not venture into areas beyond arms control. I, nevertheless, thought it was a major issue and recommended that the president not go to Reykjavík unless Daniloff was freed. But Reagan and Gorbachev were by now both eager to meet and worked hard to smooth things over. After several days of intense diplomatic activity, Daniloff was released and charges were dropped against the accused

Soviet spy. It was all carried out in a manner designed to save face on both sides.

Reykjavík was chosen as the meeting site, at least in part, to keep press coverage to a minimum. The White House thought that if a location with limited hotel accommodations and telephone outlets were selected, it would reduce drastically the number of journalists who would attend. This was wishful thinking. Upwards of 3,000 media people showed up, turning the city of Reykjavík into a logistical nightmare. All of the available hotel rooms were reserved for U.S. officials and their staffs. The Soviets solved their lodging problem by staying on a naval vessel anchored in the harbor. But the news and television people had to find overnight accommodations as far as eighty miles away. Many ended up sleeping in chairs in the few bars scattered about town. Restaurants were overbooked and had to serve meals around the clock. Moreover, reporters found that they had to book their overseas calls to their home offices well in advance and then wait in turn to file their stories. A number of them were forced to resort to a practice they despised, filing pooled reports.

The work space assigned to the U.S. delegation was small and crowded. When the president met with us before the talks, it was in the secure "bubble" at the U.S. Embassy, a ten-by-fifteen-foot glass-enclosed box. To make space available for the eight of us who had to attend, all the furniture was removed except for one chair retained for Reagan. The rest of us sat on the floor or stood cramped close together. The president quipped that the bubble looked like a fish tank. I said it looked more like a transparent sardine can.

The meetings between Reagan and Gorbachev took place in Hofdi House, reportedly a haunted manor house, which, although large by Icelandic standards, was too small to accommodate even a "non-summit." When our arms control experts wanted to caucus, the only place available was the bathroom. If we wanted to meet with our Soviet counterparts, we had to do so in a makeshift conference room in the basement. The cramped conditions made everyone irritable and edgy.

When the meetings began, Gorbachev, true to form, brushed aside subjects concerning the East-West relationship and said he wanted to deal only with arms control. As he had done in Washington, Reagan proposed that regional issues and human rights be the main topics of discussion. But Reagan met with little success.

Rather than the short, "get to know you better" meeting that Reagan would have preferred, Gorbachev announced that he had come to Reykjavík prepared "to deal" on arms control. He led off the very first session with the proposal in his early January letter, saying that all strategic nuclear weapons should be eliminated by the year 2000. The issue I had dreaded and hoped would be dismissed as a mere propaganda ploy was now on the table. Matters became worse when Reagan said that he, too, was interested in eliminating nuclear weapons.

Gorbachev, as I feared he would, took Reagan's answer as signifying approval of his proposal. After all, Reagan had given him an opening by stating that he too favored eliminating nuclear weapons. The Soviet leader then said that he was prepared to talk in detail about arms control and suggested that they be joined by Shultz and Shevardnadze. As soon as the secretary and foreign minister were seated, Gorbachev took the Americans by surprise. He reached into a folder and produced the English translation to a set of "directives" by which the foreign ministers were to be guided, in expectation that they would be agreed to at a later Washington summit. The scope and detail of the directives made it at once clear that Gorbachev had planned, all along, to present Reagan with a comprehensive set of arms control proposals. They encompassed strategic arms, intermediate-range forces in Europe, and space weapons. The proposals included a 50 percent cut in Soviet heavy missiles and put in writing Soviet willingness to drop their demand that British and French missile systems be taken into account. Finally, Gorbachev proposed that neither side should withdraw from the ABM Treaty for ten years and that SDI research be confined to the laboratory.

When we met with Reagan and Shultz after the first session, they both expressed surprise that Gorbachev had submitted such a sweeping set of proposals. Reagan said, "I'm afraid he's going after SDI."

In spite of the pressures of the talks, when Reagan, Gorbachev, and the two foreign ministers were in their restricted negotiating session, those of us not involved in the talks rushed downtown to buy souvenirs for the folks back home. The stores were well stocked with tacky pillowcases, scarves, and T-shirts displaying Reagan and Gorbachev shaking hands. Among the more clever items on sale, reminiscent of the pet rock gimmick of the mid-1970s, were cans of "Genuine Hot Air from Reykjavík."

As I was looking over the selection of souvenirs, one of my Soviet counterparts came to the counter with several T-shirts in hand. His interpreter said to the saleslady, "My boss is a negotiator and will offer you ten dollars apiece for these T-shirts marked eleven dollars."

He was astonished when she said, "Fine," and wrapped up his purchases. My Soviet friend smiled at me and said, "See, I'm learning how to negotiate in a capitalist society." When it came my turn, I offered the saleslady nine dollars for the T-shirts. "No, they're priced at eleven dollars," she said. "But," I came back, "it says here in our welcoming package that official members of the U.S. and Soviet delegations are entitled to a 20 percent discount."

"You see," I told my Russian friend, "I'm learning from Soviet negotiators that it pays to read the fine print."

At the afternoon meeting, President Reagan led off by welcoming some of Gorbachev's proposals, objecting to others, and asking for clarification of still others. Given the short time we had over lunch to study what the Soviets had put forth, we were far from ready to respond in detail. We recommended to Reagan that he stall for time and simply reiterate the American position that he had outlined in his reply to Gorbachev's January letter. When he did as we suggested, Gorbachev became very annoyed, calling Reagan's ideas "a set of mothball proposals . . . choking the Geneva talks." Anxious to calm him down, Reagan proposed that the U.S. and Soviet arms control experts get together that evening.

When we sat down in the conference room at the Hofdi House on Saturday evening, we were met with several surprises. The first was the composition of the Soviet delegation. While our team consisted of the same individuals who had attended arms control sessions in Moscow and Washington, the Soviets showed up with almost an entirely new crew. The only Soviet official present who had attended our previous meeting was Viktor Karpov.

Their delegation was headed by Marshal Sergei Akhromeyev, the deputy defense minister and chief of the General Staff of the Soviet Armed Forces. Two additional Soviet officials at the table, Georgi Arbatov and Valentin Falin, were well known as heavily involved in Soviet propaganda and public relations efforts. Their number-one authority on Soviet space systems, Yevgeni Velikhov, was also there, as was their ambassador to the United States, Yuri Dubinin.

It was obvious from the outset that the Soviets intended to use the Reykjavík meetings as grist for their public relations mills. Still, when I saw Marshal Akhromeyev at the table, I knew that the Soviets had come to Reykjavík prepared to engage in serious negotiations. I recalled hearing that when it came time to deal in the SALT I negotiations, the Soviets had temporarily replaced their civilian chief, Vladimir Semenov, with Marshal Nikolai Ogarkhov. It seemed that whenever the Soviets were ready to move quickly to cinch a deal, they put a top military man in charge. It may have been that only a military man was empowered to make concessions, or perhaps the civilian head of the negotiating team did not want to face criticism for giving up military weapons.

Marshal Akhromeyev, a short, thin, graying, bespectacled man in his sixties, at first glance appeared unassuming and unpretentious, yet he radiated confidence and authority. He was obviously the man in charge. When Karpov, their only arms control expert present, tried to intervene, Akhromeyev would politely but firmly put his hand on Karpov's arm and Karpov would fall silent. Akhromeyev spent almost no time on preliminary amenities. He said he was neither a diplomat nor a negotiator but a simple military man whose mission it was to strike a deal. It was not only what he wanted, he said, but more important, what Gorbachev wanted. He proposed that we begin with START, proceed to INF, and then move to Gorbachev's proposal to eliminate all nuclear weapons. This order suited me fine. I hoped that we could use up the available time on START and INF and thus not get to the elimination issue.

Akhromeyev suggested that we build on the progress made during START and reduce strategic weapons to 6,000 "charges," a cut of about 50 percent. Paul Nitze, who headed the U.S. team, said that he could agree, provided that the aggregate number did not include individual bomber weapons. To my pleasant surprise, Akhromeyev suggested a solution along the lines General Chervov and I had discussed in Washington. Each aircraft carrying only bombs would count as a single weapon in the 6,000 aggregate. One of our team members was not certain about the Soviet proposal and suggested that we put the matter aside for the time being. Akhromeyev agreed and turned to SLCMs.

Once again, following along the same lines that General Chervov and I had discussed in Washington, Akhromeyev proposed that we establish separate limits for SLCMs outside the aggregate of allowable weapons. This was not an ideal solution inasmuch as we would have preferred no limits at all in view of the difficulties connected with verification. It was to me, however, a great improvement over the former Soviet proposal, which would have counted all SLCMs in the 6,000 aggregate regardless of how they were armed. Our position was that we would place limits only on those SLCMs armed with nuclear warheads. Akhromeyev agreed, saying that the Soviets had no objection to limiting only nuclear-armed SLCMs. The catch was verification: how would one know which SLCMs were nuclear armed?

At this point Richard Perle, the smooth-talking but tough-minded Defense Department representative, weighed in. He argued that SLCMs should not be limited at all because it was impossible to discriminate between the large numbers of conventionally armed SLCMs in the U.S. inventory and the smaller number fitted with nuclear warheads. We had discussed this matter of SLCM verification at great length with the Soviets in Washington but had come to no agreement. At that time, they told us that the verification problem could be resolved by employing certain Soviet technical devices. These devices, when placed on helicopters and flown over naval vessels, were supposed to be able to determine whether nuclear weapons were on board. We were highly skeptical and did not want to pursue the matter. Nevertheless, the Soviets invited us to a demonstration in the Black Sea to witness the effectiveness of their devices. We declined to go, saying that such a demonstration would be a waste of time. Undaunted, the Soviets invited several U.S. scientists not connected with the government to attend the demonstration. The Soviets fully expected that these scientists, whom they had chosen because of their opposition to U.S. defense policies, would give their seal of approval to the "new" devices. But to their chagrin and to our pleasant surprise, most of the U.S. scientists who attended the demonstration reported to us that it had proven nothing.

At Reykjavík, Richard Perle and Adm. Jonathan Howe, representing the Joint Chiefs, debated the issue for several hours with Akhromeyev and Velikhov. While I was under no illusion that nuclear warheads could be differentiated from conventional weapons with anything short of full-time inspectors, I thought it important to capitalize on Soviet willingness not to include SLCMs in the aggregate. Perle took a harder line and would not agree to any compromise. Because Perle was always a hard man to argue down, even in our private sessions, I decided not to debate the matter with him in the presence of the Soviets. At this point, the U.S. team caucused, and I spoke my piece. But I was unable to get my colleagues to adopt the proposal Chervov and I had discussed. Instead, we agreed to propose to the Soviets that each side simply declare the number of nuclear SLCMs it intended to deploy. This declaratory policy would at least provide each side with a degree of predictability as to the size of the other's SLCM force. The Soviets, however, would not accept this proposal. Since it was getting close to midnight, Akhromeyev suggested that we put off the issue until another time.

During what turned into an all-night marathon, I had several occasions to speak with Akhromeyev. He was the only person in the Soviet delegation who spoke no English, and I was the only person on our side who spoke Russian. Our one-on-one informal talks showed me that Akhromeyev, contrary to his detached and business-like manner, had a lively sense of humor. When I asked him if he was one of the few remaining active-duty military men who had seen combat in World War II, he replied, "No, I was not in World War II. Do you mean the Great Patriotic War?"

"Okay, have it your way," I said. Akhromeyev then replied, *"Da, ya poslednij iz Mohikan"* (Yes, I'm the last of the Mohicans). When I asked him where he had learned that expression, he said with a wry smile, "It's an old Russian saying we picked up from James Fenimore Cooper."

On a more serious note, Akhromeyev told me that he had been wounded and had almost starved to death during the siege of Leningrad. "I was down to less than forty-five kilos [under 100 pounds], and, while I did eat dogs and rats to stay alive, I did not, as some of my fellow soldiers, resort to eating the cadavers of our fallen comrades."

At about 2:00 A.M., seven hours after we had convened, Akhromeyev declared that we had made as much progress as possible on strategic forces and should take a break. During the break, we caucused, and I raised the bomber weapons proposal that Akhromeyev had advanced. Rather than stress that I had worked out the deal with Chervov, which I knew would be a cause for suspicion and would be resented by several members of our team, especially the State Department representatives, I argued that it was a good deal because the Soviets were no longer insisting on counting individual bombs in the aggregate. Furthermore, they had indicated receptivity to establishing a maximum number of ALCMs per bomber that would be counted against the overall total. Nitze said he preferred not to re-open START issues but to go on to INF. It was just as well because subsequently the bomber and bomber weapons counting rules were agreed to in Geneva along the general lines Chervov and I had originally discussed.

When we resumed our meeting around 3:00 A.M., Akhromeyev shifted to INF. By way of background, shortly after President Reagan came into office, the administration had announced that it favored reducing the number of INF warheads on each side to zero. Defense Secretary Weinberger, who proposed the option, took it seriously. But nearly everyone else considered it unattainable and hence a "safe" way to capture the moral high ground. The only U.S. official to oppose it had been Secretary of State Haig, who thought such an option, if adopted, would be detrimental to NATO's security. He had argued that we should not advance a bad proposition that might be accepted by the Soviet Union. But since few, including the Soviets, took the proposal seriously, Haig had not pressed his case. Our original formal offer to the Soviets in Geneva was that the Soviet Union reduce its SS-20 warheads from more than 800 to 472, the number of Pershing II and ground-launched cruise missiles the United States planned to deploy in Europe. At Reykjavík, however, the United States now made a proposal that it considered quite bold: reducing the number of INF warheads on each side to 200, of which no more than 100 could be deployed in Europe. To our great surprise, Marshal Akhromeyev said he would go the U.S. proposition one better. He proposed that both sides reduce to zero in Europe. Since the "zero option" had been an earlier U.S. position, Nitze said that we would accept it, providing the Soviets reduced to zero in Asia as well. "Nyet," Akhromeyev said, "No reductions in Asia." When we pressed him further, Akhromeyev replied with a typically Western expression: "That decision can only be made by someone above my pay grade." It was clear that he had not been authorized to negotiate this issue; it was up to Gorbachev to make that call.

At about 5:00 A.M., we raised another issue, sublimits in START. Our proposals in Geneva called not only for the 6,000 limit on warheads and a 1,600 limit on strategic nuclear delivery vehicles (SNDVs) but also for sublimits that would assure that there were strict restrictions on the number of ICBM warheads, the most destabilizing weapons. Akhromeyev would not accept our sublimits proposals. We said we reserved the right to bring it up in Geneva. Akhromeyev astonished us by saying he agreed. "Each side could raise anything it wanted at the Geneva negotiations," he said.

By the time the session finally broke up at 6:00 A.M., we had agreed upon a 50 percent reduction in strategic offensive arms to take place over five years. Although the SLCM issue was still up in the air, we had taken a major step forward. The bomber and bomber weapons counting issue was finessed, left to be worked out in Geneva. On INF, we agreed to reduce to zero in Europe even though some members of our team thought our German ally would object. Others argued that having pressed hard for reductions in Europe, it would have put us in an untenable position to not accept the Soviet offer of reducing to zero. We did, however, "put down a marker" that reductions in Asia would need to be proportionate to reductions in Europe. Time had run out, and to my great satisfaction, the Soviets had not brought up the thorniest issue of all, the elimination of all nuclear weapons.

At 7:00 A.M. on Sunday morning, President Reagan was briefed on the results of our all-night meeting. He was delighted that progress had been made on START and was particularly pleased with the Soviet INF offer. He said he was glad that we had insisted that the Soviets reduce their SS-20s in Asia, reminding us that he had promised "his good friend Nakasone" that reductions of SS-20s in Asia would have to be proportionate to reductions in Europe. Secretary Shultz was bubbling over with uncharacteristic enthusiasm, happy that we had made so much progress. Reagan asked if we had discussed the Gorbachev proposal to eliminate all nuclear weapons. When Nitze replied "No," Reagan said perhaps the Soviets would not bring it up again. I hoped this would be the case, but had a premonition it would not go away.

At 9:00 A.M., Reagan and Gorbachev resumed their meeting. Shortly afterwards, they "agreed in principle" that both sides would reduce strategic forces by 50 percent. In a long session on INF, Gorbachev repeated his proposal of reducing INF warheads to zero in Europe while keeping SS-20s in Asia. Reagan said the United States would not agree. "Why not 'double zero,' why not reduce all of your SS-20s to zero?" he asked. Gorbachev gave no explanation, saying only that he could not accept it.

To my great chagrin, it was not Gorbachev but Reagan who brought up eliminating all nuclear weapons. While I knew that Gorbachev would eventually raise the issue, I was sorely disappointed when Reagan took it upon himself to do so. My premonition was proving correct. I was greatly relieved, however, that Reagan did not dwell on the issue. Instead, he introduced the alternative plan that we had proposed he use if Gorbachev pressed his proposal. Reagan suggested that both sides eliminate not all nuclear weapons but only strategic ballistic missiles. Gorbachev said that when he had brought up the matter of reducing all nuclear weapons the day before, Reagan had not rejected it. At that point, I again became nervous, believing that Reagan was about to get himself cornered.

But Reagan deftly extricated himself. He said that he, too, wished to see the eventual elimination of nuclear weapons, but he felt it necessary to have an insurance policy. This would allow both sides to retain bombers and air- and sea-launched cruise missiles until the conventional imbalance was redressed. He said he wanted to assure that there was a "coupling" of nuclear and conventional forces in Europe, and he did not simply want to make the world "safe for conventional warfare." It was a good rejoinder, one that I had brought up at an NSC meeting but did not think had registered with the president. I marveled that Reagan was able to think so clearly under pressure and was pleased that the arguments we had pressed on him had won out. Still, I was apprehensive that the president would at some point return to his dream.

Gorbachev once again reminded Reagan that he had agreed the day before to his elimination proposal. Reagan calmed my anxiety by explaining that what he had intended was that nuclear weapons be eliminated *eventually*, not by the year 2000.

Time was running out. The summit was scheduled to end at 12:30 P.M., and it was already noon. Gorbachev showed himself a skillful debater and clever tactician. He had Reagan over a barrel, and he knew it. Reagan did not want to admit to the world that he opposed the idea of eliminating nuclear weapons.

Sensing that the "elimination" issue was going nowhere, Gorbachev now became despondent. Deciding to salvage what he could, Gorbachev shifted the discussion to the need "to strengthen the ABM Treaty." I again became uneasy, recalling that Reagan had muddied the waters on this issue by suggesting to Gorbachev, in a letter on July 25, that the United States would be willing to share the results of SDI research with the Soviets. Reagan shifted gears nicely and asked Gorbachev to clarify what he meant by "strengthening the ABM Treaty." Gorbachev said he meant that research on strategic defenses should be confined to ground laboratories. Since the ABM Treaty did not cover research, Gorbachev's proposal confirmed our belief that the Soviets wanted to make the ABM Treaty much more restrictive than originally intended. Gorbachev probably did not realize that he was touching such a sensitive nerve. But then he went even further and, in Reagan's words, threw him a curve ball. The Soviet leader said that the cuts he had proposed in strategic offensive arms were all part of a package. If there was no agreement on the ABM Treaty and SDI, then there would be no reductions in offensive arms. Angered by this ploy, Reagan said he wanted to make the U.S.

position clear: he was unwilling to place any restrictions on SDI research.

"Then let's go home," said Gorbachev. "We've accomplished nothing." Anxious to avoid ending on a sour note, Reagan proposed that the Reykjavík summit be extended and an additional session held that afternoon. Gorbachev agreed, and a meeting was scheduled for 3:00 P.M.

President Reagan once more reviewed the situation with us, stating that he thought two main issues needed clearing up. To my satisfaction, he asked if he had made it clear to Gorbachev that we were willing to reduce offensive ballistic missiles but not all nuclear weapons. Adelman said he thought the matter was important, and it should be nailed down so that there could be no uncertainty. I agreed, saying that I thought Reagan should do what he could to prevent Gorbachev from trying to twist things to his own advantage. Gorbachev might have in mind, I said, reaping a propaganda bonanza by appealing to world opinion, claiming that Reagan had rejected his offer to eliminate nuclear weapons. Were that to occur, there was little doubt in my mind that Reagan's proposal to eliminate only ballistic missiles would be completely lost on the public.

Reagan's second concern was that the Soviets were intent on restricting our SDI research program to ground laboratories. Since the president was fully committed to SDI, it was relatively easy to convince him that Gorbachev was not seeking a reasonable solution. He was simply trying to kill SDI.

In the meantime, Shultz had gone to see Shevardnadze in an attempt to work out a compromise their leaders could agree on. Shultz took with him several members of our team, among them Paul Nitze, Max Kampelman, Richard Perle, and NSC advisor Robert Linhard. Shevardnadze told Shultz that the main issue was whether Reagan would agree to a ten-year period during which neither side would withdraw from the ABM Treaty. Perle and Linhard got together and wrote out on a notepad a brilliant scheme, which they passed to Nitze, Kampelman, and Shultz. It proposed that the United States would adhere to the ABM Treaty for ten years and that both sides would reduce their ballistic missiles to zero in the same period. At the end of ten years both sides would be free to deploy strategic defenses. Shultz, anxious to seize any opportunity to break this impasse on SDI, approved the proposal and passed it to Shevardnadze. The Soviet foreign minister said he did not believe Gorbachev would accept it because strategic defenses would be permitted at the end of the ten-year-period. He said, however, that he would submit it to Gorbachev.

When Shultz returned from his meeting with Shevardnadze he told the president what he had done. He pointed out that Gorbachev would get what he wanted, a U.S. commitment to abide by the ABM Treaty for ten years. I was pleased that the proposal committed the president to backing the elimination of ballistic missiles, not all strategic nuclear weapons, the issue on which he had been seesawing back and forth for two days. The president said he liked the proposal, especially the last part, which would permit U.S. deployment of SDI after ten years.

When the two leaders resumed their talks that afternoon Gorbachev told Reagan that he had been briefed on the latest U.S. proposal. He said he had a counterproposal: the elimination of all strategic nuclear weapons and confining SDI research to the laboratory. He had not considered our proposal at all; he was simply couching his original demands as a counteroffer.

"No dice," said Reagan. "I've modified my proposal but you haven't changed yours at all. I think the best we can do is study each other's proposals and take up the matter again when we meet in Washington." At this point Shultz, sensing that everything that had been accomplished at Reykjavík was about to go down the drain, asked that the sides take a break and reconsider their positions.

The president joined us in our caucus room, the Hofdi bathroom, into which a dozen had crowded. Most of us had to stand. Only the senior people got to sit on the edge of the bathtub. Richard Perle and Bob Linhard actually sat in the tub. The "throne," of course, was reserved for the president.

Reagan asked how he might smoke out Gorbachev's real intentions on SDI. He queried each of us in turn on how he could best safeguard U.S. interests. He did not get a unanimous opinion. Nitze told the president that the United States might be able to work out a way to deal with SDI research. I, on the other hand, told the president that he was doing the right thing by not accepting constraints on such research. My view was seconded by Perle. Reagan agreed with Perle and me, adding that he was convinced that Gorbachev was intent on killing SDI. Reagan directed us to redraft the U.S. proposal, saying that we could make word changes where possible to accommodate the Soviets, but we were to stick to our main points.

When the meeting resumed, Reagan read the redrafted U.S. proposal. When he got to the portion covering SDI, Gorbachev interrupted and asked if the Soviet proposal to restrict SDI testing to the laboratory had been purposely omitted.

"Yes," said Reagan.

"And what about the reduction of all strategic nuclear weapons? Did you intentionally substitute for them ballistic missiles?"

"Yes," said Reagan again.

"But I thought you were in favor of eliminating all nuclear weapons," said Gorbachev.

Once more Reagan faltered. "It would be fine with me if we eliminated all strategic offensive arms. We can turn the matter over to our people in Geneva, and they can draft an agreement, which you could sign when you come to the United States."

My worst fears had been justified. Despite his reassurances to us at lunch and despite his approval of the Perle-Linhard compromise, Reagan seemed determined to carry out his dream of doing away with all nuclear weapons. All seemed lost.

But once again, Gorbachev's strong insistence on killing SDI saved the day. Instead of picking up on the crucial issue of eliminating all strategic nuclear weapons, where Reagan had once again given him an opening, Gorbachev returned to the question of confining tests to the laboratory. "Is this your final position?" he asked Reagan.

"Yes," said Reagan

"Then we can say goodbye and forget everything we have discussed," said Gorbachev.

Reagan tried to overcome the impasse and told Gorbachev that the Soviets need not worry about SDI, that the United States was not seeking a military advantage.

"I can't do it," said Gorbachev. He shook his head and said that he had done all he could; his conscience was clear.

At this point, Reagan, exasperated, closed his briefing book. Gorbachev did the same, and they both left the room. The summit was over.

Immediately afterward, Secretary Shultz held a press conference. Bone-tired and disappointed that no consensus had been reached on the ABM Treaty and SDI, Shultz lost his previous enthusiasm for what had been accomplished. While he reported on the substantial progress that had been made on START and INF, his dark and gloomy manner was not lost on the press. They picked up on the negative aspects of Shultz's remarks on the ABM Treaty and ignored the positive elements.

As I had feared, Gorbachev began his press conference by trying to exploit the "elimination of all nuclear weapons" issue. But the gods now smiled on us. Whereas he had been skillful and agile in his debate with Reagan, he was now far less clear and not at all articulate in presenting his case to the press. For once appearing tired and confused, he failed to capitalize on the propaganda advantage that was clearly his. I was, for the first time in a day and a half, able to breathe easily. Gorbachev had saved us from a difficult predicament.

Sensing the need to dispel the gloom Shultz had created, the president outlined the results of his Reykjavík meeting to the American public on nationwide television the following evening. He skillfully and convincingly emphasized Reykjavík's positive aspects. Almost immediately the negative tone disappeared from U.S. press accounts and a palpable optimism emerged. By the end of the week, a nationwide poll indicated that 70 percent of the American people approved of the way the president had handled himself in Iceland. The "great communicator" had done it again.

I went directly from Reykjavík to Tokyo and then to Seoul and Beijing to brief Asian leaders on Reykjavík's results. My job was made somewhat easier because the Japanese government had taken the unprecedented step of airing President Reagan's television address live throughout Japan. The president was as convincing to the Japanese as he had been to the Americans. Several days later, a poll revealed that 80 percent of the Japanese approved of the way President Reagan had conducted himself at Reykjavík.

As I had anticipated, the Japanese questioned me relentlessly on the issue of Soviet SS-20s remaining in Asia. I told them that President Reagan had been firm and, in fact, quite blunt with the Soviets, insisting that there be a proportionate reduction of missiles in Asia and Europe. Knowing that great pressure had been placed on the president to separate the reductions in Europe from those in Asia, the Japanese officials said they appreciated that he had stuck by them and had not settled for the politically expedient solution. The Koreans and Chinese were also pleased that Reagan had remained firm.

In Europe, however, public opinion immediately soured on the Reykjavík proposals on intermediate missiles. The Europeans had not opposed our zero option in 1981, believing, as did most Americans, that it was made for propaganda purposes. They did not think that the Soviets would take it seriously. Now, however, the Europeans argued that going to zero would raise Soviet military superiority to dangerous levels. Rather than face the possibility of repulsing a Soviet attack with only conventional forces, the Europeans felt that a solution permitting the United States to retain some nuclear missiles in Europe was essential. Furthermore, they complained that Reagan had moved into uncharted waters involving their security without having first consulted them.

The situation was rich in irony. The Europeans did not like having Soviet nuclear missiles aimed at them, but could not bear the thought that missiles on their soil might be removed entirely. It was a situation that stood logic on its head. Only time and a great deal of diplomatic effort finally restored the Europeans' faith in America.

Notwithstanding the Europeans' unhappiness, six years of firmness and patience at the negotiating table were beginning to pay off. The Soviets had not only opened the way for the elimination of intermediate-range missiles but also had indicated a willingness to reduce strategic offensive missiles by 50 percent. Only their linkage of SDI to the ABM Treaty stood in the way of a more comprehensive agreement. All things considered, Reykjavík proved a qualified success, especially since the near disaster of agreeing to eliminate all nuclear weapons had been averted. We had not agreed to leave the Soviet Union with overwhelming conventional superiority, and we had prevented them from taking advantage of living in a closed society where they could hide nuclear weapons.

PREPARING FOR THE WASHINGTON SUMMIT

The weeks and months following Reykjavík proved a difficult time. The Soviets, seeing that their initiatives at Reykjavík would not result in quick agreements, were frustrated. They went so far as to signal that there should be no repetition of the 1986 exchange of New Year's greetings between Gorbachev and Reagan. Nevertheless, on February 28, 1987, there was a breakthrough. The Soviet Union formally notified us that they would no longer couple progress on an INF Treaty to SDI. The Soviets had apparently concluded that a deal with Reagan would be in their interest and that the only one possible was on intermediate-range forces. Shortly thereafter, Secretary Shultz went to Moscow to try to get negotiations moving. However, his efforts were set back by an unrelated event. Some months earlier, we had discovered that our new Moscow embassy, which was almost finished, had hundreds of Soviet eavesdropping devices implanted in its walls and construction beams. The secretary was incensed by the crude spying efforts. Soviet contractors had not permitted U.S. inspectors into the building while it was under construction. Now that the building was nearing completion, the slipshod workmanship of Soviet construction workers had exposed a number of the devices. I climbed into the attic with the secretary and saw for myself the hundreds of "bugs" the Soviets had planted.

The bugging of our new embassy was exacerbated by the discovery that the communications system in the old embassy had also been compromised. As a result, the United States flew several Winnebago trailers to Moscow, placed them in the basement of the new embassy, and shielded them with antibugging screens that prevented the Soviets from listening in. The penetration had been so complete that even our typewriters had been bugged. To send classified messages to Washington, we had to write them in longhand and send them by courier to Helsinki, where they were typed and dispatched over secure circuits.

During the summer of 1987, I was invited by the Soviets to a conference at the Black Sea resort of Dagomys, where I had unusually candid discussions with Minister Bessmertnykh and General Chervov. Our final meeting was in a nightclub to which Soviet *nachalniki* (high-ranking bureaucrats) were invited as a reward for exceeding their previous year's quotas. The Western-style rock-and-roll music was boomed out by a ten-piece band at a 100-decibel level. We had to shout to be heard and so soothed our throats with countless steins of beer. While it was an uncomfortable setting, at least no KGB agents could possibly hear what we were talking about. I told Bessmertnykh and Chervov that Soviet insistence on keeping 100 SS-20 warheads in Asia would prevent the United States from signing the INF Treaty. I added that the Asians, particularly the Japanese, did not like being considered second-class citizens, and they thought that if SS-20s were reduced to zero in Europe, then they should be reduced to zero in Asia as well.

Chervov, in a complete reversal of what the Soviets had earlier said, told me not to worry. He said that Gorbachev had decided to reach an INF agreement with Reagan and that the Soviet missiles in Asia would not remain an obstacle. The Japanese had already made their position known through diplomatic channels. The Chinese added to the diplomatic pressure by letting the Soviets know that they considered the SS-20 missiles in Asia to be a threat to their security. At the same time, the United States lobbied its NATO allies to pressure Moscow to eliminate its Asian SS-20s, arguing that these missiles could readily be redeployed to the European front. This pressure, when added to Gorbachev's anxiousness to sign an INF Treaty, led the Soviet leader to overrule his military advisors and to scrap the Soviet Union's entire force of SS-20s. On July 22, 1987, Gorbachev, using an unusual method to signal his intentions, told an Indonesian reporter that the Soviet Union would drop its demand to keep 100 SS-20s in Asia.

A POLITICAL FLAP

One of the more interesting and enjoyable responsibilities of my arms control advisory position was briefing former presidents on the status of negotiations with the Soviets. At least once a year, I had the pleasure of briefing Richard Nixon, who was extremely well acquainted with the issues. He always took the time to read the briefing papers that I sent to him in advance of our meetings.

In the midst of the INF treaty debate in the spring of 1987, I met Nixon at his daughter Tricia's apartment in New York City. He was vigorous and alert. He told me straightaway that he agreed with seven of the eight talking points in the briefing papers, and he wanted to concentrate our discussion on the one matter to which he took exception. Not surprisingly, Nixon disagreed with the Reagan administration's policy of pursuing separate arms control negotiations, not tying progress in one to progress in others. I explained that the Reagan administration proceeded in this fashion because it believed that comprehensive treaties were simply impossible to negotiate with the Soviets.

Nixon felt that President Reagan was making a serious mistake by not linking the all-but-signed INF accord to reductions in Soviet conventional forces in Europe. He was also concerned by the clause in the INF Treaty that allowed both sides to maintain 100 intermediate-range missiles outside the European theater, thus making treaty verification an almost impossible task. His rationale was simple. Mikhail Gorbachev needed an agreement with the West in order to reduce tensions and allow him to pursue domestic reforms. With such leverage, why should the United States enter into a treaty that did little to reduce the Soviets' overall ability to attack Europe with conventional or nuclear weapons? In essence, said Nixon, the proposed treaty made Europe once again "safe" for conventional war.

Shortly after I met with Nixon, he and Henry Kissinger, in their first collaboration since Nixon left office, published an op-ed piece in the Sunday *Los Angeles Times* arguing that if the United States struck the wrong kind of deal in the INF negotiations, it could create the most profound crisis for the NATO alliance in its forty-year history. The two senior statesmen went on to suggest that a viable INF Treaty not only needed to eliminate the 100 intermediate-range missiles it allowed both sides, but it also should tie the destruction of Soviet SS-20 and U.S. Pershing II missiles to the elimination of the huge Soviet conventional advantage in Europe.

The day after the article appeared several anonymous administration officials were quick to criticize the Nixon-Kissinger piece as not providing sufficient grounds for scuttling the treaty. One went so far as to suggest that since we had lived with Soviet conventional superiority in Europe prior to the deployment of the Pershing missiles, their removal would make no appreciable difference. It was, in my estimation, a rather hollow rationalization. The official White House line was more diplomatic, if somewhat disingenuous. Administration spokesman Dan Howard stated, "We genuinely welcome everyone's view on this issue."

Several days after the Nixon-Kissinger piece ran, I attended a breakfast meeting with reporters. They were aware that I had recently briefed Nixon on the status of the negotiations and asked me what I thought about his criticism of the Reagan arms plan. I told them that President Reagan had long supported the goal of the Nixon-Kissinger proposal, but he had sought to accomplish the same ends through means other than linkage. I added that both of the main points raised in the article had been thoroughly debated within the administration, and there was considerable support for both.

I then made the mistake of offering a personal opinion. As a career military officer, my inclination was always to view arms control agreements from the standpoint of their effect on our security. I argued, therefore, that if the reason those Pershing missiles were originally placed in Europe was to help deter a Soviet conventional attack, then until that threat was removed those missiles had a legitimate mission. I added that even though the INF Treaty was a pretty good deal, the United States needed to think of arms control in broader terms.

The following morning, all hell broke loose. A headline in the *Los Angeles Times* read, "Reagan Aide Supports Criticism of Arms Plan." The *New York Times* wrote, "Criticism of the U.S. Strategy Could Complicate Talks." Presidential spokesman Marlin Fitzwater said that my remarks were "not particularly helpful," and administration officials were "somewhat upset." President Reagan was more restrained, telling reporters "I expect diverse opinions in the shop."

At 10:00 A.M. I received the expected telephone call from Senator Howard Baker. Baker, who had recently been appointed President Reagan's chief of staff, asked me to come to his office at 11:00 A.M. When I arrived, a stern Baker asked me if the newspaper accounts were accurate. "Yes," I admitted, adding that I had made a point of distinguishing official policy from my personal point of view.

"Dammit," said Baker, "you've been around this town long enough not to make a dumb mistake like that. You get paid for supporting administration policies; if you have any quarrel with them bring your complaints to me, not the press."

I assured Baker that I had no intention of making an end run on the administration and that I would be more careful in the future.

"Be damned sure you are," said Baker.

Three years later, in August 1990, a month after I had left the Bush administration, I ran into Senator Baker at a cocktail party. I told him I appreciated the gentleness with which he had taken me to the woodshed.

"Hell, Ed," said Baker, "spanking you hurt me more than it did you. But being a military man you can understand the need for discipline and that I was just doing my job."

GEARING UP

In October 1987, Secretary Shultz and arms control experts, I among them, traveled to Moscow to work out the details of the INF agreement and, if possible, to advance START. As was our habit, we stopped off at Helsinki a day early to recuperate from jet lag and make final preparations. When we were ready to leave, Helsinki was fogged in, and we had to take an overnight train to Moscow. We were unable to get the Soviets to provide rail cars for us, but our ambassador to Finland managed to get the Finnish government to put a train at our disposal. Not only were the cars nicer than the Soviets', but we were treated to an elegant dinner as well. The Soviets, nevertheless, insisted on a separate caboose to transport the "escorts" they had detailed to our delegation. One of the escorts told me that the KGB also preferred Finnish trains.

As I often did to pass the time away, I took out my harmonica and played a variety of American and Russian folk songs. A number of our delegation joined in the singing. When we arrived in Moscow the next day, the Soviet press ran an article accusing me of playing "prerevolutionary tunes." I had no idea that my repertoire included "prerevolutionary tunes" or that they were frowned upon.

Later that day, I ran into Gennadi Gerasimov, an acquaintance of some years who had been an editor of *Pravda* but who had recently been reassigned. "Gorbachev has decided that it is more important to influence the American public than it is to inform our own," he said. "I'm now writing for the Americans and not the Soviets." Signs of changing times and things to come.

The meeting between Shultz and Shevardnadze was unproductive. When Gorbachev joined the foreign ministers, he immediately raised the topic of SDI, saying that there could be no progress on START until the United States changed its position on strategic defenses. By adding that there would be no point to a summit simply to sign an INF agreement if there was no significant movement on START, he seemed to be putting the summit in doubt. When Shultz suggested that he and Shevardnadze could sign the INF agreement, Gorbachev changed his tune. "I didn't mean I wasn't going to come," he said, adding that he wanted to visit the United States. But he said that he wanted to come only if there were substantive results to justify a summit.

Something was obviously bothering him. Trying to explain why Gorbachev was so uneasy, Jack Matlock, our ambassador in Moscow, said later that there had been a confrontation the day before in the politburo; Yeltsin had shaken Gorbachev's confidence by severely criticizing him for failing to move rapidly on internal reforms.

On October 26, three days after Shultz left Moscow, Shevardnadze said he would like to come to Washington to discuss the summit meeting. Gorbachev had obviously changed his mind and would come to a summit even if it were only to sign an INF Treaty. Shevardnadze arrived on October 30 and later that day he and Shultz announced that Reagan and Gorbachev had agreed to meet in Washington on December 7, 1987.

Meanwhile, throughout the fall of 1987 our negotiators continued to grind away in Geneva on the details of the INF Treaty. As always, the Soviets resorted to stalling in order to get a better deal. They also introduced new demands, insisting, for example, that we destroy the Pershing missiles we had built at the request of the Federal Republic of Germany and that were stored in the United States. We dug in our heels and reminded them that U.S. and Soviet bilateral agreements with other countries were not affected by any agreements between the two of us.

With only five weeks before a planned Washington summit, there were still thirty-six issues to be resolved. As they had done in the past, the Soviets tried to exploit our having agreed to a deadline by making last-minute demands and introducing new issues. Two weeks passed and the number of issues to be resolved had grown to forty-two.

Our INF negotiator, Mike Glitman, and a dedicated U.S. INF team worked night and day those last three weeks to get the treaty completed. Just days before the team was scheduled to leave Geneva for Washington, they succeeded in reducing the number of unresolved issues to four. That morning, Glitman went to the Soviet compound in an effort to resolve the final questions with his opposite number, Alexandr Obukhov. A frustrated Glitman was told that Obukhov had gone skiing. Glitman returned to the Soviet compound that evening. He was told that although Obukhov was back home, he was tired and had left instructions not to be disturbed.

The next day, two days before they were to leave for Washington, Obukhov told Glitman that he had finally received instructions from Moscow. He admitted that he had not, after all, gone skiing. By the end of the day, they were able to hammer out three of the four remaining issues. The final stumbling block concerned a photo of an SS-20 missile. Under the terms of the treaty, the Soviet Union was to turn over such a photo to the United States. Obukhov said no photos of the missile existed because it had never been displayed outside its canister. As a substitute, he provided Glitman with a photo of a canister that he said contained an SS-20. Glitman was not satisfied, repeating that the terms of the draft treaty called for a photo of the missile itself. Obukhov told Glitman not to worry, that when the Soviets arrived in Washington they would turn over a photo of an SS-20.

THE WASHINGTON SUMMIT

When the Soviet negotiators arrived on Monday night, December 7, shortly after the arrival of Gorbachev and Shevardnadze, they produced the same photo of the canister they had tried to pass off on Glitman in Geneva. That night, Secretary Shultz called an emergency session of U.S. arms control experts. The State Department representative said it was a trivial matter that should not hold up the signing ceremony scheduled to take place the next day. The Defense Department representative thought otherwise. The Senate, he argued, would not ratify a treaty whose basic provisions had not been fulfilled. Secretary Shultz decided to let President Reagan make the decision. When the issue was explained to the president, without batting an eyelash, he reportedly said, "No tickee, no laundry; no photo, no treaty." The decision was relayed to the Soviet embassy in Washington.

A number of us wondered why the signing of the INF Treaty was to take place on the first day of the meeting. Since it was to be the main event of the summit, we thought it highly unusual, especially if the Soviets, as they had done in the past, were planning to throw a wrench into the machinery at the eleventh hour. We suspected that the date had been selected by Nancy Reagan after talking to her astrologer. We later found out that this was indeed the reason why the date, and even the hour, had been specified by the president. Washington can, at times, be bizarre.

On Tuesday morning, December 8, at 7:30, only hours before the scheduled signing, Ambassador Dubinin arrived at the State Department with a photo of an SS-20 missile. The photo was of poor quality, obviously a facsimile transmitted electronically from Moscow. The CIA representative ruled that while it was a poor photo, it met the requirements of the treaty.

As we had come to expect, the Soviets tried yet one more delaying tactic. At 11:00 A.M., three hours before the 2:00 P.M. signing ceremony, they reopened the question of German missiles stored in the United States, something we thought had been settled in Geneva several months earlier. The issue was debated for two-and-a-half hours.

While experts were working at a furious pace to remove the roadblock the Soviets had placed in the way, President Reagan and several of his aides went to the Soviet embassy for lunch. We heard later that in an attempt to ease the tension, Reagan told Gorbachev a story about two cab drivers, one an American and the other a Soviet. Each had immigrated to the other's country. When asked what he wanted to do in Washington, the Soviet said he had not yet made up his mind. The American, when asked in Moscow what he wanted to do, said, "I don't know, the politburo hasn't yet decided." I was told that Gorbachev was not amused.

At 1:30 P.M., with only thirty minutes to spare, Frank Carlucci, the secretary of defense, came forward with a solution on the German missiles. Having anticipated that the Soviets might raise the missile issue at the last minute, Carlucci had discussed it the day before with high-ranking German officials. The Germans said that if the Soviets made it a sticking point, rather than hold up the signing of the treaty, they would agree to an arrangement that would be a face-saving device for all parties—Soviet inspectors could visit the sites where the missiles where stored. The signing ceremony went ahead, only a quarter of an hour behind schedule.

At the White House state dinner that evening, one would never have suspected by watching the affable and smiling Gorbachev that he had almost derailed the INF Treaty. As he sang along to Van Cliburn's rendition of "Moscow Nights," I wondered what would have happened if Carlucci had not pulled the rabbit out of the hat. Would Gorbachev have relented and signed the agreement? Or would he have walked out and let the treaty go down the tube? Probably not, but I just was not sure. Not only did Gorbachev have teeth of iron, he had what the Soviets called "Stalin's intestines," steel guts.

The next morning, Gorbachev, while riding to the White House with Vice President Bush following their breakfast at the Soviet embassy, suddenly ordered the driver to stop. He got out of the limousine at Connecticut Avenue and L Street and started shaking hands with the delighted onlookers. Gorbachev was determined to dominate the news and chalk up a public relations advantage.

Meanwhile, on December 9, we met all day with the Soviet arms control experts, trying to advance START. The meetings got nowhere. As they had in Reykjavík, they got hung up on SDI. At the end of the day, in an unusual effort to try to satisfy both sides, an ambiguous statement was crafted. It said that each side would "observe the ABM Treaty, as signed in 1972, while conducting their research, development, and testing as required, which are permitted by the ABM Treaty." This remarkable bit of ungrammatical double-talk was interpreted by each side to serve its own purposes; it was the subject of debate for months to come.

MOSCOW SUMMIT

Reagan's fourth and final meeting with Gorbachev took place in Moscow less than six months after the Washington summit. The administration spent the intervening period trying to accomplish three basic goals: getting the INF Treaty ratified in the Senate, completing an agreement on START, and advancing Reagan's broad agenda.

Even though the INF Treaty was clearly advantageous to the United States, it did not sail through the ratification process. First, a coalition of senators, led by Democrats Joseph Biden of Delaware and Sam Nunn of Georgia, used the INF ratification hearings as a forum to grind personal axes. They tried to force the United States to move from a broad to a narrow interpretation of the ABM Treaty in order to constrain SDI. This was clearly a "red herring," meant for domestic consumption. It did delay, but not prevent, ratification of the treaty.

The second holdup was the concern of another group of senators who felt that the INF Treaty's provisions were insufficiently binding. Led by Senator Dan Quayle of Indiana, this generally conservative coalition, which included Democrat James Exxon of Nebraska and Republicans John East and Jesse Helms of North Carolina, wanted to eliminate—or at least tighten up—what they viewed as loopholes in the treaty's verification provisions. They believed it important that INF not serve as an undesirable precedent for the anticipated START agreement. I was impressed by Quayle's knowledge of the issues and his ability to organize and persuade the other senators.

A number of senators and newspaper commentators were surprised that I strongly supported INF during the Senate debate. They had branded me an "inflexible hawk" because of my active opposition to SALT II and thought that I was fundamentally opposed to all arms control agreements. However, my position had always been clear: I favored entering into agreements, but only if they were equitable and verifiable. The INF Treaty met those criteria, and accordingly, I enthusiastically endorsed it. It eliminated an entire class of ballistic missiles from Europe and Asia and called for the first-ever on-site inspection of a Soviet final missile assembly plant.

As the INF Treaty was nearing completion, there were at least twenty, and probably as many as twenty-four, senators who had expressed reservations about INF's provisions. President Reagan, not wanting to see that many votes logged against what he thought was a good treaty and a major personal accomplishment, charged me with the task of reducing the number of negative votes to ten.

I convinced some senators that their complaints were unfounded. Several senators, most prominently Senator Helms, criticized the emerging treaty for not specifying how the warheads of the eliminated missiles would be destroyed. I explained that the nuclear material in these warheads could not be destroyed but would be reprocessed for other uses. The launchers of the missiles and the missiles themselves, minus the warheads, would, of course, be destroyed. I helped Senators Malcolm Wallop and Dan Quayle draft recommendations to the administration on how potential verification loopholes could be closed before the treaty was finally completed. For example, the Soviets proposed that they destroy the missiles and simply certify to us that this had been done. The senators insisted that U.S. inspectors actually witness the missiles being destroyed. The Soviets had also proposed that they be allowed to retain SS-20 launchers, which they would use "for peaceful purposes." Provisions were drafted that would require the Soviets to modify the launchers so that they could not be used to transport missiles. The Soviets were not happy with our request, but we were able to convince them that their cooperation was necessary for the treaty to be ratified. In the end, only five senators voted against the INF Treaty.

Another part of our effort prior to the Moscow summit, advancing START, went less smoothly. Although we believed that the remaining obstacles to a workable agreement had been largely resolved at Reykjavík, we were unable to get the Soviets to codify those understandings in writing. During our meetings with the Soviets in early 1988, one thing became perfectly clear: they wanted to link progress in START to U.S. adoption of the narrow interpretation of the ABM Treaty. In short, they continued to insist on holding START hostage to restrictions on SDI.

Indications that the Soviets were in no hurry to conclude a START agreement became apparent in the first few months of 1988. My informal discussions with Marshal Akhromeyev and General Chervov convinced me that they felt the need to underscore the Soviet Union's status as a superpower. To do so in the wake of a rapidly declining economic situation and internal political turmoil, they believed that the Soviet Union needed to maintain intact its large strategic arsenal.

Other Soviet military assets were not perceived as being as important as their strategic weapons. Several Soviet military officers had confided to me their willingness to reduce conventional forces because of their confidence that they could defend the Soviet Union with smaller forces deployed within Soviet borders. Furthermore, since conventional forces are seven times as expensive as strategic forces, the Soviets coveted the potential savings that would result from such forced reductions. In truth, the Soviet military hierarchy would have preferred to make no cuts at all. But when forced to choose, they decided that strategic forces gave them more political and military bang for the ruble.

In light of mounting Soviet intransigence in Geneva, President Reagan told *Washington Post* reporter Lou Cannon that the American public should not expect a START agreement to come out of the Moscow summit. The president was aware of Soviet reluctance to negotiate strategic reductions and wanted to spare himself the pain of the public's unfulfilled expectations. It was a wise political move.

To promote President Reagan's broad agenda, Secretary of State Shultz, in a series of meetings with Foreign Minister Shevardnadze, hammered away at human rights and regional issues. Progress on arms control could wait. In fact, it had always been President Reagan's position that if progress were made on the fundamental issues, arms control agreements would naturally follow.

Constant pressure on the Soviet performance in human rights was beginning to pay small, but discernible, dividends. The Soviets eased foreign travel restrictions and permitted more emigration. But there was little, if any, progress on resolving regional differences. As Shultz and Shevardnadze continued to talk past one another, the issues continued to smolder. Still, each side was able to explain its positions and outline its basic requirements for progress. At the very least, each side got to know where the other stood.

Afghanistan consumed much of Shultz's and Shevardnadze's time during their meetings. Shevardnadze had headed a special politburo commission on Afghanistan. He tried on numerous occasions to get Shultz to help him extricate the Soviets from a no-win situation. Shultz, however, was instructed by President Reagan not to enter into deals concerning Afghanistan. "They got themselves into the mess," he said, "and they should get themselves out of it." Shultz, nevertheless, signed an agreement in Geneva on April 14, 1988, in which the United States and the Soviet Union "guaranteed non-interference" in Afghanistan. But even as he was signing the agreement, Shultz decided he had better hedge. He told the Soviets that ". . . it is our right to provide military aid to the resistance."

Although it was clear that Gorbachev was going to keep his promise to remove Soviet troops from Afghanistan, Reagan was determined that the United States make no concessions to the Soviet Union for undoing the wrong he felt they had committed. Scarcely a month before the summit was to take place, the president made a speech in Springfield, Massachusetts, in which he said that the Soviets "have pledged that next month they will continue withdrawing troops from Afghanistan." But he did not stop there, adding that "the will for freedom has defeated the will for power." Gorbachev reacted immediately to Reagan's remarks, complaining to Shultz that the speech was "unacceptable coming from a leader planning to visit the Soviet Union in a month's time." Shultz, who had not been consulted on Reagan's speech, did his best to smooth Gorbachev's ruffled feathers.

The Springfield speech impressed on me once again the significant role that speechwriters play in mustering public support for presidential policies. Some of the most fierce interagency battles I witnessed over the course of my many years in government service were fought—usually behind the scenes—over what went into major presidential addresses. Several days before we left for Moscow, a speech President Reagan was to give in Helsinki came across my desk. I thought it was an excellent piece of writing, rich in imagery and strong in its reinforcement of our basic values. I sent Tony Dolan, the principal author, an "atta-boy" note congratulating him on a fine job.

On the plane to Helsinki, I again complimented Dolan for having drafted such a good speech. But Dolan was crestfallen. "Look what they've done to it," he said. State Department staff officers had deleted a critical passage referring to the "church bells that could be heard all over Helsinki." Their reasoning was that it made an odious comparison between religious freedom in Finland and the lack of it in the Soviet Union. But drawing that comparison was precisely what Reagan wanted the speech to do. Moreover, wherever the word *totalitarian* appeared, the State Department editors deleted it, saying that it cast Gorbachev in the same light as Hitler.

I disagreed with the changes and felt that Dolan's original text was not only more powerful, but more accurate. Probably remembering President Reagan's famous "evil empire" speech, State Department staffers had gone overboard in their effort to avoid offending Soviet sensibilities. They confused diplomacy with truth.

I tried to help Dolan but could not get in to see Secretary Shultz. I wrote him a note, suggesting that he obviously had not seen the original draft of the speech. If he had, I said, I was confident that he would have left it intact. To my pleasant surprise, and I hope because of my intervention, the president gave the speech much as Dolan had drafted it. It was as forceful in delivery as it was on paper.

We arrived in Moscow for Reagan's last summit at 2:00 P.M., Sunday, May 29. It was a beautiful, unusually warm day. I was struck by the large number of Muscovites sunning themselves, many of them wading in the brown muddy waters of streams and ponds. The Soviets had gone to unusual lengths to spruce up the city. The grass on both sides of the road in from the airport had been spray-painted green. In fact, in typically slipshod manner, the workmen had sprayed green paint on the sidewalks and even the walls of buildings. As if not to be outdone, other workmen spraying the walls ended up spraying whitewash on the grass.

At the first meeting of the summit, Reagan led off, as planned, by addressing human rights. Whereas Shevardnadze had been rather subdued when Shultz raised the issue during their preparatory meetings, Gorbachev surprised everyone by going on the offensive. When Reagan referred to political prisoners in the Soviet Union, Gorbachev struck back at the "inhumanity" of capital punishment in the United States. When Reagan spoke about restrictions that keep Soviet citizens from leaving the Soviet Union, Gorbachev lashed back, telling an incredulous Reagan that it was no more immoral for the Soviet Union to prohibit its citizens from emigrating than it was for the United States to prohibit Mexicans from immigrating. Gorbachev was trying to portray the Soviet Union as the moral equivalent of the United States.

Gorbachev suggested that Reagan give him a catalog of humanitarian complaints against the Soviet Union and, in return, he would provide a compendium of U.S. human rights violations. They could then, Gorbachev said, work together on reducing grievances from the combined list. For once, Reagan was speechless, outraged at Gorbachev's lame attempt to place the two nations on the same moral plane.

Reagan shifted the discussion to regional matters, bringing up not only Afghanistan, but the Iran-Iraq war, Ethiopia, Angola, and Central America. In contrast to vehemence over human rights, Gorbachev responded diffidently.

Apparently feeling it was time to relieve the tension, Gorbachev tried to emulate Reagan's attempt to break the ice at the Washington summit with his cab driver story. Gorbachev told a rather self-deprecating story about *perestroika*. A raven saw a fox running down a path in the forest. "Why not try *perestroika*," said the raven. "When I fly backwards, you should run backwards." The fox did so and backed into the open jaws of a wolf. As the fox was about to be devoured, he complained, "You tricked me." "Oh, I forgot to tell you," said the raven, *"perestroika* is for high flyers only."* Reagan laughed heartily, and Gorbachev, pleased that he too could tell a story, laughed with him.

In between official sessions, President Reagan, not to be outdone by Gorbachev's example in Washington of "pressing the flesh," took a stroll through Red Square. He made it a point to seek out several women and praised them for their "courageous contributions to Soviet society." Posing for television cameramen, he was the consummate politician—he kissed a baby. But the public relations high point of the trip came later, at a memorable speech at Moscow University. One thousand students, undoubtedly screened by the KGB for their loyalty to the Communist party, assembled to hear the president. They were prepared to be polite but not inclined to be persuaded. Reagan cut his forty-minute speech to twenty minutes, allowing more time for questions and answers. It was a polished, soft-sell sales pitch on the virtues of the capitalist system. His simple eloquence, clarity, and obvious conviction impressed the students. But it was during the question-and-answer period that Reagan won them over. The students found themselves taking part in an extraordinary event: the president of the most powerful nation on earth, the person they had been taught to revile as their archenemy, was giving them a basic course in civics, the likes of which they had never heard before and would not soon forget. One of the students questioned the ability of uninformed groups to pick candidates. Would it not be better, he asked, to let party officials examine the credentials of potential leaders and decide which ones were most qualified? Reagan explained that our primary system is a good screening process. Besides, he said, if a person elected does not live up to expectations, the voters will not elect him to a second term. Another student asked if the U.S. Supreme Court was not simply another Communist party. Did it not have the final ability to "dictate" to the executive and legislative branches which rights would be given to the people and which would be denied them? The president explained that the Supreme Court was not a dictatorship but a diverse group of independent-minded persons charged with upholding the Constitution. It was the third of three groups, he explained, the legislature and the executive being the other two, which provided checks and balances on authority. The students asked good questions, and Reagan provided equally good answers. When he finished, they gave him a standing ovation. I, too, applauded, unabashedly proud of our president.

The previous evening, I had been invited to the state dinner hosted by Gorbachev. It was a standard Russian affair—a heavy meal followed by long, boring toasts. It stood in sharp contrast to the "thank you" dinner hosted by President Reagan and the First Lady on their last evening in Moscow, which was a replica of the "beautiful people" state dinners in Washington for which the Reagans had become famous.

When the guests began to arrive, I was amazed to see who had been invited: Soviet ballet stars, athletes, clergymen, and political dissidents. Raisa Gorbachev was startled. At times she seemed to recoil and look the other way rather than shake hands with the guests, most of whom she had never met and undoubtedly never wanted to meet.

At my table were seated former Foreign Minister Andrei Gromyko and political dissident Andrei Sakharov, an odd couple if ever there was one. Also seated with us were a ballerina, a wrestler, a priest, and a surgeon. The surgeon was Doctor Svyatoslov Fydorow, the Soviet eye specialist who headed an assembly line clinic for removing cataracts. I quickly declined his offer to operate on me even though he promised he could do it the next morning and that it would cost me nothing.

The dinner was typically American: New England clam chowder followed by grilled Kansas City steaks, green asparagus, and Idaho baked potatoes, accompanied by a fine selection of California wines. For dessert—what else?—deep-dish apple pie and cheese.

There were no long-winded after-dinner speeches. Reagan simply thanked the Gorbachevs for their hospitality and, before Gorbachev could respond, signaled the orchestra to play. Reagan immediately asked Raisa to dance, forcing an embarrassed Gorbachev to clumsily shuffle around the dance floor with Nancy. Raisa spent much of the evening trying to shush the Soviet wrestler at my table who had convinced the waiter to bring him one glass after another of Jack Daniels whiskey. The Gorbachevs had been to a dinner like this in Washington, but I am certain they never expected to attend one like it in Moscow. Unlike the Soviet dinner, which ended promptly at 11:00 P.M., the guests stayed until well after midnight, long after the Gorbachevs had departed.

We had one morning left to work out the wording of the joint communiqué to be issued at the completion of the summit. Both sides readily agreed to self-congratulatory language about concluding the INF treaty, but there was a great deal of sparring when it came to deciding how to characterize START. Not able to reach agreement, they papered over the differences. Neither side wanted to be blamed for the lack of progress on reducing strategic arms.

The most difficult part of the communiqué centered on Gorbachev's desire to insert the term *peaceful coexistence* into the text. He wanted to be able to show that the Soviet Union had officially achieved superpower status, and the United States had adopted the lexicon of Soviet foreign policy as well.

The problem was compounded by an earlier Reagan misstep in which he had implied that he accepted the concept. Gorbachev had said that Soviet policy was *peaceful coexistence,* and Reagan had answered that the "United States wanted to exist in peace with the Soviet Union." The State Department's Rozanne Ridgway convinced the president that it would be a grave error to allow the term to appear in a joint statement. The situation was awkward. Obviously in a bind, Reagan brushed Gorbachev off by saying that he had misunderstood him. The term *peaceful coexistence,* Reagan said, was unacceptable in the communiqué. They debated the matter for thirty minutes beyond the time set for the final ceremony. Reagan, flanked by his advisors, stubbornly insisted that the words not appear. It was a test of wills that Reagan finally won. An angry Gorbachev, red-faced and muttering to himself, gave in.

THE REAGAN YEARS

After eight years of close association, I felt good about my relationship with President Reagan and what had been accomplished. I respected his ideas and was pleased that he had accepted a number of mine. Before he left office, he generously presented me with the Presidential Citizen's Medal. The citation read: "Edward L. Rowny has been one of the principal architects of American policy of peace through strength. As an arms negotiator and presidential advisor, he has served mightily, courageously and nobly in the cause of peace and freedom." No words could have pleased me more.

By the time Reagan left office, he could justifiably claim that his new approach to the Soviet Union had met with success. He had moved arms control away from the center of U.S.-Soviet relations and yet was still able to make progress on reducing nuclear weapons. He had succeeded in getting the Soviets to agree to an INF Treaty that called for the elimination of all ground-based intermediate-range and shorter-range missiles and in getting the Senate to ratify the INF

Treaty with only five dissenting votes. He had prevented the Soviets from killing SDI. Although a START treaty was still a distant goal, Reagan had managed to get the Soviets to agree to reduce warheads, not simply missile launchers. He had gotten the Soviets to accept on-site inspection as a method of effectively verifying arms control agreements. Reagan had also been able to turn the near disaster of Reykjavík into a success. After flirting with his dream of quickly eliminating all nuclear weapons, he had put it aside, making it an eventual, not an immediate, goal. Most important, he succeeded in getting the Soviets to address a broad agenda. The Soviets were beginning to make some improvements in their record on human rights and were seriously coming to grips with a number of regional issues, the most important of which was Afghanistan. Reagan had begun to place East-West relations on a new and proper footing. It was a fitting legacy to leave to George Bush, who was to benefit in ways that none of us could have anticipated at the time.

CHAPTER 7

President Bush: A Lack of Conviction

Most people were stunned during the 1988 presidential primaries by former United Nations ambassador Jeane Kirkpatrick's description of George Bush. "After four-and-one-half years of serving on the Reagan administration's senior foreign policy team and attending meetings with the vice president," she said, "I don't know what he feels about most issues in the world, and I don't know where he stands." She had it right. Despite having worked closely with Bush for almost a decade, I, too, was unable to say with any certainty that I knew where Bush stood on most major issues. Even in my field of expertise, arms control, I was at a loss to predict what his policies would be, let alone whether they would prove successful. This worried me greatly. After eight years as chief START negotiator and special advisor to the president on arms control, I should have had some idea of what the vice president felt about such critical issues.

In fact, the transition from the Reagan to the Bush administration was rough and agonizing, the most difficult transition I had experienced. Almost immediately after the election, aides in the Reagan White House attributed to Richard Darman the news that those who had worked for Reagan should not assume they would be reappointed. Bush was quoted as saying that he wanted new faces; he wanted his to be a Bush I and not a Reagan III administration.

The transition process in the White House was extremely slow and tedious, while at the State Department the transition team, which included Dennis Ross, Robert Zoelleck, and Margaret Tutwiler, was secretive, impersonal, and arrogant. I had the impression that James Baker's incoming team felt insecure and therefore was not looking for advice. Outgoing Secretary Shultz's people also thought this was the case. Baker's team did not avail itself of the opportunity to talk with the outgoing secretary or his staff because, as one of Baker's team told me, it was up to Shultz to call on Baker, not the other way around. This did not bode well for my potential role in the Bush administration.

During Reagan's second term, I sat in on all cabinet meetings dealing with arms control. Bush always appeared alert and attentive, but I felt that he deliberately avoided active participation in the discussions. He spoke up only to ask for more details or to clarify a specific point. When I asked why he did not play a more active role in these debates, I was told that he wanted the president to hear the views of the involved agencies and did not want to use up valuable time voicing his own opinions. He said he preferred to give his recommendations to the president in private. While I accepted this explanation, I was never able to determine the degree to which he shared his views with Reagan.

While vice president, Bush had on a number of occasions invited me to breakfast with him. He wanted to be certain that he understood basic arms control issues, and he usually asked a number of intelligent, detailed questions. After each meeting, I was generally confident that he understood the essentials of what we had discussed. But even in our private sessions, he seldom revealed his own thoughts. When I told him where I stood on some important point and asked if he agreed, he would answer with some vague remark like, "Oh, sure," or "Certainly." When I pressed further and asked if he would underscore the point with the president, he would shy away and not commit himself. This was in stark contrast to the president. I was never in doubt where Ronald Reagan stood on any issue. At first, I could not decide whether Bush's reluctance to air his opinions was a reflection of his belief that vice presidents should be seen and not heard or simply a shrewd effort on his part to keep his options open in the event of policy disputes. As time passed, I was inclined to think it was the latter. It tied into my growing belief that the vice president lacked a strategic world view.

On a personal level, my relationship with Bush was pleasant. He was always polite and courteous, but he sometimes seemed impatient and ill at ease, even in our private conversations. He frequently got up from his chair and paced the room during briefings. When aggravated or frustrated, he was apt to use benign expressions like "shucks" or "darn." While I did not appreciate Nixon's frequent use of really strong language, or even the milder expletives Reagan sometimes used, I found Bush's choice of profanities almost laughable.

On a substantive level, our relationship was less than satisfying. On more than one occasion, I was convinced that Bush was trying to understand issues solely to prevent himself from being blindsided if a subject should arise unexpectedly. When I asked Bush to include some of the points raised in my briefings in his speeches, or bring them to the attention of the press, he told me that he felt doing so would be encroaching on the president's prerogatives. Still, I felt it desirable to keep the vice president informed and let him know where I stood on important issues.

Bush managed to keep a low profile even though he was involved in several key areas, particularly foreign policy. Much to the consternation of then-Secretary of State Alexander Haig, who felt foreign policy crises were his responsibility, Reagan placed Bush in charge of the administration's Crisis Management Team in March 1981. The mission of the team, which was subsequently renamed the Special Situations Group, was to rapidly collect and integrate interagency proposals on how to deal most effectively with international crises. In October 1983, when Prime Minister Maurice Bishop of the Caribbean island nation of Grenada was overthrown and assassinated by members of his own Marxist government, the Organization of Caribbean States requested U.S. military assistance to restore law and order. As Reagan's point man in the Special Situations Group, Bush took the lead in developing a wide array of contingency plans and options aimed at resolving the crisis and rescuing the nearly 1,000 U.S. students stranded on the island. The group recommended sending a U.S. Marine battalion and a U.S. Navy task force, led by the aircraft carrier *Independence,* to the Caribbean, and plans were readied for a possible invasion. Although the president was responsible for the final decision to launch the military strike, he was away from Washington at the time, and the vice president deserves a good deal of the credit for planning and carrying out the rescue operation.

In part because of his experience as CIA director during the Ford administration, Bush was often called upon to advise or direct groups involved in intelligence or international law enforcement. Additionally, he headed two important national task forces: one to combat terrorism and another to deal with illegal narcotics. The vice president also played a vital role in convincing a reluctant Europe to accept U.S. medium-range missiles. Finally, he took the lead in calling for a treaty banning chemical and biological weapons. Throughout all of these activities, Bush was always careful not to upstage Reagan.

That Bush carried out the role expected of him came as no surprise; he had a habit of tying his political future to the rising star of those more powerful and prominent than he. Sometimes those efforts backfired—for example, when he closely affiliated his unsuccessful bid in the 1964 race for a Senate seat from Texas with Barry Goldwater's doomed presidential campaign. In general, however, Bush's loyal and low-key service was rewarded.

When Reagan's second term was coming to an end, I initially decided to remain on the political sidelines and not get involved in the forthcoming elections. After so many years in the military, I could not shake my inclination to remain apolitical. My decision to join the Reagan campaign had been an exception to that rule and I had not intended to make any more exceptions. But when Massachusetts Governor Michael Dukakis won the Democratic Party's nomination, I was forced to reconsider. I knew that Dukakis's proposals on how to deal with the Soviet Union and his views on defense issues could lead to serious dangers for the United States. I felt compelled to actively support Bush for president.

Bush had served Reagan largely behind the scenes, and until the 1988 presidential campaign, the public knew very little about where he stood on important issues. Conservatives and liberals alike began to question what—if anything—Bush stood for. The very same personal and political traits that inspired good reviews for his performance as vice president came back to haunt him. Even Lee Atwater, Bush's friend and campaign manager, said that if Bush were elected he would be a "transitional president." The clear implication was that Bush would be a lackluster leader, one who had served in Reagan's shadow and lacked an independent sense of direction. While I was sure that he would make a better president than Dukakis, Bush's personal characteristics and ill-defined policy objectives left me uncertain as to what precisely he would do if elected.

MY ROLE CHANGES

Although he beat Dukakis handily, Bush assumed office without a clear public mandate. Having run a campaign almost entirely devoid of issues, Bush appeared content to start his term by maintaining the status quo. This was not surprising coming from a man who had once described his basic creed as: "If it ain't broke, don't even think about fixing it."

Shortly after Bush was elected president, I was asked to write a memorandum giving my thoughts on how the administration should approach the Soviet Union, in general, and arms control, in particular.

I delivered the memorandum to Gen. Brent Scowcroft, Bush's national security advisor, several days after the inauguration. In it, I said that President Bush should continue the approach adopted by President Reagan in his second term, emphasizing regional issues, human rights, and bilateral problems. If these issues were resolved, I wrote, arms control would follow. In a brief discussion with Scowcroft, I said that we should support Gorbachev's policies of *glasnost* and *perestroika* but not tie ourselves too tightly to Gorbachev. Leaders of the Soviet Union would come and go; it was the enlightened policies that we should support. I also suggested that President Bush should support early German unification, which I said would occur within the next several years.

Some time later, Scowcroft called and said that he and the president had read my memorandum, agreed with most of it, and found it helpful. Scowcroft said that the one thing he disagreed with was the timing of German unification. "Germany will not," he said, "be unified in this century."

As is expected of political appointees during a change in administrations, I submitted my resignation as special advisor on arms control. For several weeks, I received no reply. My counterpart, Paul Nitze, after turning in his resignation, also remained in the dark as to his future. Not content to rest in a state of limbo, Nitze pressed the issue and demanded that Secretary of State James Baker clarify his status. It was soon apparent that Baker did not want Nitze to continue as his principal arms control advisor at the State Department. Nitze left, making little effort to conceal his bitterness.

Desirous of clarifying my own status, I tried to speak to Baker, but I was told that he was busy and that I should talk to his deputy, Larry Eagleburger. I had come to know Eagleburger well over the years, and we had an open and straightforward relationship. Eagleburger said that both Secretary Baker and President Bush wanted me to stay on to advise them on arms control, but they differed from Secretary Shultz and President Reagan on how they wished to receive advice. Baker wanted to funnel all his arms control advice through one of his principal deputies, Reginald Bartholomew. Eagleburger asked if that posed any problems for me. I told him that I would prefer to work directly for the secretary, but in view of Baker's wishes, I was willing to explore the matter. Bartholomew confirmed to me that Baker wanted him to consolidate arms control opinions within the State Department and submit recommendations to the secretary. He proposed that if my views differed from his on any given issue, I could submit my dissenting views as an addendum to his recommendations and that he would not alter or comment in any way on my contrary opinions. I told him and Eagleburger that I thought this was a crazy way to do business and far from an ideal arrangement. Nevertheless, I said that if this was how the secretary of state wished to operate, I would be willing to give it a try.

Another indication of the change in my status occurred in early March 1989, when Larry Eagleburger asked me if it was true that I had had lunch with John Sununu, the White House chief of staff.

"Yes," I said.

"Well, cut it out," Eagleburger said. "Baker doesn't like end runs."

"I didn't end run Baker," I said, explaining that I met with Sununu and other key cabinet officials as a matter of courtesy to keep them informed on the broad issues before us.

"Well, Baker doesn't like it," said Eagleburger. "Don't do it any more."

After that day I had only one more private discussion with Sununu: I asked him whether I should remain in my post or quit.

As for my relationship with the president, Eagleburger said that I would continue to function in much the same manner as I had with President Reagan. If I disagreed with Secretary Baker on an arms control issue, I was to submit my counterproposals to the president through Brent Scowcroft. However, I was no longer to sit in on cabinet meetings. Eagleburger said that Bush would hold few if any cabinet meetings on arms control, and those would be attended only by the secretaries of state and defense, the chairman of the Joint

Chiefs of Staff, and the national security advisor. Agency views on arms control, as well as mine, were to be discussed, summarized in writing, and submitted to Scowcroft through his deputy, Robert Gates. I would, of course, be invited to sit in on Gates's "deputies' meetings," along with Bartholomew and the principal deputies of other key agencies.

I told Eagleburger that I thought this was a most unusual way for me to fulfill my role as special advisor to the president. I would, in effect, be advising the bureaucracy, not the chief executive. I went to see Scowcroft and told him that if the president did not want my advice, I would rather retire than become another staff officer. Scowcroft confirmed what Eagleburger and other White House aides had told me—President Bush did not like large or frequent cabinet meetings. He insisted, however, that the president wanted my views on critical issues, and they would be treated as seriously as if I had presented them in person.

Over the next several months, I kept my reservations about the process to myself and worked the way Bush and Baker preferred. True to his word, Bartholomew furnished me with copies of his recommendations to Secretary Baker, and when I disagreed with them, I appended my dissenting views. I found that I disagreed with only about one recommendation out of four or five, but my differences were on the more important issues such as how to define new types of missiles and missile throw-weight. We also came to loggerheads over how to deal with warhead "downloading," the Soviet proposal to deploy fewer warheads on MIRVed missiles without destroying the additional warheads the missiles were capable of carrying.

At Gates's deputies' meetings, as Eagleburger and Scowcroft had indicated, I was called upon to give my views whenever I disagreed with those of the State Department or any other agency. I then submitted those views in writing to General Scowcroft but addressed them to the president. Scowcroft told me that he always forwarded my dissenting opinions to the president, and on occasion, I received a note from Bush thanking me for my comments. From time to time, I went to see the national security advisor to reinforce or elaborate on my views. While I was always treated courteously, Scowcroft seldom told me what he would eventually recommend to the president. This rather indirect way of providing advice was not very satisfying even though the president followed my recommendations on several crucial issues, most notably on the Strategic Defense Initiative and, at least initially, my insistence that the Soviets be prohibited from testing their heavy missiles.

Yet I still felt out of the loop—and with good reason. In July 1989, Shevardnadze came to Washington with a team of arms control experts to try to make progress on START.

The evening before the meeting was to begin, I noticed that my package of briefing papers failed to include a pass to the eighth floor of the State Department where the meetings were to take place. Thinking it was an administrative oversight, I had my assistant call Stapleton Roy, the State Department administrator. It was no oversight; he said that my name did not appear on the roster for the meeting. He said that to get on the list someone in Secretary Baker's front office would have to give approval.

The next morning I went to see Reginald Bartholomew. He told me the decision to put names on the list was above his pay grade. I told him that was ridiculous, since he was Baker's principal coordinator on arms control. Nevertheless, Bartholomew would not act. I then went to Eagleburger's office, but he was not in.

I decided to take the bull by the horns and went to the Ben Franklin Room of the State Department where the Soviets were assembling. A guard attempted to stop me, but I brushed past him and went in to talk to the Soviet visitors. Later, when we sat down for the first plenary meeting, one of Stapleton Roy's assistants brought me a pass, apologizing for the "mistake." I, of course, knew it had been no mistake. It was an early indication that Secretary Baker was excluding outside influences and consolidating his grip on the administration's foreign policy process.

Later that day, Marshal Sergei Akhromeyev, deputy defense minister of the Soviet Union, told me that he feared there would be a coup against Gorbachev by the military and hardline conservatives. It was the first inkling I had that the Soviet military might act. I reported this to the State Department and the CIA, who did not take it seriously. The State Department dismissed my concern; they felt that Akhromeyev was merely playing for sympathy, hoping we would soften our stance and offer the Soviets additional concessions on START.

TWO SETS OF ADVICE

In the early days of the administration, the president received conflicting advice from his principal aides on whether he should actively pursue arms control. One group, led by Secretary of State Baker, held that agreements on arms were important catalysts to achieving our foreign policy objectives and should be pushed with vigor. A second group, led by Secretary of Defense Dick Cheney, pointed out that the Soviet Union was continuing to spend more than 25 percent of its GNP on military forces and that our own expenditures of less than 6 percent put us in a poor bargaining position. Better to wait, this second group believed, until the sagging Soviet economy forced the Soviet Union to cut back its forces and only then press for agreements. The president, preoccupied with getting his team in place and trying to gauge the direction in which the public wanted him to move, did nothing. That was consistent with what I perceived as Bush's tendency: when in doubt, resort to fence-sitting.

The same two groups gave President Bush opposing views on the degree of support he should put behind Gorbachev. The group led by the State Department argued that *perestroika* was succeeding and that Gorbachev should be praised and encouraged; those in the group led by the Defense Department said that Gorbachev's reforms were not going deep enough to bring about real changes and therefore U.S. support for the Soviet Union's leader should be restrained. President Bush characteristically tried to have it both ways. His original statements showed that he favored the first group. But subsequently Bush wanted to be "cautious and prudent"—two of his favorite words. He summed up the latter approach in a speech on May 21, 1990.

> If the Soviets advance solid and constructive plans for peace, then we should give credit where credit is due. And we're seeing sweeping changes in the Soviet Union that show promise of enduring, of becoming ingrained. At the same time, in an era of extraordinary changes, we have an obligation to temper optimism—and I am optimistic—with prudence.

It was vintage Bush.

BUSH THE MAN

Throughout my decade-long relationship with George Bush, the impressions that I formed early on about his character, style, and personality were constantly reinforced. He seemed the archetypical well-heeled, blue-blooded, WASP New Englander whose service to God, country, and Wall Street was a function of birthright. While he was ambitious and hardworking, his energies were often channeled in dubious directions. For example, his 1988 presidential campaign made even some veteran political operatives blush in embarrassment at its lack of substance. He seemed devoid of the powerful sense of purpose that so characterized Ronald Reagan. When it came to specifics, Bush was hard to pin down. He was vague to the point of being vacuous, lofty to the point of being unreachable. In some respects, he was an anachronism, a philosophical throwback to the heady days immediately following World War II when America's rise to international preeminence was managed by men like Averell Harriman, Robert Lovett, and Dean Acheson, whose mentor and role model was the venerable Henry Stimson, Roosevelt's secretary of war. In their book, *The Wise Men: Six Friends and a World They Made,* Walter Issacson and Evan Thomas describe these men as "sharing a vision of public service as a lofty calling and an aversion to partisan politics. They had a pragmatic and businesslike preference for realpolitik over ideology." The authors could just as easily have been talking about George Bush.

Shortly after agreeing to stay on as Bush's arms control advisor, I decided to look for reasons that might explain the characteristics I had observed in Bush and help me determine whether he could be expected to change during his tenure as president. The more I learned about his past from talking to those who had known him over the years, the more I came to believe that George Bush was pretty much set in his ways.

Coming as he did from a patrician background, Bush, like his father Prescott, was inspired by the belief that the debt his class owed society should be repaid through public service. Much of his idealism he owed to his mother, who distanced herself from her husband's business and political interests and devoted herself to raising her children in a protective atmosphere, stressing morality and religion. She told her son never to boast or to refer to himself in the first person, something he always remembered. It was not until the 1988 presidential campaign that Bush, at the insistence of his speech writers, referred to himself as "I."

As a young man, Bush followed in his father's footsteps. He first went to Phillips Andover Academy and put off going to college so that he could become a U.S. naval aviator in World War II. Like his father, who was decorated for valor in World War I, Bush distinguished himself in combat. In holding his crippled bomber on course to its target on Chichi Jima, a Pacific island, Bush for the first time revealed a trait that has become one of his greatest strengths: he is at his best when faced with a crisis. His record as the youngest commissioned pilot in the U.S. Navy is exemplary. He flew fifty-eight combat missions, was shot down twice, and received three Air Medals and the Distinguished Flying Cross for his service in the Pacific theater of operations.

After the war, Bush entered Yale, the perfect base for establishing many of the personal contacts that would eventually play a large role in his future success. He was good in sports and in his studies, making Phi Beta Kappa. He graduated with honors in economics in 1948. Determined to emphasize his independence and desirous of playing down his privileged birth, Bush turned down a job offer from his father's prestigious Wall Street firm and struck out on his own to Texas. The pioneering spirit that characterized Bush's departure from the relative security of the East Coast establishment to the rough-and-tumble Southwest was common in the days immediately following World War II. The war had changed America. Veterans like Bush, imbued with the exhilaration of having survived in combat, often ignored traditional social boundaries and sought challenging opportunities in new settings. But his was no Horatio Alger story. With the help of a substantial loan from his uncle, he started an oil rig business. In his intense search for a winning enterprise, Bush risked all the money he had and backed Richard LeTourneau, a pioneer in developing offshore oil rigs. LeTourneau, who was my executive officer in West Africa in 1942, told me that Bush was an extremely hard worker who had an intense determination to succeed. The risk paid off handsomely, and in 1954 he became president of the Zapata Off-Shore Company. Within a decade Bush was financially secure enough to launch a career in government.

While working in Texas in the mid-1950s, George Bush told his friend and business associate Fred Chambers, "I really feel that some day I want to go into public service. I think I'd like to get into government. I don't know if I want to be a politician, but I'd like to hold office." A former close advisor explained this apparent contradiction: "He's basically embarrassed to be a politician. It's tacky. He has to do those horribly embarrassing things and he finds it distasteful, except as a competitive exercise." His dilemma was obvious: a strong desire to hold public office, but an equally strong unwillingness to deal with the nuts and bolts of politics.

Bush's contradictions and complexities showed up in other ways. He was gentlemanly and gracious in small social gatherings, but shy and uncomfortable when facing large numbers of strangers. He was extremely loyal, often to a fault, and expected the same kind of loyalty from subordinates. When that loyalty was not forthcoming, his generous and gracious side disappeared and an unforgiving and vindictive George Bush came to the fore. In 1980, when it became clear that he would not win the Republican presidential nomination, some of his supporters abandoned his political ship. At this point Bush, quoting Lyndon Johnson, said, " 'They painted their asses white and ran with the antelopes.' I remember that, and I remember who some of them are."

From his earliest days in politics, Bush's decision-making style reflected his father's influence. Prescott Bush had gained a reputation for high standards of conduct while serving in the U.S. Senate, but he had shown enormous caution on legislative issues. The elder Bush rarely made a decision until all options were exhaustively examined and he was forced to cast a vote. He avoided partisan rancor, and gained entry to the upper house not as a result of a victorious campaign, but by political appointment after the death of Senator Brian McMahon.

George Bush was almost an exact copy of his father. He was most uncomfortable when it came to making up his mind. His first real exposure to partisan political "hardball" came in 1964, when he ran for the U.S. Senate in Texas. For the first time in his life, Bush had to wade knee-deep into a partisan quagmire and declare where he stood. In a somewhat naive attempt to establish his Republican credentials, Bush went against his moderate inclinations and aligned himself with the ill-fated Goldwater presidential campaign. When Lyndon Johnson won in a landslide, Bush, along with other Goldwater supporters, went down to defeat. Ironically, although Bush had willingly signed on to Goldwater's archconservative platform, he later blamed his defeat on conservative "nut fringe zealots." It is ironic that in 1992 he finds himself forced to perform a delicate balancing act between the factions of his own party and always seems concerned about an attack from the right wing.

Two years after his failed bid for the Senate, Bush ran for a congressional seat in Texas. He was helped substantially by Senator John Tower and vowed to someday return the favor. Tower was also instrumental in designing Bush's successful "Southern strategy" in the 1988 Republican primaries. Bush tried to repay his political debt after becoming president by naming Tower secretary of defense, but the Senate blocked the appointment.

Bush was more careful in the congressional race than he had been in seeking the Senate seat. Running as a moderate, he won handily. This brought the transplanted New Englander into national prominence and in 1970, after another failed senatorial campaign, this one run at the behest of Richard Nixon, he was appointed U.S. ambassador to the United Nations. Ironically, Nixon originally had intended to reward Bush's loyal sacrifice of his secure congressional seat with a mid-level job at the White House. Bush, however, lobbied for the UN position, using his establishment credentials as the bait. Nixon had always been at odds with the New York, Wall Street, "TriLateral Commission Republicans," but he was keenly aware that he needed their political support if his policies were to be realized. Knowing this, Bush emphasized his natural rapport with this group and offered Nixon entree to the influential New York cocktail and dinner party circuit.

Bush cut his eyeteeth on foreign policy while at the United Nations. His tenure there was unremarkable save for what some saw as his about-face on the question of whether to grant mainland China membership. Although he had previously been a vocal supporter of Taiwan as the legitimate representative of the Chinese people, he quickly changed his position to support Nixon's two-China policy. His loyalty was duly noted not only by Nixon but also by Vice President Gerald Ford.

In 1972, under mounting pressure from the Watergate scandal and desperately in need of political allies, Nixon appointed Bush chairman of the Republican National Committee. Although Bush was reluctant to take the post, his natural inclination to serve when called upon by the president was too powerful to overcome. Even his wife, Barbara, tried to get him to turn down the assignment. Reflecting upon the Watergate debacle in later years, Bush admitted that had he been in Congress at the time, in light of the evidence uncovered by the congressional investigation, he would have voted for Nixon's impeachment. In September of 1974, only a month after he became president, Ford rewarded Bush's faithful service by appointing him U.S. representative to the People's Republic of China.

In that post, Bush added to his reputation for not rocking the boat. When I asked several people who knew Bush in those days, they could not recall his ever having taken a firm stand on any issue. Later, when asked how much autonomy he had in his Chinese post, Bush tersely replied, "None."

In 1976, President Ford appointed Bush director of the Central

Intelligence Agency, a job which in certain ways suited him to a "T." It put Bush at the head of an organization noted for its Ivy League character and one that by definition played to his strengths as a behind-the-scenes advisor and secretive manager. Bush enjoyed the job, and was given credit for restoring agency morale at a most controversial time in its history. When several members of the CIA were accused of lying under oath to Congress about the agency's operations in Chile, Bush fought the Justice Department's effort to launch a criminal investigation. Even though President Ford eventually ordered Bush to give the investigators the information they sought, Bush's stock within the CIA soared.

BUSH'S BASIC PHILOSOPHY

After Jimmy Carter was elected president in 1976, Bush decided to concentrate on winning the presidential nomination in 1980. Bush won in the caucuses, but the big test was in New Hampshire. He performed poorly in a state debate, and Reagan won the New Hampshire primary by a two-to-one margin. Bush got a boost when he won the Michigan primary. But, overall, Reagan was surpassing Bush with the GOP faithful. With a Reagan victory looming, Bush withdrew from the race and subsequently became Reagan's vice president and, in 1988, his successor.

Aside from his rather vague establishment Republican internationalism, Bush has consistently displayed a lack of strategic vision. After his successful campaign for the White House, one long-time Republican operative remarked, "We have seen from this campaign that George Bush likes to win. The question is, on behalf of what?" Bush's tour in Congress and his subsequent stints as U.S. ambassador to the United Nations, representative to China, and director of the CIA do not provide much help in answering that seemingly simple question. Bush has enormous faith in American greatness, but he tends to project that vision onto countries that are vastly different from our own, both ideologically and culturally. He once described his basic philosophy as "promoting democracy everywhere." At first I did not quite understand what he meant. But in a speech to the U.S. Coast Guard Academy on May 24, 1989, he made his philosophy clearer:

> Democracy isn't our creation, it is our inheritance. And we can't take credit for democracy, but we can take that precious

gift of freedom, preserve it, and pass it on, as my generation does to you, and you, too, will do one day. And perhaps, provided we seize opportunities open to us, we can help others attain this freedom that we cherish.

Over time, I discerned that what he meant was that he would like to see leaders in other countries freely elected, who would subsequently rule by "consensus." He seemed to take for granted a country's ability to absorb and adopt our complex democratic philosophy. He displayed an abiding confidence in the rationality of world leaders and seemed to assume that American middle-class ideals were shared by other societies. He ignored intractable differences and historic enmities. He idealistically assumed that anything was possible if he simply made some broad pronouncements and then left the details to his aides. I have always considered this inability to see the world in realistic terms as one of George Bush's biggest weaknesses. Insulation from day-to-day concerns seems to be his hallmark.

From our earliest conversations, I heard a great deal from Bush about what he called his policy of *inclusion*. I later learned that this was his term for what most people call *networking*. From his earliest political days in Texas, Bush determined that the best way to succeed was to engage in personal diplomacy and cultivate a large circle of friends. Even in those days, people joked that they were among Bush's closest one thousand friends. His theory was that if he got to know a sufficiently large number of important and influential people, those friendships would stand him in good stead later in his career. He apparently believed that if he knew the right people, he would not have to worry about coping with difficult issues. One of his favorite expressions was, "Friends don't argue, they compromise." At times, Bush was able to put this theory to work in the White House, and it paid him large dividends. Cashing in on his good relationships with global leaders helped him to oust Manuel Noriega from Panama and to establish the international coalition that was crucial to the defeat of Saddam Hussein's military forces in Iraq. But he seemed not to understand that it took more than establishing personal bonds to formulate sound policies.

Consistent with his bent for networking, Bush was constantly on the lookout for opportunities to make personal contacts with influential people in and out of office. For example, when he visited

Poland in July of 1989, he insisted on meeting with Lech Walesa, who at the time still headed the Solidarity trade union.

A great deal of Bush's inclusion and coalition building is pursued by telephone. He took AT&T's advice literally to "reach out and touch" fellow world leaders. He made as many as five or six telephone calls a day to such luminaries as Great Britain's Margaret Thatcher, Helmut Kohl of Germany, French leader François Mitterrand, Canada's Brian Mulroney, and Pope John Paul II. This intensive personal diplomacy, which one wag has called Bush's "Rolodex Diplomacy," has advantages and some pitfalls. Bush's staff has to study carefully the transcripts of his telephone conversations to guard against accidental or misleading policy statements. Sometimes Bush has had to change or clarify in writing what he said over the phone. For example, arrangements for the Malta summit in December 1989, which he had initiated with a phone call to Gorbachev in June, had to be followed up with three handwritten letters clarifying his position. Aides told me the letters following Bush's phone conversations were full of statements like: "What I meant was. . . ."

I often wondered how other world leaders reacted to Bush's personal approach to diplomacy. In speaking to some of their subordinates, I learned that the British, Canadians, and Germans liked Bush's way of communicating informally, while the French, Japanese, and Soviets were highly uncomfortable with his departure from protocol. My Soviet contacts told me that Gorbachev found Bush's lack of formality highly disconcerting.

On occasion Bush took informality a step further. He liked to arrange to meet his guests in unorthodox settings, even though it made for some awkward situations. For example, when President Hosni Mubarak of Egypt came to the United States in the spring of 1989, Bush invited him to a Baltimore Orioles' baseball game. Mubarak was totally confused. Later that year, Bush invited François Mitterrand, who liked pomp and circumstance, to his vacation home in Maine. Mitterrand was reportedly miserable in the casual surroundings.

Bush is also fond of writing informal notes and always has a stack of note cards handy. As he raced through his daily diet of six morning newspapers, he would dash off notes to friends as well as strangers whom he felt were deserving of support and recognition. It was a rare day, I was told, that he did not write a dozen such notes. On the way home from his European trip in May 1989, he wrote some forty thank-you notes to staff members who helped him while abroad. When the staffers compared their notes, they discovered that the president had made an effort to personalize each one. I was the recipient of a number of such notes, often after our breakfast meetings.

Barbara Bush, too, has a warm and human side. I had heard stories that she had been included in White House strategy sessions and that she had given decisive, steely advice to her husband and close advisors; but I never witnessed anything like this. Once, when my wife and I attended a reception at the vice president's home, there was such a long receiving line that my wife, who had suffered a stroke, had to sit down. When I got to the head of the line, Mrs. Bush asked, "Where's Rita?"

"She couldn't stand in line so long and is seated on the other side of the room," I replied.

Mrs. Bush immediately grabbed two secret service men and had them run interference in front of her as she pushed through the crowd toward my wife. She sat down next to my wife and for the next five minutes, while the receiving line waited for her to return, she carried on a friendly conversation. Later, in October 1988, within hours of my wife's death, a messenger arrived at my door with a handwritten expression of sympathy from the vice president and his wife.

In the foreign arena, Bush's unfocused style precludes policies based on a long-term strategic sense of how to achieve and maintain the elusive new world order that he professes to seek. For example, while he brought the 1991 Persian Gulf war to a swift conclusion, it is not yet clear that he will be able to build on his military success and bring about greater stability in the region.

Although I was no longer in government at the time, I happened to be visiting a friend in the White House two days after the ground war in Iraq started. Several members of the press commented on the unfairness of U.S. troops' firing upon retreating Iraqi vehicles. They did not recognize that all the Iraqis had to do to avoid being fired upon was to run up a white flag or abandon their tanks and armored personnel carriers. But this criticism so affected Bush's sense of fair play that I was told it was a major factor in his decision to terminate the war early. Subsequently, his search for a new solution to the age-old conflict in the Middle East went nowhere despite a great investment of time and political capital. His ad hoc approach and failure to develop and carry out concrete ideas within a conceptual framework will become ever more relevant as Bush begins to deal with increasingly important international economic issues.

Bush is a believer in linkage of a kind that is consistent with his upbringing. It is not Nixon's type of direct linkage, which held that the Soviets should cooperate in Vietnam in exchange for U.S. cooperation in arms control. Rather, Bush's linkage is a gentlemanly quid pro quo: "You scratch my back, and I'll scratch yours." For example, he indicated a desire to trade off the long-held U.S. negotiating position of not allowing further testing of Soviet heavy ICBMs, without specifying what he expected the Soviets to give up in return. This resulted in our agreeing to the testing of Soviet heavy ICBMs while not receiving a corresponding Soviet concession. Bush's apparent willingness to sacrifice long-held and important U.S. positions is seen by his critics as further evidence that Bush lacks conviction.

The fact is that Bush is a man without a plan. He is not an architect who conceives of a long-range strategy; he is a problem-solver who slowly and deliberately collects facts, gets advice from a variety of sources, and carefully weighs the options. He makes decisions only when forced to, cautiously moving from one crisis to the next. He is a tinkerer who looks for pragmatic, near-term solutions rather than integrating elements into a grand design. He prefers to let the outcome of one problem carry him over into the next that comes his way.

Dan Murphy, a retired admiral who was Vice President Bush's first chief of staff, later compared Bush's approach to his job as president to the way a ship captain operates:

> The captain on the bridge of a ship isn't up there creating a strategy. He's already got the strategy when he's at sea. When he's out there running things, he's not worrying about novel ideas or some new initiative. He'll do that when he gets his job done.

Murphy apparently assumed that the president's main job is steering the ship. In fact, an effective president has to hold down two jobs simultaneously. In addition to running the ship of state, he must determine where it is headed. It is a task that needs to be dealt with before the president heads out to sea. In modern management terms, Bush prefers to be the chief operating officer (COO) rather than the chief executive officer (CEO). But the people who elect a president expect him to fill both roles.

Bush, however, does have one quality that helps lessen the impact of his lack of long-range strategy. Like Nixon and Reagan, and unlike Carter, he has a good understanding of the role of force in the conduct of foreign affairs. This attribute may have resulted from his having been a combat pilot in World War II and perhaps from his observation of Reagan's experience with the Soviets during the cold war. Although he had to work hard to overcome the stigma of his early "wimp" image, his uncompromising sense of international responsibility has helped him rise to the challenge when the situation called for the use of force. So, while generally indecisive in political action, he is more apt than his predecessors to use military force to reinforce diplomacy and international order. This aspect of his character was evident in Panama and again in his prompt dispatch of troops to the Persian Gulf after Saddam Hussein invaded Kuwait.

Despite his narrowness of strategic vision, there have been times when Bush surprised us by looking ahead, such as the time in early 1989 when he asked the State Department to review U.S. security policy. After four months of intensive study, State Department officials arrived at a half-hearted recommendation that our relations with Moscow should be "status quo plus," without specifying what the "plus" should be. *New York Times* reporter Thomas L. Friedman wrote that for all its labors, the State Department had "produced a mouse." Bush was dissatisfied with State's lack of imagination. He said he wanted something new and creative that would put him one up on Gorbachev, who was gaining much public support for his offers to accelerate the conventional forces in Europe (CFE) process. (CFE was the ongoing set of negotiations that dealt with the reduction of conventional, that is, nonnuclear, forces.)

Gorbachev had offered to unilaterally remove equipment and troops from Eastern Europe. We learned after the fact that Bush dealt with Gorbachev's initiative by convening a small group of advisors, designed to guarantee secrecy and cut the Washington bureaucracy out of the process. The group was made up of chief of staff John Sununu, Brent Scowcroft, James Baker, Dick Cheney, and Adm. William Crowe, chairman of the Joint Chiefs. In less than two weeks, they came up with a scheme for troop reductions that has been variously described as "eye-catching," "dramatic," "radical," and "dazzling." On May 11, shortly before a planned NATO summit, Baker presented the outline of the plan to Gorbachev in Moscow. Gorbachev said he was receptive, giving Bush the green light he was looking for. On May 14, at a White House meeting, Bush asked the same small group to produce a specific proposal that he could present to NATO. Scowcroft recommended a 20 percent cut in U.S. military manpower, while Baker thought that a 25 percent cut would be more appealing. Speaking for the military services, Admiral Crowe said that the chiefs could accept only a 20 percent reduction. Bush then asked Secretary of Defense Dick Cheney if he could live with a 20 percent cut. When Cheney agreed, Bush said, "OK, we have a consensus. Let's go." The proposal was fleshed out by the group and presented to NATO. Those of us who were cut out of the policy loop were surprised at Bush's initiative, especially since the White House had previously told us that the only cuts the United States was willing to make were in weapons and not in manpower.

This action showed, once again, Bush's dissatisfaction with involving the Washington bureaucracy. He prefers to work with a small handful of carefully selected advisors, reflecting his obsession with secrecy.

His visceral hatred of leaks is almost the stuff of legend. For example, Bush had wanted his 1989 decision to hold a summit with Gorbachev at Malta a tightly held secret. Not even Dick Cheney, the secretary of defense, reportedly knew of the plans until they came out in a story by David Hoffman in the *Washington Post*. Bush was enraged and embarked on what was described as a full-scale witch hunt to discover the source of the leak.

While as a negotiator I, too, abhorred leaks, there is a serious drawback to Bush's penchant for working with small groups. It prevents him from receiving differing points of view and offers little opportunity to carefully evaluate opinions that only a larger group of advisors can provide. It also may later reduce support for his decisions from key members of the executive agencies and in the Congress.

Bush's process for arriving at the troop cut proposal demonstrates his love of surprise. Until he has arrived at a decision, Bush likes to keep his own views secret from even his closest advisors. We have seen this trait at work in his surprise choice of Senator Dan Quayle as his running mate. Although predisposed to caution and prudence, Bush likes to occasionally come forth with a bold stroke. At times I felt he did this to counter his public image as a man who is unimaginative, overcautious, and reactive. This is a risky game to play, however, because there is usually little margin for error.

Bush on the whole was restrained and emotionally detached from issues he dealt with. Yet, there were a few times when he seemed to act on the basis of sincere conviction, for example, in his involvement with U.S. policies on chemical and biological weapons (CBW). In 1984 President Reagan decided to give more visibility to CBW by

designating his vice president to attend a Geneva conference on curb-
ing such weapons. While I expected Bush to approach the task seriously, I did not anticipate the passion with which he tackled it. When
he pored over photos of chemical warfare casualties in the Iran-Iraq
War, it caused him to choke with rage and brought tears to his eyes.
"This is bad," he said, "as bad as nuclear war. There must be something we can do to make people realize what devastating weapons
are available to irresponsible leaders in the Third World."

When other Reagan aides and I pointed out to him that a ban on
chemical and biological weapons is virtually unverifiable, he told us
we were timid and unimaginative. He chastised us and charged that
we were treating the matter too casually. Never had I seen him so
worked up over an issue. He prevailed on the Office of Management
and Budget to find money for studying how a chemical and biological
warfare ban could be verified. He told the secretary of state to have
our ambassadors raise the issue at the highest levels, and he personally strengthened the statements that were prepared for his delivery
at the Geneva conference. He seemed a man seized with the mission
of personally ridding the world of weapons he described as "an
affront to humanity." I had to wonder if this was the same man, a
man lacking in passion and conviction, that I had observed so often.
I concluded that this was simply among the exceptions to the rule.

Over the years that I worked with George Bush, I found that he
disliked giving detailed explanations of his policies. When he grasped
a point, which he usually did quite quickly, he assumed that others
understood it too. This unwillingness to explain carefully or to repeat
policy positions was perceived as evidence that he lacked a strong
point of view and was unsure of himself. I am quite certain, however,
that Bush sees himself differently. Joseph C. Whelan of the Library of
Congress put it well when he wrote that Bush's style:

> . . . presumed a special, and unique knowledge and compe-
> tence above that of the common folk, a sort of belief in the
> "divine right" of leadership, a "father knows best" attitude
> that downgrades the popular intelligence in diplomacy but
> endows the patrician elite with a special enlightenment. It is,
> in brief, a style more elitist than populist, more aristocratic
> than democratic. . . .

At the same time, I believe that the president thinks that it is more
important to be a conciliator than an advocate. Ever since his childhood, when he was known as "Have Half" for his insistence on

sharing his toys with his brother, Bush was schooled in the tradition of compromise.

THE COLD WAR THAWS

During the first half of 1989, it became clear that communism was collapsing. The Soviet Union seemed no longer an imposing military threat. The Warsaw Pact was coming unraveled, and the Soviets were, out of political and economic necessity, beginning to remove their troops from central Europe. It seemed the perfect time for Bush to seize the initiative and drive a hard bargain on arms control. Instead, Bush remained impassive; he simply instructed Secretary of State Baker to explore with Foreign Minister Shevardnadze whether progress was possible.

In early autumn 1989, Baker invited Shevardnadze to Jackson Hole, Wyoming, for five days of talks. Like his boss, Baker believed that if he could get his Soviet counterpart away from the conference table and out into the wide open spaces of the American West, he could improve their personal relationship, which in turn would lead to progress on resolving outstanding arms control issues. Secretary Baker invited me to come along and participate in the meetings of the arms control experts. The setting was indeed magnificent, and the weather cooperated nicely by providing several rare warm fall days, which the Soviets call "Grandmother's Summer"—the equivalent of our Indian Summer. It permitted the foreign ministers to hold most of their meetings outdoors.

Baker and Shevardnadze, both in an upbeat mood, reported that good progress was being made. The Soviets dropped their insistence that there be a separate treaty on defense and space, which they had previously linked to completing the START Treaty. The Soviets did, however, build in one of their typical loopholes. Linkage would be dropped, they said, if "both sides would continue to comply with the ABM Treaty as signed in 1972." The Soviets were harking back once again to their insistence on the narrow interpretation of the ABM Treaty. It was their way of putting us on notice that they had no intention of abandoning their policy of stifling U.S. strategic defense developments. Shevardnadze also said the Soviets were willing to conclude an agreement on sea-launched cruise missiles separate from the START Treaty. Here again, however, there was a catch. Shevardnadze said SLCMs could be dealt with in the same manner that the Backfire bomber had been handled in SALT II. He should have known better and realized that this was a nonstarter; we had no intention of seeing another "Backfire solution," which would simply exclude SLCMs from the treaty.

Despite these proposals laden with conditions favorable to the Soviets, Secretary Baker praised what he called "positive developments." It was the standard language diplomats use when they want to put a good face on a poor state of affairs, hoping that the situation will improve if only described in a favorable light. Over the years the United States and Soviet Union had developed an entire lexicon of terms to obfuscate the true character of ongoing negotiations. For example, stating that an *agreement in principle* had been reached usually indicated that no agreement was actually codified. The phrase *frank discussions* usually meant that both sides disagreed sharply and no agreement was possible. A *businesslike exchange* usually signified that there had been a thorough but futile negotiation. In Wyoming, Baker went one step further. He said, "We have, in my view, moved from confrontation to dialogue and now to cooperation." Shevardnadze, delighted with Baker's hyperbole, and not to be outdone, stated, "I will say without any exaggeration, these talks have placed Soviet-American dialogue at a new stage." Both Baker and Shevardnadze had indulged in serious exaggerations.

At the conclusion of the talks, Baker threw a lavish barbecue dinner and presented each member of the Soviet delegation with a red bandanna and a Texas-style hat. Baker did even better by Shevardnadze, giving him a custom-made pair of cowboy boots. Shevardnadze, who had learned in advance that Baker had taken the trouble to find out his measurements and to have the boots made, reciprocated with a highly unusual gift. He gave Baker an antique and obviously valuable icon, saying that he knew Baker was deeply religious. It was an ironic situation; the avowed atheist offering the professed believer a religious gift. Although Shevardnadze was profuse in his thanks for the boots, an astounded Baker was almost speechless and accepted the icon with a simple thank you.

The Soviets thoroughly enjoyed themselves, riding horseback and hiking through the beautiful Wyoming countryside. Some even went to explore the supermarket in downtown Jackson Hole. Ivan Zlotnich, one of the Soviet interpreters, was amazed that "out here in the wilderness" he could find fresh vegetables, fruits, fish and meats, even frozen foods. Interested in taking home souvenirs, he asked a young Wyoming saleslady, "Do you know any Russian?"

"No," she said, "I know only one word—vodka."

"Haven't you ever heard of *perestroika?*" he asked.

"No," she said to the astounded Zlotnich, "I'm a teetotaler."

When I told this story to Senator Malcolm Wallop of Wyoming, he assured me that not everyone in his state knew so little about world politics.

NOT IN THIS CENTURY

In October 1989, while in Bonn having dinner with my friend, Vernon ("Dick") Walters, U.S. ambassador to Germany, he told me that German unification was rapidly approaching. I told Walters he should be careful about what he said, recounting my telephone call from Scowcroft in which he said, "Germany will not be unified in this century."

"I am not surprised," said Walters. He told me that he had urged the State Department to plan for the unification, but he was told that it would not happen for five years. "I told them," said Dick, "that it would happen in more like five months." He told me that he had expressed his views during a background briefing for the press. When reporters asked State Department officials if Walters was stating U.S. policy, he was rebuked. The reporters were told, "Walters is speaking for himself." The events that followed proved Walters's prediction much closer to the target.

Less than a month later, on November 8, 1989, the Berlin Wall came crashing down. For several years, President Reagan had been publicly insisting that the wall should come down and now, suddenly, a huge political plum had fallen into Bush's lap. Soviet troops would soon be leaving the occupied countries of the Warsaw Pact, and the dream of a democratic Eastern Europe would soon become a reality. Bush was able to reap the harvest Reagan had sown. The day the Berlin Wall came down, I recommended to the White House that the president go to Berlin and make an "Ich bin ein Berliner" speech, following up on President Kennedy's speech almost three decades earlier. I said that Bush could stress the coming unification of Germany and be supportive of the independence of Poland, Hungary, and Czechoslovakia.

I was told that the president would not go to Berlin, that in fact he wanted to play down the crumbling of the Berlin Wall because he did not want to appear to provoke Gorbachev or push him into moving more rapidly. I thought it was an opportunity missed. All Europe was awaiting the reaction of the United States. When it finally came, it was overly cautious and restrained, seemingly typical of this president's style.

The most serious threat to U.S. security, escalation of a conventional war in Europe into a U.S.-Soviet nuclear confrontation, was greatly diminished by the crumbling of the Soviet empire. The Soviet Union was rapidly transforming from a menace that had to be contained into a nation on the verge of collapsing under its own weight. But to Bush, the instability that might follow a possible breakup of the Soviet Union posed a greater threat to world peace than the status quo ante.

In the fall of 1989 Hugh Sidey of *Time* magazine reported that President Bush had begun writing notes to Gorbachev on "a routine basis instead of limiting them to times of crisis. The letters contained subtle hints that Bush would stand up publicly for the Kremlin reformer." By late November, several weeks after the Berlin Wall came tumbling down, Bush finally made up his mind what to do. In his Thanksgiving Day television address to the nation, Bush said, "I am reaching out to President Gorbachev, asking him to work with me to bring down the last barriers to a new world of freedom."

Because of the rapidly changing events in Europe, President Bush decided the time was ripe to have his first meeting with President Gorbachev. Like Reagan's first meeting with the Soviet leader in 1985, the summit was to be a "get to know one another" affair, intentionally designed to avoid substantive discussions. At Bush's suggestion, the meeting was held on the island of Malta during the first three days of December 1989. The original idea of meeting in Malta was suggested to Bush by his older brother, William, who was impressed with the island's charms. An international businessman, "Bucky" (William's nickname) had been sent to Malta some months earlier as the president's personal goodwill representative. George Bush thought that holding meetings aboard U.S. and Soviet warships off the island would offer privacy and protection from the throngs of journalists who normally cover such events. Because arms control was not to be addressed in detail, and because space on the U.S. Navy cruiser *Belknap* was limited, those of us advising Bush on arms control were left behind in Washington. We were to stand by the telephone in the event any questions came up. Although Gorbachev raised some arms control issues in Malta, we received no calls.

It was just as well we did not go because foul weather put a large crimp in the planned activities. Malta suffered a storm the likes of which had not been seen in the Mediterranean in a decade. On the opening day of the summit, high seas and sixty-mile-per-hour winds kept Bush from leaving the *Belknap* for his scheduled meeting with Gorbachev on the Soviet warship *Slava*. On the second day, an impatient Bush, literally throwing caution to the winds, took off for a meeting with Gorbachev that had hastily been rescheduled despite the bad weather. The session was to have been held on the Soviet pleasure ship *Maxim Gorky*. By deciding to brave the elements, Bush's critics said, he was trying to live down his lingering wimp image. The admiral's barge in which he made the trip was seen on television bouncing around in the harbor like a cork in a bathtub. After five failed attempts to board the *Maxim Gorky*, Bush made it on the sixth try. He could have saved himself the trouble because Gorbachev had not risked leaving the safety of the *Slava*. Nicholas Brady, Bush's longtime friend and treasury secretary, later recalled a similar incident that had occurred some years earlier on a fishing trip he had taken with the future president off the coast of Florida. Brady wrote: "The damn waves were eight feet high, and everybody else's eyes were as big as saucepans. But it didn't seem to bother Bush at all."

When the two leaders finally got together, Bush immediately moved to bolster Gorbachev's image in the Soviet Union and internationally. Making certain that reporters were within earshot, Bush told Gorbachev: "You are dealing with an administration that wants to see the success of what you are doing.... The world will be a better place if *perestroika* succeeds." Gorbachev replied through his spokesman, Gennadi Gerasimov, that the talks were excellent and that "the cold war is over." This was the first official statement on either side announcing the end of the cold war. To some of Bush's advisors, however, the statement seemed premature and overly optimistic; there were still major trouble spots. Alarmed that the rhetoric overstated the case, John Sununu took steps to dampen the euphoria. He told several reporters, who could be counted on to get the message to the Soviets, that American offers to help *perestroika* could evaporate if the Soviets did not clean up their act in Central America.

Bush intended to stay away from substantive discussions on arms control, but Gorbachev brought up strategic arms (START) and conventional forces in Europe. The discussions on START were desultory and resulted in an acknowledgment from both leaders that no progress had been made; important issues remained unresolved. As for the discussions on conventional forces, the results were better. Bush accepted Gorbachev's suggestion that a twenty-three–nation conference be scheduled in Berlin to clear up the remaining obstacles to a CFE treaty.

Toward the end of the Malta meeting, Baker and Shevardnadze tried for three hours to produce a joint statement on START indicating that some progress had been made. But they got nowhere because, in fact, there had been no progress. In an otherwise gloomy atmosphere, aside from the prospect of progress on CFE, there was another small ray of hope. Some gains had been made in an area close to Bush's heart: chemical weapons. The two leaders pledged to end all CBW production and to destroy most of the existing stocks within a ten-year period. Bush insisted on a hedge, however. The United States would keep 500 tons of chemical weapons until all other countries capable of producing such munitions signed an agreement prohibiting their existence. The idea of maintaining a stockpile did not sit well with critics at home or abroad. Several weeks later, President Bush yielded to the pressure and dropped his insistence that the United States keep a stock of chemical munitions in reserve. Instead, he announced a policy that had a good ring to it as a public relations ploy but was still quite safe. The United States would destroy all chemical stocks if the other chemical-producing nations signed a verifiable treaty banning chemical weapons. It was a safe proposal because it would be some time, if ever, before a verifiable treaty could be worked out.

The two leaders did agree that Baker and Shevardnadze would meet in January 1990 to tackle the three largest stumbling blocks in START: counting rules for air-launched cruise missiles; nondeployed missiles; and missile telemetry encryption. However, the leaders' intentions went unfulfilled; the foreign ministers made no progress at the January meeting. Bush had once again made the mistake of believing that Gorbachev, faced with the collapse of communism in Europe, would rush to conclude a strategic arms agreement. He compounded the mistake by prematurely announcing that START would be initialed at a June summit in 1990. He did not listen to the advice of those of us who had been through the experience of SALT II. In the past, external events had put little or no pressure on the Soviets to soften their approach and expedite arms agreements, and there was little evidence that the Soviets would now change their habits. Setting a deadline once again put pressure on U.S. negotiators to make concessions in order to fulfill raised expectations.

In February 1990, Secretary Baker was planning a visit to Moscow to talk to Shevardnadze about START. I, along with others, had helped prepare briefing papers for the trip and I naturally expected to be included in the party.

The night before the group was to leave Washington, however, my name was not on the roster. Perplexed, I went to see Eagleburger. It turned out he was away on a mission. I tried to see Secretary Baker and was told he was busy. I wrote him a note, asking for clarification about why I was not included on the roster. Although I was assured Baker read my note, he never replied. I did not make the trip.

It was now more clear to me than ever that Baker would negotiate differently from his predecessors. Instead of taking an interagency group to his meetings with the Soviet foreign minister, he relied solely on Bartholomew and his State Department advisors. It did not matter that I had been appointed to advise the secretary of state and the president.

This incident marked the beginning of the end of my job as special advisor to the president and secretary of state. President Bush had turned almost complete control of arms control policy-making over to Secretary of State Baker. This made it increasingly awkward for me to render an independent opinion, since it would amount to second-guessing Secretary Baker. My having been excluded from the trip to Moscow made it obvious that the mantle of arms control had shifted from the imperial president and all his advisors to the imperial secretary of state.

BAKER REACTS TO SAFIRE COLUMN

I saw further evidence of such imperialism when, in May 1990, Secretary Baker summoned me to his office. As I entered, I could see he was visibly upset; his knuckles where white and his hands shook.

"Did you see the Safire column in the *New York Times* this morning?" he asked me.

"Yes," I said. Safire was highly critical of Baker's performance during a recent meeting he had with Shevardnadze about START. He wrote that Baker had "caved in to basic Gorbachev demands all the way down the line."

"I don't like this one damned bit," said Baker. "Did you leak the information to him?"

"No," I said.

"But you know Safire," he said, "and you should be writing op-ed pieces and going on TV talk shows to enhance the administration's image."

"I don't get an opportunity," I replied. "The last six requests I've had from TV shows and the last two op-ed pieces I've written have been killed by your office."

"Is that right?" Baker asked Eagleburger, his deputy, who was in the room with us.

"Yes," he said.

"Then unmuzzle Rowny. Let him get out the administration's view on these matters."

But nothing changed. My subsequent requests to appear on television shows and an op-ed piece I submitted for clearance were all turned down.

FURTHER DEVELOPMENTS

Despite my misgivings about the advisability of another meeting between Bush and Gorbachev, the two got together at a Washington summit held from May 30 to June 3, 1990. As I had predicted in January, the meetings yielded no breakthroughs, and the treaty was not initialed. Determined to make it a significant public relations event, Bush surprised us by announcing steps to increase U.S.-Soviet trade. Before the summit, Bush had wisely announced that he would take no steps to improve trade with the Soviet Union until it passed legislation codifying the right of the Soviet peoples to emigrate freely and until there was a letup of political pressure on the independence-minded Baltic states. In Bush's haste to show support for Gorbachev at the summit, however, he retreated from his earlier conditions. He was now highly anxious to bolster Gorbachev and gave him a concrete bonus to take home to the economically hemorrhaging Soviet Union.

Although Gorbachev was grateful for Bush's help with his domestic problems, he did not reciprocate by being more forthcoming on arms control. In the past, it had been Gorbachev who raised the issue of arms control; this time it was Bush. Gorbachev spurned Bush's advances; moreover, he flatly refused Bush's invitation to visit him at his Kennebunkport, Maine, vacation home. Bush then invited Gorbachev to spend several days at Camp David. The Soviet leader once again demurred and would agree to only a ten-hour session, insisting that he had to get back to Washington to attend to other business. Although it was never made clear what "other business" was more important than meeting with the president of the United States, it may have been that Gorbachev was having difficulties with the politburo and military officials. Whatever the reason, Gorbachev was now playing hard to get.

During my service in the Bush administration, I continued the practice, initiated during the Reagan administration, of briefing Pope John Paul II on the status of arms control. Because a number of Catholic bishops in the United States were opposed to U.S. military policies, I felt it beneficial to let the Pope know the rationale behind our positions.

At my briefing of His Holiness in 1990, I thought that I would try to impress him by speaking in his native language. I had spoken Polish with my grandmother, with whom I lived from the time I was six until I was sixteen. Although I had forgotten most of what I had learned, I thought that with some practice I could get away with the four or five sentences I had memorized. But in the middle of the second or third sentence, I slipped into Russian, which I had studied at Yale and had used during the negotiations in Geneva.

The Pope, feigning anger, stood up and said with a stern voice, *"Et maintenant, mon general, nous parlerons en Anglais"* (And now, general, we shall speak in English). A little later the Pope, knowing of my running battle with the Catholic bishops in America over their call for a nuclear freeze, asked me, "And how, my dear general, are you getting along with your bishops?"

"Holy Father," I said, "I thought they were *your* bishops."

"Bardzo dobrze" (very good), he replied in Polish.

MY DEPARTURE

In early June, after the Washington summit, I felt that my usefulness as an arms control advisor to the president was becoming marginal. Although there had been no clear-cut differences between the president and myself on major issues, it was the way I was required to give my advice to him that was not to my liking. I felt that I was no longer a major player on the president's team and that my views were not being taken sufficiently into account. I was sure the administration wished I would go away, but it probably had not asked me to resign because it would cause trouble among conservatives. I went to seek the advice of John Sununu, at the time the president's chief of staff. He told me he was not surprised how I felt, adding that he marveled that I had served so long under such awkward conditions. He said that Secretary Baker was Bush's principal, and at times only, advisor on arms control and that he overshadowed the other three principal advisors, Brent Scowcroft, Richard Cheney, and Chairman of the Joint Chiefs of Staff Colin Powell. When I asked Sununu if there was some way I could improve my situation, he said he did not think so. I said that under the circumstances I would submit my resignation, effective June 30, 1990. Much to Sununu's relief, I told him that I would not make an issue of my departure or take it to the press. He said it was a wise decision, adding that if I were to indicate that I was resigning in protest over the way I was being treated, the administration would make some token effort to paper things over. But in the long run, he said, nothing would change. On my last day in office, White House press secretary Marlin Fitzwater made a simple announcement that I had resigned. Several reporters asked him questions that he referred to me. When asked if I was resigning in protest or because of major policy differences with the Bush administration, I said only that I thought it was time for me to leave. President Bush's reaction was predictable. He sent me a nice note, thanking me for the "contribution [I had] made to U.S. arms control policies."

FINAL ROUNDS OF START

In the fall of 1990 and in the early months of 1991, President Bush was preoccupied with Operation Desert Storm, and work in Washington on the remaining START issues took a back seat. Shevardnadze had resigned abruptly on December 15, 1990, and was replaced as foreign minister by Alexandr Bessmertnykh, the Soviet ambassador to the United States. All of Baker's careful nurturing of Shevardnadze had been for naught. Baker should have known better; our relationship with the Soviet Union, or with any country for that matter, is not primarily determined by personal rapport between high-level officials. It should be more a function of basic national interests.

President Bush had scheduled a summit with Gorbachev for early January 1991. Although I was no longer a part of the administration, I let several of my friends close to the president know that I thought a meeting at that time was not a good idea. The Soviet Union had used force in seeking to crush the independence movements in Lithuania and Latvia, and I believed that Bush should show his disapproval by not meeting with Gorbachev. The president did, in fact, cancel the meeting, but the reason he gave was that he was too busy dealing with the Gulf War crisis. While I was pleased that Bush did not meet with Gorbachev, I thought he had sent the wrong message to Gorbachev and the international community.

Several days later, the Soviet Union tried to get a piece of the action in the Gulf War through some political maneuvering. Although the Soviets had committed no forces to the effort, they attempted to convene a meeting in which they would play a major role as intermediaries between Iraq and the allied coalition. President Bush, having read their intentions correctly, deftly and firmly thwarted their efforts. By refusing to pay much attention to the demands of the Soviets, the president was able to keep them on the sidelines. It was a diplomatic triumph.

Following the cessation of hostilities, the administration floated a trial balloon. Marlin Fitzwater said that Bush would be willing to meet with Gorbachev at a summit, whether or not a START treaty was ready for signature. The idea of holding summits as a matter of routine, regardless of progress on arms control, was a policy I had consistently favored. In my opinion, it was better not to tie summits to expectations of success in negotiations because the Soviets invariably used these heightened expectations of reaching agreement as a way of extracting concessions. However, leaders of the inside-the-beltway arms control community felt differently and immediately told the media that Bush should make completion of START a precondition for the summit. Within hours after his original statement, Fitzwater changed his tune and said that the president preferred to go to a summit when START was ready for signature. The next morning, reporters asked Bush which of his spokesman's statements they should believe. "Both of Fitzwater's statements are correct," Bush said.

Later in the spring of 1991, the president made several statements assuring the public that the outstanding, unresolved START issues were "merely technical." In fact, the remaining issues were clearly substantive; they concerned such matters as inspection of "suspect sites" and how to define new types of missiles. The president's statements raised the question of whether he was being adequately briefed on the critical differences between U.S. and Soviet negotiating positions.

By mid-June 1991, Washington was rife with rumors of an impending summit. But acting chief START negotiator Linton Brooks reported that there were approximately sixty issues—most minor, but some major—still awaiting resolution.

In early July, several days prior to the opening of the G-7 economic summit in London, President Bush wrote to Gorbachev asking that he send a high-level representative to Washington empowered to make final decisions on the remaining START issues. To the utter dismay of our negotiating team in Geneva, Bush telegraphed to Gorbachev that he wanted to wrap up START in a hurry and reportedly provided Gorbachev with the U.S. "bottom line" on each of the major issues. Gorbachev sent Foreign Minister Bessmertnykh to meet with Secretary Baker. Under the circumstances, it is not surprising that when Bush left for London all but one of the issues had been resolved. The remaining stumbling block concerned how to define new types of missiles. The Soviets were apparently ready to agree, but were obviously playing to the public galleries in order to build suspense and highlight the summit. At the last minute, during a luncheon following the G-7 meetings, Bush and Gorbachev agreed to a "new types" definition. The two leaders declared that the last obstacle to START had been overcome and that the treaty would be signed at a Moscow summit held from July 29–31, 1991.

The START agreement was signed in Moscow on July 31. It received relatively little attention in the media, since most press and television coverage centered on Gorbachev's attempts to build political support for his economic agenda. During the press conference following the signing of the START Treaty, President Bush characterized the agreement as the first of its kind because it called for an actual reduction of strategic arms. Gorbachev also praised the treaty but cautioned that it would encounter difficulties in the ratification process. Within twenty-four hours after its signing, the START story dropped off the front pages of most newspapers. Several editorial writers praised the agreement for reducing weapons. As usual, others felt that so many nuclear weapons still remained in the arsenals of both sides that the treaty was of little significance.

BUSH'S BOLT FROM THE BLUE

Less than two months after the signing of START, Bush sprang another of his surprises. On September 28, 1991, he took to television to announce that events in the Soviet Union had reduced the threat to U.S. security and went on to outline one unilateral arms control initiative after another. He took American B-52 and B-1 bombers and our force of 450 Minuteman II missiles off strategic alert. He said that he intended to remove from Europe—and destroy—all nuclear artillery shells and nuclear-armed short-range ballistic missiles. He also promised to remove and place in storage 50 percent of the tactical nuclear weapons, including nuclear-armed cruise missiles, from U.S. surface ships and attack submarines. He cancelled the development of U.S. land-based mobile missiles and offered to scrap U.S. land-based MIRVed systems if Gorbachev would follow suit.

Bush's speech was immediately hailed by world leaders as a "bold and imaginative initiative." U.S. lawmakers on both sides of the aisle quickly joined in indicating approval.

The next day Gorbachev responded. He said that although his initial reaction was positive, he needed time to examine Bush's proposals more closely before he could embrace them outright. Yet, in the next breath, he reminded the world that he was still a shrewd negotiator. He called on the United States to give up nuclear testing and said that any significant reduction in Soviet land-based MIRVed missiles would have to be reciprocated by a corresponding reduction in U.S. sea-based MIRVed systems (SLBMs).

The president's initiative was a repetition of the style of his May 1991 proposal to withdraw U.S. weapons and troops from Europe. As then, Bush maintained the strictest secrecy and consulted only a few of his key advisors. His love of surprise and penchant for drama disarmed potential detractors and drew attention away from the substance of the proposal. The key question remained: could the plan survive substantive review? At any rate, the manner in which it had been put forth sacrificed critical bargaining leverage by preemptively divulging our intentions.

Scarcely a week later, Gorbachev delivered his formal reply. In a tersely worded statement, he went Bush one better. Instead of reducing stocks of strategic warheads to 6,000 weapons, as called for in the proposed START Treaty, he would reduce the Soviet force to 5,000. But, as always, there was a catch. The United States would have to liquidate its nuclear weapons from forward-based tactical aviation units—our insurance policy for European security.

The moves and countermoves went well beyond the provisions of the START treaty and diminished its importance considerably. But in late November 1991, the Bush administration submitted the treaty to the Senate, where, as of this writing, its fate remains uncertain. Among other reasons, several key senators feel that START has been overtaken by the swirl of events. After all, the treaty was signed by the president of a now-nonexistent government and is supposed to apply to Soviet weapons now in dispute and divided among four new nation-states.

Throughout his administration, Bush made a conscious decision to tie Gorbachev's political star closely to his own by emphasizing their close personal relationship. I tried to advise that this was a mistake. It tended to cast Bush in the role of defender of the status quo rather than as a leading advocate of freedom; it also made U.S. initiatives dependent upon the fate of Gorbachev.

In an effort to alter this perception, Bush traveled to the Ukraine on August 1, 1991, to make his case before the republic's parliament. But his presentation only made matters worse. In his speech before the Ukrainian legislature in Kiev, Bush cautioned the Ukrainians against "those who seek independence in order to replace a far-off tyranny with a local despotism." The obvious and odious implication was that continued association with Gorbachev was preferable to the republic's calls for independence. It led many independence-minded Ukrainians (as well as many in the West) to question Bush's understanding of developments and his commitment to true democratic reform in the Soviet Union. Just before the Ukrainian vote on independence in late November of 1991, Bush shifted gears and said he would move expeditiously to recognize Ukrainian independence. When the people of Ukraine went on to vote for independence by a 9 to 1 margin, Bush's eleventh-hour conversion seemed pitifully late.

By the end of 1991, after the unsuccessful coup against Gorbachev in August, the Soviet Union had disintegrated and was reincarnated as the Commonwealth of Independent States (CIS). Moreover, the Communist party had ceased to exist in the land where Lenin once reigned. Gorbachev, in whom George Bush had invested so much, was unceremoniously removed from power.

Bush's over-reliance on Gorbachev as the sole individual capable of leading the Soviet Union into the twenty-first century defied logic and demonstrated bad advice and misunderstanding of political developments in the Soviet Union. Bush's emphasis on personal diplomacy obscured what is at the root of the political transformation in the former Soviet Union—the people. The Soviet populace had to bear the brunt of seventy-five years of corrupt and misguided rule. They alone had the capacity to turn the tide toward a more rewarding and enduring democratic future. While a capable, charismatic, and devoted leader can play a significant role in promoting democratic change, it would have been wiser to put more faith in the power of the idea of freedom. In the end, it was the people who showed through their actions that they were capable of making a difference.

Today, no one believes that the CIS has a future. In the spring of

1992, it appears to be a mechanism to carry out the dissolution of the former Soviet Union, after which the CIS may well disappear. In early June 1992, Presidents Bush and Yeltsin achieved a momentous breakthrough in strategic arms reductions. Over the next decade, strategic weapons will be reduced to 3,500 to 4,000. More significantly, the two sides agreed to eliminate all land-based MIRVed missiles. These are great achievements. Still, so long as the Russian Republic possesses a stockpile of nuclear weapons capable of devastating the United States, we cannot afford to be complacent. Prudence demands that we pursue policies that enhance internal, and ensure international, stability.

But faced with domestic economic problems and demands on his time and energies in an election year, President Bush will find it difficult to stay abreast of and to deal with U.S. policies relating to the rapidly changing scene in the former Soviet Union. This is ironic, indeed, for a man whose first love is foreign affairs.

BUSH'S FUTURE

As President Bush winds up his first term in office, it is not certain that he will be a two-term president. The problem seems to be the complexities and contradictions of his character. He has high principles that were ingrained in him during childhood; he believes it is his duty to serve the people. Yet, his beliefs do not appear to go much beyond that. Uncomfortable when dealing with domestic affairs, he seems unable to lead the nation when for the first time in decades its biggest problems are domestic and not foreign. Even in foreign affairs, the arena of his greatest interest, he lacks a strategic sense and has no clear concept of what a "new world order" should be. Nor does he stimulate his advisors to help him define "this vision thing." He chooses instead to rely on a few close advisors to generate the limited ideas that eventually form the basis of his policies. Except when there is an international crisis, he often appears ambivalent or overly cautious when events might be helped by prompt action. Aside from his broad commitment to democracy, he has no strong ideological convictions, relying on predominantly ethical norms to guide him in decision making. Yet, ultimately he finds almost everything negotiable within certain ill-defined parameters. His bottom line is rarely delineated. As *New York Times* columnist James Reston pointed out:

He always seems to win "great victories" and then wonders what, if anything, he got out of them. He invaded Panama and got Manuel Noriega, and now he doesn't know what to do with him. He . . . [got] Saddam Hussein, [but] that scoundrel is still presiding over the wreckage of Iraq, including its nuclear institutions.

President Bush's lack of convictions was evident not only in his dealings with the Soviet Union on arms control but in his policy toward China, where his stated goals did not square with his actions. While professing to support freedom and democracy, he also renewed China's most favored nation status. This did not mean that he approved of the Tiananmen Square massacre or the subsequent crackdown on dissidents, but it showed, once again, that he is a man who is willing to sacrifice long-term objectives for short-range political expediency.

I believe that George Bush is governed by a constant inner struggle between what he believes is good in the long run and what he perceives is best at a given moment. Sometimes, because of the circumstances of his birth and upbringing, he behaves like an idealist. At other times, because of his experience in the school of political hard knocks, he behaves like a realist. On the one hand, he often seems to feel that it is enough simply to espouse a set of generalized high ideals. He believes that being in favor of such ideals and occasionally expounding them with a rhetorical flourish is all that is required of the leader of a country blessed with an abundance of natural resources and strong democratic institutions. On the other hand, because he lacks depth and conviction, he usually reacts to events in ways that suggest he has the instincts of a realist who thinks in short-range terms. President Bush's contradictory idealistic beliefs and realistic actions are nowhere more clearly evident than in his process of governing and his method of running for office. These contradictions have left Americans wondering who George Bush really is and what it is he believes in. I have to admit that despite more than ten years of dealing with him, I am left wondering, too.

CHAPTER 8

Negotiating in a Changing World

I believe that this book demonstrates that in arms control negotiations with the former Soviet Union, U.S. representatives in general, and our presidents in particular, performed poorly. Yet, despite our negotiating failures, the U.S. policy of containment, backed by a strong military posture and our nuclear deterrent, prevented the Soviet Union from furthering its historical expansionist goals. The U.S. policy of "peace through strength," particularly during the Reagan years, bought the time needed for the Soviet Union to collapse under its own weight. Because of our military strength, the Soviets were unable to take advantage of our shortcomings in negotiating, sparing us the consequences of our own incompetence at the bargaining table. The sad fact is that our political leaders and their designated representatives, despite decades of experience, learned little about how to negotiate successfully with the leaders of the Soviet Union.

For more than forty years, the primary focus of world politics was the bipolar relationship between the United States and the Soviet Union. During this time, many nations willingly conceded American primacy in world affairs as a logical extension of our nuclear umbrella. Now, anxiety over the possibility of nuclear war has in large measure been superseded by more pressing political and economic matters in an increasingly multipolar world. No longer is the threat of superpower nuclear confrontation the glue that binds the Western alliance together. The end of the cold war and the fracturing of the Soviet Union make it imperative that the United States redefine its international priorities.

Our negotiators must learn to operate in a more complex and competitive world arena. In this emerging world, negotiations will become more, not less, important. It is crucial that we learn to bargain better than we did during the years of superpower arms negotiations.

A NEW POLITICAL WORLD

The emerging world is far different from any that could have been imagined only a few years ago. Once asked what the chances were that the Soviet Union would forsake communism, Nikita Khrushchev quipped, "Those who wait for that must wait until a shrimp learns to whistle." On November 6, 1991, on the eve of the 74th anniversary of the Bolshevik Revolution and only a few months after the abortive August coup sealed the fate of the former Soviet Union, Boris Yeltsin signed an edict banning the activities of the Communist Party of the Soviet Union (CPSU) in the Russian Federation. The shrimp had learned to whistle, and the world had reached a profound turning point.

For decades, the struggle between East and West not only formed the basis of U.S. military, foreign, and economic policy, but it also had become woven into the very fabric of our daily life. Schoolchildren were once drilled on safety procedures in the event of nuclear attack; thousands of American lives were lost in battle with Soviet proxies, and trillions of tax dollars were spent containing the aggressive Soviet Union. The cold war was the lens through which the United States and the industrialized democracies viewed the world.

Mikhail Gorbachev's rise to power and his six-year reign at the head of the Soviet Union began to soften the contours of that struggle. His policies of *glasnost* and *perestroika* were the building blocks of his vision of a more modern and dynamic Soviet Union. He sought to turn his people inward so that they could examine and conquer the corruption and rot created by the excesses of his predecessors. But

Gorbachev failed to realize that the cure for his country's ills was a remedy that would kill the party. When reality finally confronted a flawed political ideology that had long since lost its relevance to the people of the Soviet Union, there could be only one outcome.

In November 1989, when the most powerful icon of political repression, the Berlin Wall, fell, it set in motion independence movements in Eastern and Central Europe. For all intents and purposes, the contest was over; the American policy of peace through strength had been vindicated. Few at the time understood that this event marked the beginning of the end of the Soviet Union itself. The world, it seemed, had become accustomed to the notion of a superpower nuclear stalemate. The idea that two short years later the Soviet Union would no longer exist was then as unthinkable as it is now self-evident.

It was generally believed at the time that the ideological struggle between East and West might be tempered, but that it would remain a fixture of global politics. George Bush unwittingly alluded to this belief when, in announcing the formation of an international coalition to challenge the Iraqi invasion of Kuwait, he resurrected the Wilsonian concept of a "new world order." The president's new world order was, however, based on decidedly old assumptions. His basic hypothesis was that the Soviet Union would survive in some modified, albeit less bellicose, form. The superpowers would then act in concert and lead the world toward a more enlightened and peaceful future. Bush gave little thought to the possibility that there soon would be only one superpower, and that the term itself would require redefinition. But almost in the blink of an eye the cold war came to a close, signaling the end of the superpower era and the end of U.S.-Soviet relations as the central focus of world affairs.

Still, the sudden transformation of the Soviet Union into the Commonwealth of Independent States and independent sovereign republics marks only a first step toward solving the problems of the former Soviet Union. More than seven decades of Communist authoritarian rule has taken a toll on the region's political, economic, and spiritual well-being. The move toward political freedom has also given new life to centuries-old ethnic, religious, and nationalist antagonisms that were repressed during the era of centralized Soviet rule. Democracy and economic reform—the captivating promises of the new leaders—are proving complicated and elusive.

The possibility that this brave new political experiment will degenerate into a Yugoslavia-like civil war is an ever-present concern.

Violence is a common by-product of political and economic turmoil. The United States must now develop short- and long-term strategies for dealing with the region's changing political landscape while remaining conscious of the fact that we cannot do for others what they are unprepared to do for themselves.

It is essential that the primary goal of U.S. policy be to help codify the changes in political structure currently taking place in the former Soviet Union. Contrary to President Bush's initial response to the decline of the Soviet Union, our best interests are not served by encouraging political and economic control based on domination by the Russian Federation. We must be acutely aware of the centrifugal forces at work on the various republics and careful not to show blind preference for Yeltsin's Russian Federation at the expense of other independence-minded republics. The future stability of the region depends on both political and economic development and a diffusion of power. As Henry Kissinger has pointed out, it would be in America's interest for a confederation to emerge that is strong enough to ensure the security of its people but not cohesive enough to initiate aggression.

The most worrisome and difficult problem to be worked out concerns the control of the region's strategic nuclear arsenal. Although these weapons are ostensibly under the joint control of Boris Yeltsin and the leaders of the other three states possessing strategic weapons—Kazakhstan, Belarus, and Ukraine—Yeltsin is in sole possession of the codes that would permit the weapons to be launched. Still we are far from certain that procedures and control arrangements will be worked out to provide for maximum restraints on the possible use of the nuclear weapons. It will be some time before all strategic weapons located outside the Russian Federation are destroyed or turned over to Yeltsin's control.

Additional problems exist because of the region's remaining oversized conventional military forces. Although some of the former Soviet republics have asked to become members of NATO, and organizations like the Conference on Security and Cooperation in Europe remain in place, it is not clear whether these institutions are capable of dealing with the domestic and international threat posed by the existence of the large military forces in the former Soviet Union. One possibility for mitigating this potential threat would be for the U.S. military establishment to apply its managerial and logistical assistance to the task of reducing the region's armed forces in a coherent fashion. Our experience in developing and maintaining an all-volunteer force, national guard, and reserve components could be of great value to the republics coping with this issue. However, we should be under no illusions; this is not a problem that will be easily resolved. Few matters are more sensitive or more apt to collide with stubborn nationalist sentiments than the transformation of a country's traditional national security structure. Such efforts will require greatly enhanced communication and mutual confidence. And this can occur only through more imaginative and intense negotiations.

The fragmentation of the former Soviet Union also complicates the nuclear proliferation problem. Numerous press reports have indicated that not only are former Soviet nuclear scientists "for sale," so are nuclear materials. Indications are that Boris Yeltsin and the other republic leaders are intent upon preventing the dispersal of the former Soviet Union's nuclear stockpile. But with approximately 27,000 nuclear weapons of all types spread out over almost 9,000 square miles, the possible loss or illegal diversion of some of these weapons cannot be dismissed. A determined and comprehensive effort must be launched to identify, locate, and destroy these weapons before they fall into the wrong hands. It is, of course, impossible to put the nuclear genie back into the bottle, but it is clearly in the interest of the United States and the states of the former Soviet Union to work together to prevent nuclear proliferation.

This possible proliferation of nuclear weapons is one of the most important foreign policy problems facing the United States. The possession of weapons of mass destruction by nonnuclear nations has been a constant U.S. concern since the power of the atom was revealed. Two decades ago experts predicted that twenty-five to thirty nations would possess nuclear weapons by 1990. Fortunately, that prediction proved to be too high. Today, five nations possess nuclear weapons and five more nations are generally believed to have them. Recent estimates from the CIA, however, indicate that approximately twenty countries have or are in the process of developing nuclear weapons. Holding down the number of nations possessing these weapons presents a daunting challenge to U.S. policymakers and negotiators.

A similar challenge confronts U.S. officials in their efforts to curb the worldwide acquisition of chemical and biological weapons. These "poor man's atomic weapons" can today be produced by any nation possessing a pharmaceutical industry. At last count, more than seventy countries had the capability of manufacturing chemical and biological arms. In the late 1980s, President Bush spearheaded an effort to ban such weapons by offering to destroy the entire U.S. stock of these arms, but there is a major obstacle. The same technologies used to make such weapons are critical to nations intent upon improving their standard of living. Moreover, an international ban on CBW weapons would be virtually impossible to verify. Despite these difficulties, it would be unconscionable for the United States not to strive to limit, if not prevent, their spread.

No less important and equally complicated is the need to prevent the spread of the development and production of medium-range ballistic missiles. To appreciate why this is crucial, one need only recall the shock the world felt when Saddam Hussein launched crude but terrifying SCUD missiles at Israel and Saudi Arabia during the 1991 Persian Gulf war. Already, China, North Korea, and others produce ballistic missiles for sale on the international arms market. While keeping track of these transactions poses formidable intelligence challenges, there is yet another complication. The technology employed in building ballistic missiles also has legitimate civilian applications, such as the development of weather and communications satellites. Negotiating agreements among the United States, its allies, and the republics of the former Soviet Union to limit, or at least to monitor, the spread of these technologies should have a high priority.

Negotiations will also be required for dealing with the rekindled ethnic and nationalist hostilities in the Third World, which were largely kept in check by the cold war. The fear of nuclear escalation encouraged the superpowers to defuse regional crises before they reached critical mass. With the end of the bipolar superpower confrontation, irredentism and violent nationalism will in all likelihood sharply increase. Saddam Hussein's attack on Kuwait is an example. The overwhelming emphasis placed on U.S.-Soviet bilateral relations over the past forty years has left us ill-equipped to deal with the diplomatic challenges presented by a widespread and diverse array of smoldering antagonisms.

The end of the cold war and the persistence of serious domestic economic problems have led some in the United States to call for an American retreat from the international scene. We should concentrate on solving America's problems, they argue, and leave the countries of the world to their own devices. Let our allies and our friends pay for the peace that we have maintained for the past forty years. This view is both short-sighted and self-defeating. Economic considerations do demand that America not act with the same international largesse as in the past, but isolationism is not the answer. As Operation Desert Storm clearly showed, the United States is the only country capable of marshaling the political, economic, and military resources needed for selective actions to counter challenges to collective security and economic health. We should remain aware that future regional conflicts may demand U.S. intervention and that we must maintain adequate force levels and the capability to project our military power where needed. To retreat at a time we are the premier world power would be as wrong as it is irresponsible.

A NEW ECONOMIC WORLD

While political changes are reshaping the globe, the world is changing even more dramatically in the realm of economics. The rapid growth of instantaneous communication brought about by the revolution in satellite and computer technologies has made the planet a smaller place. Data and ideas now travel the globe in ways only dreamed of ten years ago. No spot on earth is more than twenty-four flying hours away by jet, and that time may eventually be cut in half. The development of mammoth tankers and container ships has greatly reduced transportation costs and increased the speed with which raw materials, fuel, and manufactured products are transported around the world. These commodities are moved rapidly and economically to places where cheap labor turns them into finished products for world consumption. The world is becoming a single interdependent marketplace.

At the very time that the remnants of the Soviet empire are rediscovering a sense of nationalism, Europe is on the brink of making national boundaries a thing of the past. By tearing down regional barriers to trade, the European Community is on the verge of fundamentally altering traditional concepts of international commerce and free trade. Changes are also occurring in Asia. Even Japan—a nation whose culture has placed a higher priority on the need for order than on the benefits of a disorderly, unfettered marketplace—is reluctantly but unmistakably bowing to the new economic dynamism of a world trading system. The Japanese are beginning to understand that they must import as well as export finished products.

These developments pose serious challenges to American economic competitiveness. They also underscore the point that the end of the superpower era means the end to traditional concepts of national strength. No longer is military might the primary determinant of power. The future will be dominated by those countries that find the proper balance between economic vitality and political and social cohesion. The United States must deal with this shift both at home and abroad. We must carefully devise negotiation strategies and develop negotiators who can operate successfully in this new economic world.

While the ten guidelines that I devised for negotiating with the Soviet Union will likely remain useful for negotiations with the newly independent republics of the former Soviet Union, in dealings with other countries, some of these guidelines will be more useful than others. The degree of their applicability will depend on the culture and the value systems of the diverse nations with which we will be negotiating. Still, the three most important rules will continue to apply to all negotiations to which the United States is a party: the need to have clear-cut objectives, to exhibit patience, and to maintain confidentiality during negotiations.

In dealing with the Soviet Union on arms control, there were many examples of the failure of our presidents to establish clear-cut objectives. For example, President Nixon set as a goal the conclusion of a SALT Treaty. Yet, he repeatedly linked that goal to another objective: winding up the Vietnam War. President Reagan adopted objectives that emphasized the reduction of destabilizing weapons. Yet Reagan lost sight of his objectives and substituted for them his "dream" of ridding the world entirely of nuclear weapons, a desire that, fortunately, was thwarted by the turn of events at Reykjavík.

In negotiating solutions to political problems, it is often necessary to think in terms of both short- and long-range objectives simultaneously. For example, in the case of an international border dispute, the immediate objective is to negotiate an alleviation of tensions so as to prevent the violent escalation of the crisis into full-blown conflict. Once that short-range objective has been met, the parties can then turn to the more difficult and longer-range goal of resolving the underlying political issues that precipitated the crisis in the first place.

The same is true in negotiations on international economic matters, although it is often hard to develop and maintain a balance of short- and long-range objectives. For example, the primary short-term objective of American companies seems to be to maximize quarterly shareholder profits, but that goal is often at odds with the long-term goal of developing products that will keep a company ahead of its competitors. It is certainly at odds with the collective economic goal of the U.S. government to maintain and expand the nation's economy by encouraging corporations to reinvest their prof-

its for future payoffs and to provide jobs. When engaging in international economic negotiations, the private and public sectors must
work together to reconcile their conflicts and establish mutual and
unambiguous objectives.

The difficulties of squaring short- and long-term objectives were
nowhere more evident than in President Bush's visit to Japan in
January 1992. His initial announced objective was the long-term
goal of reducing trade barriers and promoting free trade. Yet by
taking twenty-one top U.S. industrialists with him, including the
leaders of the three largest U.S. auto manufacturing companies, President Bush shifted his emphasis to the short-run objective of "jobs,
jobs, and jobs" for Americans during a recession. The end result was
confusion verging on political disaster for the president.

Impatience is another distinctly American trait that often prevents
the United States from achieving long-range international objectives.
Energized by the pioneering spirit of our ancestors, we are taught from
an early age that no obstacle is too great if we but apply American
ingenuity and hard work. We are dedicated problem-solvers who will
stop at nothing to accomplish the task at hand. If forward movement
in a negotiation falls victim to the intransigence of our partners, we
become frustrated and tend to lose sight of why we came to the table
in the first place. Counting on our impatience, the Soviets placed obstacles in our path, causing us to grant them one concession after another. Apprehensive that we might be denied the satisfaction of
"making a deal" and fearful that we might be held responsible for the
failure to reach an agreement, we lost sight of our objectives and conceded too much. The result was a SALT II Treaty that the U.S. Senate,
fortunately, would not approve. Unlike negotiators from other cultures, our deal-makers tended to view the process in terms of days and
weeks, not months, years, or even decades. It is essential that future
American negotiators realize that there is a direct relationship between
practicing patience and achieving long-term objectives.

Secrecy is a key ingredient in any successful negotiation. By nature,
Americans have a hard time keeping secrets. We tend to be open and
frank and, as a consequence of our history, culture, and form of
government, are generally uncomfortable with secrecy. But no single
development can more seriously disrupt an ongoing negotiation than
the premature exposure of one's bottom line. Perhaps the most egregious example of this American shortcoming was Secretary Vance's
presenting the Soviets with both our fallback position and our comprehensive proposal in March 1977. It was the beginning of a steady

stream of U.S. concessions that resulted in a SALT II Treaty that had to be withdrawn from Senate consideration.

Disregard for the importance of confidentiality in negotiating puts us at a decided disadvantage. This is not to suggest that we should give up our cherished values of honesty, openness, and candor. What it does suggest is that American negotiators must recognize the disadvantages of being too open and that skillful negotiators can achieve their goals without sacrificing their values. Oftentimes, a judicious silence is the best policy.

THE IMPORTANCE OF CULTURAL DIFFERENCES

While the three rules of having objectives, practicing patience, and maintaining secrecy apply universally, my other rules for dealing with the Soviets need to be modified for use in different situations. Whatever modifications are made must, above all, take into account the cultural sensitivities of those on the other side of the table. Asians, for example, are especially protective of their ancient culture and resent what they regard as the encroachment of Western values on their unique societal norms. The lingering effects of Western colonialism can have unexpected ramifications for American negotiators. The Chinese, for example, often expect special treatment from Westerners as natural compensation for nineteenth-century political and economic exploitation. They have learned that inculcating guilt among Westerners can be a powerful tool for exacting concessions. Multinational corporations are particularly vulnerable to this tactic inasmuch as anticolonial sentiments in most of the developing world are directly linked to generally accepted notions of past economic abuse. To be successful, Western negotiators must not feel bound to pay for the mistakes of their forefathers.

Between the time I left the military and joined the Reagan administration, I went to work for an international consulting firm and experienced firsthand the impact a society's cultural traits and values can have on negotiations. My job was to explore for a U.S. airline the possibility of extending flight operations to Seoul and Moscow. I decided to go first to Moscow. True to form, the Soviets took several weeks to work out appointments with government officials. When I arrived in Moscow I was met by an Intourist guide who told me that my first appointment had been cancelled and would not take place for two days. That was only the beginning of my troubles. In our first conversations, the Soviets made it clear that they would brook no competition with their national airline Aeroflot. Passengers wishing to purchase tickets on a U.S. airline would have to go to the second floor of the Russia Hotel, an establishment that restricted the access of ordinary Russian citizens. Further, the Soviets would only allow ticketing on a U.S. carrier if all seats on Aeroflot flights on that day were sold. Finally, they specified that all tickets had to be purchased in hard currency. The prospects for working out a deal were, to say the least, not very promising.

In contrast, it took me less than a week to line up appointments in Seoul. I was met at the airport by a deputy minister of trade and put up in a first-class hotel at their expense. The Koreans had done extensive research into my background and treated me as as war hero because I was one of the planners of the Inchon invasion. That evening my hosts wined and dined me, avoiding any discussion of business. The next three days were spent on the golf course, with more lavish entertainment every evening. At no time was business brought up. After a brief discussion on the fourth day, my hosts surprised me by saying that they were amenable to allowing my client's planes to land in Seoul. The details, they said, could be worked out later.

Although my client decided not to go ahead with either location, the episode stayed in my mind. Clearly, the Koreans and Soviets had completely different approaches to negotiating. The Korean emphasis was not on dictating terms or ironing out specific details of a contract but on developing a good relationship. They felt that if we could work together toward similar goals the details were secondary. The Koreans, accordingly, had spent most of the time trying to discover whether a partnership was a realistic possibility.

While trust and goodwill were of little importance to the Soviets, they are crucial elements in dealing with much of the rest of the world. In Western Europe, trust and goodwill are valued as highly as they are in America. In Asia, they take on an even greater importance. As a consequence, the first step in negotiating with Asians is to explore whether a personal relationship can be expected.

The Japanese, for example, embark immediately on an extensive program of entertaining their counterparts. I once asked a Japanese friend how he justified the expense of such lavish entertainment. He told me that the Japanese do not pay their executives as much as we do. Furthermore, the Japanese entertainment budget is no larger than our legal budget. Besides, he said, they get more fun from what they pay for than do we. During this entertainment phase, in trying to get to know their opposite numbers, the Japanese resort to asking disarming questions. They are not looking for specific information; they use this approach to broaden the discussion in order to learn in roundabout ways their negotiating partner's views and the degree of conviction with which they are held.

Simultaneously, the Japanese begin the process of seeking a consensus. This search takes place at two levels, one among themselves and the other between themselves and their negotiating partners. Their internal process is very different from ours. In the United States, we have hierarchical structures in which decisions flow from the top down. But the typical Japanese corporation or ministry generates unity through a process known as *ringi*. In this process, memorandums are circulated and discussions are held concurrently at several levels. The Japanese attempt to arrive at a solution that takes into account all points of view and meets the diverse needs of the group. While the process is lengthy, it provides the Japanese with a unifying device that fits their culture and value system. During the time they are engaged in this process we must be extremely patient; signs of impatience can seriously disrupt negotiations. By the time the Japanese reach a consensus among themselves, they will have decided whether they should continue the negotiations.

If the Japanese determine that they will be unable to reach an understanding with us, they usually signal their displeasure in some face-saving manner, often only dropping subtle hints to indicate how they feel. Instead of openly arguing, they resort to obliquely suggesting an alternative course of action. Or they may simply fall silent for long periods of time, hoping that we will notice that they are reluctant to proceed.

Developing a relationship involves more than determining whether a negotiating partner can be trusted. The concept of trust is a complicated and elusive one, which often hinges on the belief that the trusted person will behave in the manner we expect. But the patterns of thinking, especially in Asia, are fundamentally different from our own. Accordingly, when dealing with Asians, Americans must not jump to the conclusion that stylistic differences mean that we cannot trust them. We must try to understand these cultural differences, even though they are so numerous and hard to fathom that even long and close study will not explain them all. An American negotiator must, therefore, approach his task with a basic attitude that in addition to trying to understand his counterpart, he must be sensitive, flexible, and patient.

The strong desire among Asians, and especially the Japanese, to avoid the appearance of disagreeing often causes them to send signals that inexperienced American negotiators find contradictory. American negotiators should be careful when they hear the Japanese say *"hai,"* which literally means "yes." It is also the rough equivalent of our "go on" or "I hear you." Thus, *"hai"* is often used simply as a conversation marker by Japanese to indicate that they are listening. Expressions such as *"so desu ne"* (that's right) and *"wakarimashita"* (understood) are also often used in the same vein. When the Japanese want to let us know that they agree, they usually say *"kekko desu"* (it's agreed) or use some other equally unambiguous expression. It is important that Americans listen carefully.

Unlike Westerners, the Japanese rarely employ bluster or theatrics during negotiations. Whenever a Japanese outburst does occur, it is usually an indication that a negotiating partner has not been sensitive to their needs and has gone too far. A good American negotiator will sense when this is about to happen and hasten to defuse the situation before it leads to a serious breakdown.

Although it is usually better to avoid bluster when dealing with the Japanese, as with all rules, there are exceptions. On rare occasions, a display of anger by a skillful U.S. negotiator can have beneficial results. An example occurred in Geneva in 1978 during negotiation of the Multilateral Trade Agreement. Robert Strauss (now our ambassador in Moscow and then the chief of the U.S. trade delegation) thought he had achieved a meeting of minds with his Japanese counterpart. But his opposite number suddenly announced that no such agreement existed. Strauss, astonished and quite agitated, picked up a carafe from the conference table and smashed it against the wall. The Japanese negotiator, taken aback by Strauss's sudden outburst, quickly reversed himself. He said he would stand by the previous agreement and apologized for having caused the "misunderstanding." This departure from normally expected conduct showed the Japanese that there is a limit to American patience. But this approach can only be used when the U.S. negotiator is confident of the outcome. Strauss had devoted careful attention to building a good relationship with his Japanese counterpart and was secure in the knowledge that his partner was intent on concluding a deal.

Even the experienced President Nixon, who had a good grasp of the subtleties of international negotiations, experienced difficulty with the traditional Asian styles of negotiating when he met with Japanese Prime Minister Eisaku Sato over the issue of textile imports.

Whenever Sato encountered a point on which he felt he could not agree, he smiled and said simply, *"Zenssho shimasu"* (I'll do my best). Nixon, mistakenly believing that Sato was agreeing with him, was quite angry when he learned that Japanese exports to the United States would continue to rise. Nixon's response was to issue an order restricting imports of Japanese textiles. What Nixon failed to understand was that Sato's "I'll do my best" was not a commitment but simply his way of saying that he did not have the authority to make the decisions called for. These misunderstandings frequently poison U.S.-Japanese trade negotiations.

Chinese negotiators operate in ways similar to the Japanese, but there are subtle differences between the two. The Chinese, not having been so commercially involved with the West as the Japanese during the past several decades, negotiate in a more traditional, ritualistic style. Even more than the Japanese, they look upon a friendship as carrying with it an obligation to reciprocate. Moreover, they have a more deeply ingrained concept of the extended family. An old Chinese proverb holds: "Under heaven, one family." They tend to look for things that benefit not only themselves but other Chinese as well. An interesting example occurred when an American pharmaceutical firm sought a new source of licorice after its supply had been cut off by the Soviet invasion of Afghanistan in 1979. The president of the company, accompanied by two other Americans and a Chinese go-between, chartered a forty-seat plane for US$4,000 to fly them to the town of Lining to inspect the trees, the roots of which were to be boiled into licorice extract. The Americans wanted to proceed immediately to inspect the trees but the town officials insisted that they spend several hours at a lavish lunch, complete with toasts. Finally, the inspection took place and the Americans offered a generous price for a sizeable purchase of the extract. When the American party returned to the airport, to their surprise they found that the Chinese airline had sold the other thirty-six seats on the plane to local passengers who were already on board. The overhead racks, space under the seats, and aisles were full of bundles, melons, and even live chickens. The president of the American company refused to board. He had chartered the plane and was not about to share it. Local officials of the airline produced a copy of the contract. In the fine print it said that the airline could take on other passengers so long as it did not interfere with the mission of the chartered flight. The American president relented and said he would permit the Chinese to fly on his flight provided the airline would reimburse him for an amount equivalent to the additional fares from the local passengers. As a matter of principle, he did not want the airline to profit twice from the same flight. The airline officials would not give in and the American party would not embark. It was getting late and the plane had to take off because the runway had no lights. Finally, airline officials ordered the Chinese passengers off the plane, and it took off. The president of the company was quite pleased with himself. He thought he had concluded a good deal for the licorice and had won out on principle with the airline. But the deal never materialized. The airline had not been allowed to do things its way, and the Chinese stuck together as one big family.The episode was a good example of how the Chinese tend to rely heavily on group relationships. This group emphasis explains why the Chinese express disapproval when an individual is singled out for praise. The Chinese consider a person vain if he misinterprets an expression of politeness as a compliment. Thus, our negotiators should never praise an individual but rather reserve praise for the group as a whole.

Negotiating in Eastern Europe is quite another story, as an experience of mine demonstrated. In 1980, while out of the government, I was approached by a leading American producer of frozen fish products who wished to engage me as a consultant. He had contracted with the Polish Trade Ministry to buy a large amount of fish fillets each month. When the first shipment arrived, however, it contained only fish heads and tails. When I looked at the contract, I spotted the difficulty immediately. The contract simply specified "fish" and not "fish fillets." The Poles, following the Soviet practice, had built a loophole into the contract that permitted them to sell my client a lesser quality product for the same price. My advice was simple: before concluding a deal with Soviet-style negotiators, read the fine print.

When I recounted this episode to a Japanese friend, he told me that he had had similar experiences when dealing behind the Iron Curtain. He assured me that the Japanese would never stoop to the practice of deliberately creating loopholes in an agreement. From my own experiences, I am inclined to agree.

WORDS OF ADVICE

In international negotiations, Americans should generally strive to be more reserved than in domestic negotiations. When dealing with Asians, for example, Americans often insist on talking shop during the entertainment phase of a negotiation. Asians interpret this as an overly materialistic approach; it is damaging to the more traditional Asian step-by-step progression of discussions.

While small talk at the beginning of negotiations is a necessary component of building a relationship, some subjects, which Americans feel they can discuss freely with strangers at home, are not fit topics of discussion abroad. For example, in Arab cultures, it is improper to inquire about female family members. By way of contrast, Latin Americans love to discuss their families, especially their wives and daughters. Although it may sound trite, I have found that the weather is a safe topic for small talk the world over.

Proper forms of address and the observance of local rules of etiquette are quite important. Only after someone has gained their complete confidence do Europeans and Asians tolerate being called by their first names. They generally suspect the motives of those who fail to address them by their official titles or full names. American negotiators must take care to show respect for position and status, especially since our egalitarian culture causes us to be less sensitive in such matters. In Europe and Asia, for instance, greater respect is shown older persons. A younger man who fails to defer to an older one, even though the two have the same relative status within their respective societies, usually finds himself rebuffed. Germans are often reluctant to conclude negotiations on a serious matter with anyone under sixty years of age. To get around this obstacle, some American officials bring in senior partners or retired associates to have final face-to-face meetings with German counterparts.

Typically, Americans see the negotiating table as a place to work out agreements. We expect to sit down and engage in horse-trading and regard the process as an exercise where parties strive to make fairly even exchanges. In contrast, Asians typically do not like to sit at the table and engage in set-piece negotiations; they prefer to do most of their dealing in an informal atmosphere. Irrespective of where talks are held, any perceptions on the part of the Japanese that their American counterparts are "wheeling and dealing" can irreparably harm a negotiation. Asians consider such behavior crass and unacceptable. American negotiators must realize that Asians regard normal Western behavior as unduly aggressive and confrontational.

In their domestic dealings, American negotiators habitually open with a position fairly close to the desired outcome. We like to allow ourselves a little room for give-and-take, but not much, because we want to appear fair and reasonable. Europeans follow the same pattern. Asian negotiators usually open with a position even closer to the desired outcome, because they are brought up to avoid social conflict. In contrast, the Soviets opened negotiations with extreme positions almost guaranteed to produce conflict. While American negotiators like to first propose a solution and then flesh it out, Asians avoid this approach altogether, preferring instead to start with principles that will lead to a solution.

American and European negotiators like to compromise, settling matters roughly halfway between their own and their counterpart's position. But Asians find compromising difficult; they usually try to arrive at agreements by making concessions on issues removed from the subject being discussed, thus avoiding a loss of face. Asians generally compromise only if they are not seen to be doing so. They are unlike my former Soviet counterparts, who did not like to compromise, period.

American negotiators regard a signed agreement as final and binding; a deal is a deal. Asians usually do not regard a signed agreement as final, especially if they subsequently conclude that they did not enter into a reasonable deal. In such cases, they resort to adopting a new approach and try to reach an agreement on different terms; they do not share our belief in the sanctity of contracts.

Like my former Soviet counterparts, Asians are eleventh-hour negotiators. But their motives for engaging in last-minute talks are quite different. Soviet negotiators waited until the last minute as a tactic to extract concessions. Asians bring negotiations to a close late in the game simply because they devote so much time to building the relationships they consider essential.

All of this shows that Americans and negotiators from other cultures operate by different sets of rules. That is why American negotiators who want to deal successfully on the international level need to study the history, social values, and culture of their counterparts.

INTERNATIONAL NEGOTIATING
IN THE FUTURE

Clearly, the world's center of gravity is shifting—politically, militarily, and economically. In the political arena, we will need to negotiate to maintain friendships, strengthen alliances, and build coalitions. In the military field, we will need to continue to negotiate with those who possess strategic arms, primarily to build confidence and enhance stability. We will also need to negotiate to prevent nuclear proliferation, to curb the spread of ballistic missiles, and to achieve a worldwide ban on chemical and biological weapons. Above all, we will need to negotiate better in the field of international economics to ensure that Americans get a fair shake from the European Community and Asian nations in a world of growing economic confrontation. Hopefully, we will show more skill than we demonstrated in dealing with the Soviets. We certainly should, because this time our economic future is at stake. Our survival may no longer depend upon this skill, but American jobs and our well-being will depend on how well we do. We must remember that, unlike us, some people think it only takes one to tango.

Index

ABM (antiballistic missile) system, 46
  Safeguard, 24
  SALT I, 39, 40
ABM Treaty, 38, 44, 45, 188–89
  domestic reaction to, 46–48
  Gorbachev on, 187
  Jackson Hole talks and, 231
  observance of, 200
  violation charge, 82–83
ACDA (Arms Control and Disarmament
    Agency), 110, 140
Adelman, Kenneth, 155, 175, 188
Afghanistan, 203–4
Air-launched cruise missile (ALCM), 70–
    71, 184
Akhromeyev, Sergei, 55–56, 181–82, 184,
    185, 217
Almond, Edward (Ned), 9, 10
Andropov, Yuri, 156
Arab cultures, 262
Arbatov, Georgi, 109, 113
Arms control negotiations. *See also*
    Rowny, Edward L.; SALT; SALT I;
    SALT II; START
  and back-channel communications, 22–
    23, 36
  bait-and-switch tactics, Soviet, 115
  Carter naiveté and overzealousness,
    93–94
  criticism by *Los Angeles Times,* 195
  Ford policy toward, 67
  and Gorbachev directives at Reykjavík,
    180, 181
  at Helsinki, 27, 42, 43
  Nixon "linkage" and Soviets in, 21, 22,
    23

and unilateral proposals by Bush,
    242–43
Arms control summit, 37, 38, 39, 40, 41
Asia
  people of, 256, 257, 258, 259, 261–62,
    263
  Rowny's missions to, 174, 176, 190–
    91
  SS missiles issue, 176, 178, 191, 193,
    194
Atomic bomb project, 5
Atwater, Lee, 213

Back-channel communications
  and arms control summit, 40
  Kissinger and, 22–23, 35, 36, 37, 73,
    74
Baker, Howard, 126, 128, 196
Baker, James
  on arms control, 218
  and control over arms control policy,
    237
  at Jackson Hole talks, 231–32
  at Malta summit, 236
  and military manpower cuts, 228–29
  and Safire column, reaction to, 237
  and START, 242
  working style of, 215
Ballistic missiles, 68, 71, 252. *See also*
    Intercontinental ballistic missiles
    (ICBMs)
Bartholomew, Reginald, 215, 216, 217
Beam, Jacob, 40
Beletsky, Ivan, 38, 52–53, 54, 79–80,
    118

Belknap, U.S. cruiser, 234–35
Beria, Lavrenti, 80
Berlin Wall, 233, 249
Bessmertnykh, Alexandr, 177, 193, 240, 242
Biden, Joseph, 201
Bilats. *See* Informal discussions
Boatner, Hayden, 15
Bombers, 68
  Backfire, 70, 73, 75–77, 97, 121–22
  B-1, 108
Brady, Nicholas, 235
Brezhnev, Leonid, 69, 109
  and Carter, 133
  doctrine, 42
  and Ford, compared, 83
  and Nixon, 44
  and SALT II, 57–58, 105, 121–22
Brooks, Linton, 241
Brown, George, 95–96, 97, 109–10
Brown, Harold, 96, 98, 99, 107–8
Brzezinski, Zbigniew, 103, 104, 105
  background of, 99
  and linkage, 100
  on PRC ties, 115
Burt, Richard, 152–53
Bush, Barbara, 226
Bush, George, 210–46
  background of, 219–20
  and dissidents, 246
  future prospects, 245–46
  and leaks to press, 229
  and linkage, 227
  at Malta summit, 234–36
  and new world order, 249
  personality, character of, 218–23
  philosophy of, 223–31
  political career of, 220–23
  speeches
    on democracy at Coast Guard Academy, 223–24
    in Ukraine, 244
    TV address on unilateral arms control, 242–43
  as vice president, 211–13
  World War II experiences of, 219–20
Bush, Prescott, 221
Bush, William ("Bucky"), 234

Cannon, Lou, 203
Carlucci, Frank, 199–200
Carnesale, Al, 102
Carter, Amy, 111–12
Carter, Jimmy, 93–133
  and Brezhnev, 133
  character traits of, 101–3
  and naiveté on arms control issues, 93–94

new team under, 96–101
  problem-solving approach of, 102–3
  and SALT II, 122, 132–33
Casey, Bill, 126
  and foreign policy issues, 139
  and personality as CIA head, 137–38
CBW. *See* Chemical and biological weapons
Cease-fire
  in Korean War, 14, 15
  in Vietnam War, 47
CFE. *See* Conventional forces in Europe
Chambers, Fred, 220
Charter 77, 133
Chemical and biological weapons (CBW), 229–30
  and limitation difficulties, 251–52
  at Malta summit, 236
Cheney, Dick, 218, 229
Chernenko, Konstantin, 158
Chervov, Nikolai, 177–78, 182, 184, 193
Church, Frank, 127–28, 131
CIA (Central Intelligence Agency). *See also* Casey, Bill
  and Bush, 222–23
  and Rowny, working for, 137–38
Clements, Bill, 34
Cold war, 231–33, 235
Collins, J. Lawton, 12
Committee on the Present Danger, 123, 125, 126, 128, 131
Commonwealth of Independent States (CIS), 244–45, 249, 250. *See also* USSR
Communism, 231–33, 244, 248
Conference on Security and Cooperation in Europe (CSCE), 83
Congress, U.S.
  and Ford, 65, 83–84
  and SALT, 49, 122–31
Congressional Record, 130, 131
Conventional forces in Europe (CFE), 228, 235–36
Coors, Joseph, 138
Crisis Management Team. *See* Special Situations Group
Cruise missiles, 105, 108. *See* Air-launched cruise missiles (ALCMs); Ground-launched cruise missiles (GLCMs); Sea-launched cruise missiles (SLCMs)
Czechoslovakia, 173–74

Daniloff, Nicholas, 178
Defense
  Brown, H., measures of, 107–8
  Carter, spending increases of, 129
  Nixon, measures of, 24

Reagan, measures of, 141
  and "Schlesinger Doctrine," 67
  and SDI, 136
Defense and Space (D&S), 158, 159
Deferral option, 103, 104
Democracy
  Bush on, 223–24
  USSR strides toward, 244
Derazhnya and Pervomaysk (D&P), 82
Détente, 41–42, 83–85
Deterrence, 60, 67
  Kopit play and, 131–32
  Reagan on, 136
Detinov, Nikolai, 143
Dialectical materialism, 107
Directives, 180, 181
Disarmament. See Arms control negotiations
Dobrynin, Anatoli
  at arms control summit, 38, 40–41
  and back-channel communications, 35–
    36, 40–41
  and Kissinger, 22, 23, 26, 27
Dolan, Tony, 204
Dukakis, Michael, 213

Eagleburger, Larry, 215
Earle, Ralph, 110, 114, 120–21
Economics in a changing world, 253–56
End of the World (Kopit), 132
Enhanced Radiation Weapon (ERW). See
  Neutron bomb
Escher, M. C., 132

Fallaci, Oriana, 31
Fallback position. See Deferral option
Fitzwater, Marlin, 195, 240, 241
Ford, Gerald, 64–92
  accomplishments of, 91–92
  and Brezhnev compared, 83
  and Congress on foreign aid, 83–84
  and Kissinger, 65, 66, 73, 74, 87–88
  and Mayaguez incident, 90
  media's criticism of, 89–90, 91
  personality traits of, 84, 90, 91
  and Schlesinger's firing, 86
  and Soviet rapport, 92
  at Vladivostok summit, 70–74
Foreign Affairs, 24, 26
Forward-based system (FBS), 71–72
Fosdick, Dorothy, 101
Friedman, Thomas L., 228
Fydorow, Svyastoslov, 207

Garn, Jake, 163
Garthoff, Raymond, 36
Gates, Robert, 216

Gelb, Leslie, 101, 111
Geneva, Switzerland
  SALT II site, 49
  summit, 167–72
    aftermath of, 174
    linkage issues raised in, 168
    Reykjavík compared to, 185
Gerasimov, Gennadi, 197, 235
Germany, 214, 233, 262
Glasnost, 166, 170, 171
Glenn, John, 126, 128
Glitman, Mike, 159, 198
Goodpaster, Andrew, 5, 32–33
Gorbachev, Mikhail, 165, 166
  accomplishments of, 248–49
  appearance and attributes of, 172, 200
  Bush's support for, 218
  on elimination of nuclear weapons,
    174–75, 180
  and human rights issue at Moscow
    summit, 205
  at Malta summit, 234–36
  on military forces, 157
  and military manpower cuts, 228
  on nuclear war initiative, 172
  and Reagan at Geneva, 167–72
  and response to unilateral arms control,
    243
  at Reykjavík, 178–92
  and unsuccessful coup, 244
Gorbachev, Raisa, 171, 207
Göring, Hermann, 18
Grenada, 212
Gromyko, Andrei, 60–61, 158, 168
  and MIRVs verification, 81
  at SALT I summit, 42, 45
  and Vance proposals, SALT II, 104–5
  and Vladivostok summit preparations,
    67, 70
Ground-launched cruise missiles
  (GLCMs), 156

Haig, Alexander, 140
  after assassination attempt on Reagan,
    151
  personality of, 148–50
  resignation of, 151
Handy, Thomas, 5
Hatfield, Mark, 127
Havel, Vaclav, 173
Hayakawa, Senator, 101
Heavy missile limitation, 106
Helicopters, 16, 17
Helms, Jesse, 130, 163
Helsinki, Finland
  and arms control negotiations, 27, 42,
    43, 44
  stopover at, 196

Hoffman, David, 229
Howard, Dan, 195
Howe, Sir Geoffrey, 153
Howze, Hamilton ("Ham"), 16, 17
Howze Board, 16, 17
Human rights issue, 168, 203
  at Moscow summit, 205
  Raisa Gorbachev on, 171

INF (intermediate-range nuclear forces),
    142, 157–58, 160, 184–86, 192–
    94. See INF Treaty
Informal discussions
  Bush style of, 225
  at Geneva summit, 170
  at Reykjavík, 178–92
  during SALT II negotiation procedure,
    51
  at START, 177
INF Treaty, 197–98, 199
  conclusion, 207, 208–9
  Rowny's endorsement of, 201
  ratification issues, 200–202
Inman, Bobby, 140
Interavia, 75
Intercontinental ballistic missiles (ICBMs),
    27, 28
  SALT I, 38, 41
  silo size dispute, 43, 44
International relations. See also U.S.-USSR
    relations
  Bush and force role, 228
  in a changing world, 248–64
  cultural differences and, 256–57
  Nixon doctrine and, 24–25, 26
  and Rowny's ten points of negotiation,
    7–9, 254–55
Issacson, Walter, 219

Jackson, Henry M. ("Scoop"), 42, 100,
    101, 103
  on equal aggregates number, 70
  and influence in arms control involve-
    ment, 1, 19, 96
  and influencing Rowny's recruitment by
    Reagan, 135
  and Jackson Amendment, 46–47
  on PROFIT, 15
  and SALT II, 120, 122, 124, 128, 131
Jackson Hole, Wyoming, 231–32
Jackson-Vanik Amendment, 74
Japan
  invasion of (World War II), 5
  people, 257–58, 259, 262
  postwar, 5, 6, 9
  Reagan relations, 176–77
Japanese Self Defense Force (JSDF), 9

Javits, Jacob, 130
JCS (Joint Chiefs of Staff)
  and equality issue in Soviet negotia-
    tions, 69
  and Kissinger, 59–62
  in Korean War, 11–12
  and SALT II, 18–19, 48, 56–57
Johnson, Harold K., 17
Johnson, U. Alexis
  and Kissinger, 32, 48
  and SALT II, 50–51
  and Semenov, 78, 81
Jones, David, 110
Jordan, Hamilton, 95
Joshua, Winifred, 84
Joy, C. Turner, 15

Kalb, Bernard, 32
Kalb, Marvin L., 32
Kampelman, Max, 158–59
Karpov, Viktor, 106
  background of, 143, 144
  and SALT II, 120–21, 143, 144
  and START, 142, 144–45, 157–58,
    160
  style of, 110–11
KGB, 156
Khrushchev, Nikita, 248
Kirkpatrick, Jeane, 178
  on Bush, 210
Kissinger (Kalb and Kalb), 32
Kissinger, Henry
  at arms control summit, 40
  and back-channel communications,
    22–23, 35, 36, 37, 40, 57, 73,
    74
  background of, 28–36
  careerism of, 32
  and China relations, 24
  and détente, 41–42, 85
  and FBS issue, 72
  and Ford, 65, 66, 73, 74, 87–88
  and influence on SALT involvement,
    18, 19
  on INF Treaty, 195
  JCS and, 59–62
  and "linkage" under Nixon, 22
  on MIRVs, 62, 69, 81
  at Moscow summit, 62
  on new political order in former USSR,
    250
  and Nixon, relationship with, 28, 31–
    32, 34–35
  and Nixon's views on arms control,
    26–27, 194–95
  personality and temperament of, 33–34
  publications of, 30, 31, 58
  and SALT I summit, 42, 43, 45, 46

and SALT II negotiations, 56, 58, 63
and Vietnam War cease-fire, 47
and Vladivostok summit, 67–68, 69–70, 71, 72, 73
Klein, Herb, 46
Klosson, Boris, 38
Kohl, Helmut, 156
Kopit, Arthur, 131–32
Korean War, 10, 11, 12, 14
Kraemer, Fritz, 33
  on Kissinger, 28, 29, 30, 33
  on Nixon, 35
  in World War II, 28–30
Kraemer, Sven, 123, 131
Kremlin, 61–62
Kvitsinsky, Yuli, 156, 160

Laird, Melvin, 25, 42, 64
  and article on ABM Treaty, 82–83
Latin Americans, 262
Laxalt, Paul, 163
LeTourneau, Richard, 220
Lincoln, George ("Abe"), 3, 4, 5, 6
"Lincoln's Brigade," 3
Linhard, Robert, 188, 189
Linkage
  and Bush, 227
  and Nixon, 21, 22, 23
  and in SALT II, 74
Los Angeles Times, 195
Lugar, Richard, 129

MacArthur, Douglas, 5
  in Korean War, 10, 11, 12, 13
  in postwar Japan, 6, 9
McFarlane, Robert ("Bud"), 162, 163
McGovern, George, 127, 129
McNamara, Robert, 16, 98
MAD (Mutual assured destruction).
  See Deterrence
Madison Group, 123, 124, 125, 126, 128, 129
Makharov, Sergei, 54–55
Malmstrom Air Force Base, Montana, 82
Malta summit, 225, 229, 234–36
Manhattan District Engineer. *See*
  Atomic bomb project
Marshall, George Catlett, 5
Mathias, Charles, 79, 127
Matlock, Jack, 197
Maxim Gorky, 235
MBFR. *See* Mutual and Balanced
  Force Reductions
Military buildup

Shchukin on Soviet, 157
Weinberger and U.S., 148
Minuteman III, 38, 44
MIRVs. *See* Multiple independently
  targetable reentry vehicles
Mitterrand, François, 225
Moorer, Thomas, 18–19, 42
Morris, Roger, 30
Morrow, Douglas, 9
Moscow summit, 42, 60, 61, 62, 204–8
Moynihan, Daniel Patrick, 127
Mubarak, Hosni, 225
Multiple independently targetable
  reentry vehicles (MIRVs)
  limits on, 27
  and Moscow summit, 62
  and SALT I, 38, 39
  and SALT II, 56
  verification of, 81–83
Murphy, Dan, 227
Muskie, Edmund, 129–30
Mutual and Balanced Force Reductions
  (MBFR), 1, 18

National security. *See* Defense
National Security Memorandums
  (NSDMs), 66, 163
NATO (North Atlantic Treaty Organization), 1
  article V on attack of, 71
  and INF, 142
  and military manpower cuts, 228–29
  and Steinhoff, Johannes, 18
Negotiation. *See also* Soviet style of negotiation
  and back-channel communications, 22–23, 35, 36, 37
  in a changing world, 247–64
  cultural differences and, 256–61
  etiquette, 262
  equality in
    U.S.-USSR negotiations, 68–70
    Vladivostok summit, 70
  humor in, 80–81
  and leaks to press, 145–46
  mind games in, 77
  non-paper, 54
  Reagan's style, 146, 147
  and regional disputes, 167–68, 253
  and Rowny
    first experience, World War II, 4
    ten points of, 7–9, 254–55
  small talk, 78, 262
Nessen, Ron, 73
Networking policy, 224–25
Neutron bomb, 108–9
New York Times, 153, 195

Niemczyk, Jay, 173
Nitze, Paul, 142, 156, 162
  and differences with Rowny, 161–62
  resignation of, 214
  and START talks, 182, 185
Nixon, Richard, 21–63
  and defense systems, 24
  doctrine of, foreign aid, 26
  and Eisaku Sato, 259–60
  Ford's pardon of, 65
  on INF Treaty, 194–95
  and Kissinger relationship, 28, 31–32,
    34–35
  and Kissinger's views on arms control,
    26–27, 194–95
  and "linkage" policy in foreign affairs,
    21, 22, 23
  and PRC, relations with, 24–25, 27
  and Rowny's briefing of, 194
  at SALT I summit, 44–45
  and SALT II negotiation failure, 62–63
  secrecy and distrust, 22, 35
  and Vietnam War, 25, 26, 27, 39, 41
  and Watergate scandal, 57, 60, 61
Noriega, Manuel, 246
Norstad, Lauris C.
  "dream sessions" of, 6
  nuclear policy revision of, 16
Nuclear testing debate, 54–56
Nuclear war, 172
Nuclear weapons, 71
  elimination of
    per Carter, 94
    per Gorbachev, 174–75, 180
    per Reagan, 164, 186–87, 190
    Yeltsin's control of, 250, 251
Nuclear Weapons and Foreign Policy
    (Kissinger), 30
Nunn, Sam, 126, 128, 129, 201

Obukhov, Alexandr, 160, 198
Occupation forces
  Korean War retraining of, 10
  in postwar Japan, 9–10
Ogarkhov, Nikolai, 76

Paderewski, Ignacy Jan, 173, 174
Pavlichenko, Vladimir, 77
Peaceful Nuclear Explosions (PNE), 54–56
Perestroika, 170, 171, 205, 218, 235
Perle, Richard, 101, 189
  on ABM Treaty, 188
  and Burt, 152–53
  on SLCMs, 183
Pershing II missiles, 156
Persian Gulf War (1991), 226, 252
Playboy, 113, 169

Poland, 173–74
Political dissidents. See Dissident groups;
    Rowny, Edward L.
Politics in the emerging world, 248–53
Pope John Paul II, 239
Pravda, 113
PRC (People's Republic of China)
  and cultural differences with, 256,
    260–61
  in Korean War, 13, 14
  Nixon and, 24–25
  U.S. relations and, 115
  U.S.-USSR issues and, 37, 194–95
Press, the, 152, 153, 154
  and criticism of Ford, 89–90, 91
  and games reporters play, 111
  and Reagan's "evil empire" speech,
    154–55
  at Reykjavík, 179
  on START delegation, 155
PROFIT (Professional Improvement
    Time), 15, 16
Proxmire, William, 127
Puller, Lewis ("Chesty"), 13

Quayle, Dan, 201, 202, 229

Reader's Digest, 82
Reagan, Nancy, 165, 171
Reagan, Ron, 169
Reagan, Ronald
  advisors to, 138–39
  appraisal of, 208–9
  assassination attempt, handling, 151
  and defense measures, 141, 142
  and elimination of nuclear weapons,
    186–87, 190
  and "evil empire" speech, 154–55
  first term of, 134–63
  and Gorbachev at Geneva, 167–72
  hosts Gorbachev in Washington, 192–
    94, 198–200, 238
  and human rights issue at Moscow
    summit, 205
  and Japanese, relations with, 176–77
  personality of, 135–36
  at Reykjavík, 178–92
  second term of, 164–209
  speeches
    at Moscow University, 206
    in Springfield (Mass.), 203–4
  and TV address on Reykjavík progress,
    191
  and understanding Soviets, 134–35
Regan, Donald, 141
Remotely piloted vehicles (RPVs), 115
Reston, James, 245

Reykjavík (Iceland) meeting, 178–
    92
    bathroom diplomacy, 179, 189
    and delegation changes, 181
    Geneva, comparison to, 185
    press conference, 190–91
Ridgway, Rozanne, 167, 208
R.N. (Nixon), 27
Rockefeller, Nelson, 31, 65, 88, 89
Rogers, Bernard, 120
Rogers, William, 22, 23
Rostow, Eugene, 140
Rowny, Edward L. See Asia; CIA;
    Jackson, Henry M. ("Scoop");
    Negotiation; Nixon, Richard;
    SALT II
    and Akhromeyev, 184
    Army career, 3–6, 9–19
    arms control negotiations
        and proposals under Carter, 97,
            100, 101
        under Reagan, 141
        U.S. performance, evaluation of,
            247, 254
    and Baker, J., 163, 237
    and Beletsky, 118
    and Bessmertnykh, 193
    and Brezhnev, 58
    and Bush, 211, 215, 216, 239–240
    and Carter, 116–17
    and Casey, 124–25, 140, 162
    and Chervov, 193
    dissidents, meetings with, 173–74,
        207
    and Haig, 149, 150
    harmonica playing, 52, 196–97
    and INF Treaty, 201
    international relations, 3, 6, 7–9,
        254–55
    and Jackson, 135
    and Japan, 176–78
    and Johnson, U., 54, 79
    and Karpov, 77
    and Kissinger, 58
    and Nitze, 161–62
    Presidential Citizen's Medal, 208
    PROFIT sessions, 15–16
    and Reagan, R., 135–37, 140–41,
        146, 160
    and Shchukin, 156–57
    and Shultz, 159–61
    and ten-point negotiation list, 7–9
    and Trusov, 117–18
    and U.S. Senate, relationship with,
        163
    and Vance, 117
    visits Moscow on break, 117–
        18
    at Yale, 6–7

Rowny, Rita, 226
Roy, Stapleton, 217
Rumsfeld, Donald, 66, 87, 88, 90

Saddam Hussein, 245, 252
Safeguard ABM system, 24
Safire, William, 32, 237
SALT (Strategic Arms Limitation Talks),
    1, 19
    ABM Treaty, domestic reaction to,
        46–48
    back-channel communications and, 36,
        57
    encryption of telemetry issue, 115, 116
    ICBMs and, 27–28
SALT I, 38–46
SALT II
    concessions to ease ratification of,
        119–20
    demise of, 122–31
    and linkage, 74
    and negotiations, 56–59
    and procedure, 49–52
    and Rowny joins team, 48–54
    and shape-up under Carter, 103–7
    signing of, 121–22
    and Vladivostok, 70–74
Sato, Eisaku, 259–60
Schlesinger, James, 59–60, 66, 67, 69
    and Backfire bomber, 76
    and détente, 84
    doctrine, 67
    firing by Ford, 85–86
Scowcroft, Brent, 87, 214, 215, 216,
    233
SCUD missiles, 252
SDI (Strategic Defense Initiative, or Star
    Wars), 136, 158, 171, 172, 187,
    188, 189, 190, 202, 209
Sea-launched cruise missiles (SLCMs),
    177–78, 182–83, 231–32
Seignious, George, 114
Semenov, Vladimir, 52
    and Earle, 110
    and Johnson, A., 78
    and Mathias, 79
    and quotes from classics, 81
    on seating arrangements, 50
    and Smith, 37, 45
    on timing, 80
Senate, U.S.
    on INF Treaty ratification, 200–202
    and SALT II defeat, 126–31
Senate Armed Services Committee
    (SASC), 123, 124, 131
Senate Foreign Relations Committee
    (SFRC), 124, 129, 130
Shchukin, Alexandr, 112, 116

Shevardnadze, Eduard, 177
  human rights and regional issues,
    203
  and Jackson Hole talks, 231–32
  and Malta summit, 236
  and Shultz, 188–89
  and START talks, 217
Shultz, George, 162
  and Gromyko, 158
  and human rights and regional issues,
    203
  and press conference on Reykjavík
    progress, 190
  and Shevardnadze, 188–89
  style of, 152
  and Weinberger, 152
Sidey, Hugh, 234
Sino-Soviet relations, 25, 37–38
Slava, 235
Slocombe, Walter, 97, 101
Smith, Gerard, 36, 37, 42, 43, 44, 45–
    46
Sokolov, Oleg, 167
Solidarity, 173
Solzhenitsyn, Aleksandr, 89
Sonnenfeld, Helmut, 36
Soviet style of negotiation, 110–11, 114,
    115, 263. *See also* U.S.-USSR rela-
    tions
  on Backfire bomber, 75–77
  on equality issues, 68–69
  examples of, 78–81
  and hindering SALT II signing, 121–22
  at Jackson Hole, 231–32
  and Karpov on START, 144, 145
  and Nixon "linkage" policy, 22
  and the "party line," 53, 110
  prior to Washington summit, 197–98,
    199
  and Reagan, 134–35
  at Reykjavík, 178–92
  at SALT II, 52–54, 57–58, 74, 104–
    7
  on SALT II ratification, 120
  shortcomings of, 255
  and social functions, 117–18
    Bible incident, 112–13
    nightclubbing, 193
    during SALT II, 52
    souvenir hunting, 180–81
    at summit meetings, 241
    at Vladivostok, 72
Soviet Union. *See* USSR
Special Situations Group, 212
SS missiles, 106, 193, 194
  in Asia, 176, 178, 191, 193, 194
  photo issue of, 198, 199
Starodubov, Viktor, 143
START (Strategic Arms Reduction Talks),

    142, 144, 145, 157–58, 177–78,
      185
  and Akhromeyev's proposals, 182
  and delegation changes, 160
  final rounds of, 241–42
  and hit list, 155
  and linkage issues, 202
  Malta summit, 235, 236
  signing, 242
  value after USSR break up, 243
Steinhoff, Johannes, 17–18
Stevenson Amendment, 74
Stoessel, Walter, 149
Stone, Richard, 129
Storytelling
  Gorbachev on *perestroika*, 205
  Haig, 149
  Reagan, 146, 147, 199
Strategic delivery systems, 68, 71
Strauss, Robert, 259
Submarine-launched ballistic missiles
    (SLBMs), 41, 43, 46
Sununu, John, 215, 235, 239–40

Television address
  Bush, use of, 234, 242–43
  Reagan on Reykjavík progress, 191
Terrorism, combat of, 213
Third World, the, 84, 252
Tho, Le Duc, 47
Thomas, Evan, 219
Tower, John, 138, 159, 221
Trade in a changing world, 253
Trusov, Konstantin
  and backfire bomber issue, 75, 76–77
  and dialectical materialism example,
    107
  on equality, 69
  and FBS issue, 71–72
  on Ford, 91
  and hidden meanings, 78–79
  on MIRV silos, 82
  on religious practice, 113
  and Rowny, in Moscow, 117–18
  SALT II, 52–53
Trusov, Mrs., 113

Ukraine speech, 244
United Nations (UN), 10
United States
  in a changing world, 250, 252
  foreign aid, 26, 83–84
  U.S. embassy in Moscow, bugged,
    192–93
U.S. foreign policy. *See also* International
    relations
  Bush and force role, 228

and détente, 41–42
and Ford on Soviet arms control, 67
issues under Reagan, 139, 154
Kissinger's enhancement of, 32
"linkage" of Nixon, 21, 22
nuclear policy
  proliferation prevention, 251
  revision work of, 16
  and "Schlesinger Doctrine," 67
ten points of negotiation, 7–9, 254–55
U.S.-USSR relations. *See also* International
  relations
back-channel communications, 22–23,
  36
Backfire bomber negotiations, 75–77
Bush on, 228
Carter's naiveté and overzealousness,
  93–94
China issue, 37
détente, 83–85
equality issues, 68
  and U.S.-USSR negotiations, 68–70
  and Vladivostok summit, 70
Ford policy, 67
Gulf War, 241
human rights and regional issues,
  203–4, 205
Moscow summit (1988), 205–8
Nixon "linkage," 21, 22, 23
nuclear testing debate, 54–56
Reagan and Gorbachev, 165–66,
  167–72
Reykjavík, 178–92
SALT I, deployment strategies, 38–
  46
SALT II, 50–52, 56–59, 104–7
START, 142–45
in Vietnam War, 27
Vladivostok summit, 71–73
USSR. *See also* Commonwealth of Independent States (CIS); *Glasnost;
  Perestroika;* Soviet style of negotiation; U.S.-USSR relations
break up, 234, 244
environmental degradation, 55
events leading to demise, 248–49
human rights and regional issues,
  203–4
regional disputes issue, 167–68
religious practices, 112–13
ten points of negotiation, 7–9

Vance, Cyrus, 95, 98
concessions on SALT II, 119
and Gelb, 111
on PRC relations, 115

on Rowny's projected retirement, 117
SALT II deferral option, 103, 104–5
Vietnam War
cease-fire, 47
escalation of, 39, 41, 47
helicopter use in, 17
"linkage" point in U.S.-USSR negotiations, 22, 23
resolving under Nixon, 25, 26, 27
Vladivostok summit, 105
U.S. military aid in, 26
Ford and, 70–74
issues, 68, 70
verification, 72–73

Walesa, Lech, 173
Wallop, Malcolm, 163, 233
Walters, Vernon ("Dick"), 233
Warheads, 38
Warnke, Paul, 100–101, 110, 114
War Powers Act, 65
Warsaw Pact
Rowny debriefing countries after super-
  power meetings, 172–73
unraveling, 231–33
Washington Post, 140, 155, 229
Watergate scandal, 56, 59, 60, 61
Weinberger, Caspar, 138, 162, 167
INF, 185
influence on Reagan, 147–48
on missile elimination, 175
and Shultz, 152
Werbel, Gerald, 108
West Point, 3
Wheeler, Earle ("Bus"), 17
Whelan, Joseph C., 230
White House Years (Kissinger), 31
Willoughby, Charles A., 10, 13
*Wise Men: Six Friends and a World They
  Made, The* (Issacson and Thomas),
  219
Wood, Joseph ("Smokey Joe"), 3, 4
World Restored, A (Kissinger), 30

Yale University, 6, 7–9
Years of Upheaval (Kissinger), 58
Yeltsin, Boris
banning communism, 248
control of strategic nuclear arsenal, 250,
  251
Gorbachev, criticism of, 197

Zero option, 185–86
Zlotnich, Ivan, 232